FROM SQUEAKY CLEAN TO DIRTY WATER

From Squeaky Clean to Dirty Water

My Life with the Sixties Garage Rock Trailblazers the Standells

By Larry Tamblyn

BearManor Media

2022

Published in the United States of America by:

BearManor Media

4700 Millenia Blvd.
Suite 175 PMB 90497
Orlando, FL 32839

bearmanormedia.com

Printed in the United States.

Typesetting and layout by PKJ Passion Global

ISBN—979-8-88771-020-4

Larry, 2015, Festival Beat XXII, Parma Italy.

PROLOGUE

Larry Tamblyn is the founder and original lead singer of the Standells. Best known for their hit 'Dirty Water', The Standells released a string of snotty, aggressive garage singles in the mid to late 1960s which are now regarded as proto-punk classics. The Ramones, Sex Pistols, Stooges, Guns 'N Roses are among the many rock performers who cite the Standells as an inspiration. 'Sometimes Good Guys Don't Wear White', 'Why Pick on Me', 'Riot on Sunset Strip' – the songs of the Standells have been covered by everyone from Bruce Springsteen, Aerosmith and U2 to Spacemen 3, Minor Threat and a million punk bands. "Dirty Water" is listed in The Rock 'n Roll Hall Of Fame's 500 Songs That Shaped Rock And Roll. The song is the official victory anthem of the Red Sox, played at every home game win. The Standells have left an indelible mark in the history of Rock 'n Roll.

INTRODUCTION

On Sunday, October 24th, the Standells performed at Game 2 of the 2004 World Series between the Boston Red Sox and the Saint Louis Cardinals. Just a few hours shy of game time, it was a chilly 46 degrees at Fenway Park, the birthplace of legends Babe Ruth, Ted Williams, Cy Young, and Johnny Pesky. Red Sox fans were beginning to drift into the stadium, oblivious of the frigid weather, always the most vociferous baseball followers, their most joyous times tied directly to Red Sox wins, anxiously awaiting their team to begin warm-ups, and gazing in pride at the Green Monster, the fabled edifice that was part of the original park erected in 1912. How could you not love Fenway Park? Unless, of course, you are a Yankees fan.

We've always had quite the following in Massachusetts. Most every sports team in that state uses our song when they win a game. In fact, on my wall, I have a declaration signed by the Massachusetts General Court declaring "Dirty Water" to be the "undisputed victory anthem of the Boston Red Sox." We're even mentioned during the Duck Boat tours. The cruises go along the Charles River, and tourists learn about the historical landmarks of the city like Faneuil Hall and the Freedom Trail. They also hear about famous residents, such as John F. Kennedy, Samuel Adams, Alexander Graham Bell, Henry David Thoreau, and Oliver Wendell Holmes. To be spoken of in the company of such prolific historical Bostonian figures is an honor. Not one of us had ever imagined our group would reach a position of prominence again, let alone one of historical significance. Not bad for a bunch of musicians from Los Angeles.

It was an honor of a lifetime to accept the Red Sox's invitation to perform at the game. In addition to me, all of the original performers of "Dirty Water" were in attendance: drummer and lead singer Dick Dodd, bassist Gary Lane (real name Gary McMillan), and guitarist Tony Valentino. As we stood beneath the Green Monster, anticipating the thrill of stepping into baseball history, my thoughts drifted to how we had all changed over the years. Our outward appearances were different, of course; we all had gotten rounder and grayer. For myself, I had long before outgrown the carefree young bandleader and original lead singer who couldn't be bothered with the business of music. While I once had placed too much faith in others who made promises they failed to keep, I was now fully involved in the business and booking of the Standells.

In the sixties, Dick Dodd was a tall, good-looking dude with an ample head of dark hair, self-assured, reliable, and a great friend — someone who would give you the shirt off of his back. The former Mouseketeer and teen heartthrob was now in poor health, overweight with thinning hair, undependable and mendacious. After decades of heavy smoking and performing in small smoke-filled bars his once crisp, sexy voice had become gravelly. Years of drug and alcohol abuse had also taken their toll; he had become a shadow of his former self. Now when Dick sang "Dirty Water," it sounded like a completely different song, sung by a raspy lounge lizard.

Next to Dick was shy, aged but still handsome Gary Lane. The years had been more kind to him. He was happily married to his first and only wife, Edie. Being a barber agreed with him. An avid baseball fan, Gary was thrilled beyond measure to be in Fenway. At least, that's what we were told. With Gary, emotions were always a bit tricky to read. Along with his many other attributes, including his capable bass playing, Gary maintained his wry sense of humor.

Lastly, eyeing the attractive women in the stands, was bushy-haired Tony Valentino. Even after fifty years in this country, Sicilian-born Emilio Bellissimo (his real name) still spoke with a thick broken accent. Tony was certainly not the same good-natured, self-effacing friend who had co-founded the group with me in 1962. The once-suave Casanova who never had a problem enticing even the most virginal young woman into bed was now left only with reminiscences of past conquests. The happy-go-lucky, fun-to-be-with friend I had known had grown into a quarrelsome pain-in-the-ass to work with, and a constant complainer – most definitely not good company to be around. He had long ago lost his affable youthful appeal and was now burdensome with his persistent obstinance. Perhaps there had been hints of this all along, if so, I'd chosen to ignore them.

I remembered much happier times with Tony… like the day in the early sixties when we were driving up the California coast and some guy pulled up next to us at a stoplight, rolled down his window and asked, "Hey, do you know where Sonoma Beach is?"

Tony's dark profuse eyebrows rose in bewilderment. "Whaaaat?"

The guy spoke a little louder, "Sonoma Beach."

Tony's face reddened. "No!" he shouted. "*You* are sonoma-bitch! Vaffanculo!"

And with that he raised his index and little finger at the man, the European symbol for "fuck you."

The guy looked rather puzzled, opened his mouth as if to say something, but decided instead to drive off. When I told him that the guy was only seeking directions, Tony smacked his head in sudden realization, saying "Stupido!"

We both began laughing so hard we had to pull over to the side of the street.

The laughs and fun times were years behind us, along with our friendship.

As the memory faded, the excitement and anticipation building for our entrance, a curious thing happened. I was standing next to the event manager who held a copy of the show schedule. As we were going over the performance details one last time, a large drop of blood suddenly and mysteriously plopped onto the schedule, highlighting the Standells' name in red. We looked up in shock, not knowing what we would see. Sure enough, high above us atop the Green Monster sat a hawk in the midst of consuming his dinner. His meal? One of Fenway's finest – a large rat. I understand they are quite plentiful at Fenway – any local Red Sox fan will attest to that.

Oddly enough, it typified many of the bizarre incidents that happened to us over the years. It brought to mind one particular adventure that occurred over forty years earlier, in 1962.

At that time, the Standells consisted of Jody Rich, the eldest member, on bass, Benny (King) Hernandez, a handsome Latino youth, on drums, Tony on guitar, and me, the 19-year-old keyboardist/guitarist and lead singer. Tony had only been in the country for five years, but with his thick wavy head of hair, he was as suave as they came.

One of our first gigs as a band was at the Oasis Club in Honolulu, Hawaii. We did two shows every evening, following a Japanese burlesque show complete with actors, dancers, a comedian, and, of course, a stripper. Believe me, Miki Moto was a very tough act to follow. Boos and catcalls were quite common early on; the raucous male audience vociferously resented us for interrupting their masturbatory fantasies. As time passed, though, we began to build up a following for ourselves, especially among women.

The four of us lived in an apartment building in Waikiki Beach. Jody and Benny shared one bachelor apartment, Tony and I shared another. Unbeknownst to Tony and me, there was a third member of our household; one with four legs and fur who didn't take kindly to late-night partying. He was a small Pacific Rat, *Rattus Exulans*, whom we later named Fred. Little Fred presented us with a BIG problem. He got into our food and made quite a pig of himself. Regardless, we could have come to some sort of detente with him if food had been the only issue. The biggest hindrance was regarding the girls. Fred intruded into our sex lives, and *that* was inexcusable. Tony and I had no problems meeting local and tourist women on the beach and inviting them up to our room. However, getting them into bed was another story completely – our furry roommate made that an impossibility. Fred intruded into our sex lives, and *that* was inexcusable.

It took Tony and me considerable time and effort – and scheming – to cajole the wahines into entering our small, run-down apartment. Approaching them as young, confident studs on the sandy Waikiki beach was the first step. Inviting them to our room for Mai Tai's was the second. Once inside, we would surreptitiously dim the lights and then turn on the record player, already stacked with pre-selected seductive music – with "This Magic Moment" by the Drifters always on the bottom of the stack. The Mai Tais were expertly mixed and served. Our every move was timed to perfection. Soft lights, romantic music, sweet drinks, giggles… It was at this critical juncture that things would take a turn for the worst. Like clockwork, Fred would emerge from his hole behind the built-in oven and brazenly strut across the room, creating total havoc in the process. The now-terrified girls would then make a hasty retreat out the front door, leaving us profoundly frustrated, horny, and seething in anger at this pernicious little beast.

Over a period of two months, Fred's ill-mannered and ill-timed appearances continued, always at the most inopportune moments, always with the same results: the girls' speedy exits and us yelling obscenities at Fred. There was very little we could do; inevitably, he always scooted back to his safe hole-in-the-wall behind the stove.

However, his good fortune was about to change.

Tony, like me, had grown weary of Fred's behavior, and on one particular evening after the gig, a curvaceous red-headed tourist invited him to spend the night with her in her hotel room. I returned home from the club alone. After grabbing a snack from the fridge, I disrobed down to my skivvies (Jody insisted that we refer to all such clothing in military terms). With nothing better to do, I flipped on the TV and happened to catch the movie *The Girl Can't Help It*, starring Tom Ewell, Edmond O'Brien, and the titular Jayne Mansfield. As a teenager, I was inspired by almost every black R&B performer, including Little Richard who performed the title song, and had wet dreams about Mansfield, so I couldn't resist watching it.

To this day, I can't fathom how Fred was enticed to come out of his hiding place during the hard-driving rock song theme from the movie *The Girl Can't Help It*. Perhaps he thought things were getting a little racy with Little Richard belting out, "And if she's got a figure made to squeeze," thinking it was time for him to once again break it up before things got hot and heavy. Regardless, Fred made what I considered to be a fatal mistake. He chose this moment to make his appearance from behind the oven. Bolstered by his past performances, he had become more emboldened than ever. This time, though, he overstepped his boundaries. Fred raced right by me and ran into Tony's side of the room. A built-in sliding divider conveniently separating our two beds (a major selling point to us when we found the place) presented me with a golden opportunity.

Fred must have counted on the usual hysterical distractions to make his getaway. However, unlike the previous occasions, I was alone. My attention was now focused entirely on him. I quickly slammed the divider shut, isolating the rat bastard from his safe hidey-hole. Fred had entered No Rat's Land. My loathing of Fred had grown into an uncontrollable rage over those past two months. I dashed into the kitchen, grabbed a butcher knife, and then ventured into Tony's side of the room, sliding the divider shut behind me.

This was it, I thought, *the final conflict*. After months of raw emotions and raging hormones, it was Larry vs. Fred: Mano a Rattus. Fred was the prey and I was the great white hunter. He had tormented me in the worst possible way; he'd deprived me of my manhood. Now I would deprive Fred of his *rathood*. It was payback time!

With the partition closed, Tony's side of the room was dark. At first I wasn't able to see where the little demon had fled. Where would a sneaky, conniving rodent hide? In one motion, I flipped over Tony's bed. Sure enough, Fred scampered out and darted under a dresser. *Aha! The game's afoot!* I was a primitive warrior in tight white loincloth, saber in hand, wailing like a banshee in fevered pursuit of this four-legged cretin. I was on a mission of vengeance and honor – nothing was going to stand in my way. I pushed over the dresser. Fred scurried out, disappearing under an end table. This too was toppled. The rat frantically sought shelter under every nook and cranny he could find. All hiding places were either sealed off or overturned. With nowhere left to go, Fred raced into the bathroom and across the tile floor to the bathtub… where his last hope of escape ended. He could go no further.

Trapped like a rat, Fred turned to make his last stand. Raising the knife overhead, I lowered myself into a primal squat, coming face-to-face with my whiskered nemesis. I menacingly waved the blade at Fred, who, in turn, defensively flashed his razor-sharp incisors at me, in sort of a menacing grin.

It was at this point that I realized with a shudder my absolute vulnerability – my groin was completely exposed, with very little to shield me from Fred's fangs! While Fred was a considerably small target; I, on the other hand, presented the rat with a comparatively large and opportune target; I was in immediate danger of a *ratsectomy*.

Slowly I backed out of the bathroom, and closed the door, leaving it cracked open a tiny bit, and began re-thinking my battle plan. While I was pondering my next move, Fred made the decision for me, a momentary lapse in judgment on his part that would prove to be Fred's undoing.

Unaware that I was stealthily observing him, Fred climbed up on a small table next to the toilet and crawled inside an empty Kleenex box. Here was the moment I had been waiting for! The coup de grâce! Revenge was at hand! I rushed into the bathroom, grabbed the container and threw it into the toilet. Yes, I knew that the thin cardboard box would slowly dissolve in the water, and yes, Fred would be forced to sink or swim. Unfortunately for him, the only exit was down the drain and into the sewer where he belonged. I shut the lid, triumphant in the knowledge I was the supreme victor in this battle; Fred would eventually meet his maker in Davy Jones' Locker!

With a satisfaction that I hadn't known in quite some time, I straightened the place up, walked back through the divider, and crawled into bed. It wasn't long before I fell into a peaceful slumber, dreaming of other conquests to follow, now that Fred was no longer an issue.

Several hours later, I was soundly awakened by the most wretched scream I'd ever heard. Admittedly, I must take the blame here. I could have at least left him a note on the refrigerator. With his pants down around his knees, Tony stumbled over my bed in absolute hysteria.

"Somteeng's in the toilet!" he screamed. "Eet's alive!"

To say Tony was an emotional Italian was to say that the Pope is Catholic. When Tony sat on the pot, he'd felt movement from below, sending him into a full-blown frenzy. It took some soothing assurances and encouragement of deep breathing to calm Tony down enough to explain to him my jubilant conquest of Fred. After much cajoling I finally persuaded him to return to the bathroom to see for himself.

Slowly we crept up to the toilet. Sure enough, during the night the carton had slowly lost its viscosity. There was only a corner of the box left protruding from the water, on which Fred's two hind feet were perched. The remainder of his body was stretched to the side of the bowl, his body barely clearing the water. There were teeth marks all around the underside of the lid, through which Fred had frantically and vainly tried to escape. Fortunately for Tony, his ass was a little out of reach for the little fiend to sink his chops into. Oh, how Fred must have suffered; oh, how I should have felt complete satisfaction and vindication at this delicious turn-of-events. But after looking at those two sad little eyes, I just couldn't force myself to flush the toilet. Yeah, I was a soft touch, especially with animals… even malicious ones.

I wrapped my hands in a towel, and when I reached for Fred he almost leapt into my arms, relieved that his hellacious night of torture had come to an end. Tony and I then carried him outside. We walked a good distance from the building before releasing him. He skittered off down a walkway, and before rounding a corner, stopped, turned, and bared his teeth. He seemed to say, *you may have won the battle, but I'm going to win the war.*

I never actually saw Fred again, but on more than one occasion when I had a female overnight guest, I could have sworn I saw movement out of the corner of my eye. Of course, it may have been my mind playing tricks on me, but I remembered the sneer Fred gave me as he rounded the corner.

I'd hate to think the hawk at Fenway was somehow exacting his revenge for the wrath of Fred. I mean, now that I've aged a bit, I kind of have a soft spot in my heart for the little guy.

Besides, who else could say that his moral compass was Fred the Rat?

CHAPTER 1

Nothing can compare to the old Broadway musicals of the 1930s – lavish sets, extravagant costumes, and sometimes hundreds of performers on stage. Back then, my father Eddie Tamblyn was a well-known stage actor and dancer. Because of his youthful exuberance, he mostly did juvenile roles in such musicals as *Good News* and the Fanchon and Marco traveling unit of *Follow Thru*. It was on the latter that he met Sally Aileen (Triplett), a chorus girl. Later, in between shows, they did "follow thru" and were married.

Dad went on to act in many early low budget movies, such as *College Cuties, Sweetheart of Sigma Chi* and *A Shot in the Dark* (not the same story as the Peter Sellers movie of the same name). Eddie also had a small, uncredited dance scene in the first Fred Astaire and Ginger Rogers film *Flying Down to Rio*. This is perhaps why I am so enchanted by the old musicals. It's in my blood!

Gradually the performing jobs became more and more scarce, to the point where Dad would sit by the phone every day, waiting for it to ring. It seemed that New York stage musicals were drying up; Dad was getting older and the juvenile roles were no longer being offered to him. Days and even weeks went by without so much as a call. By then my oldest brother Warren had been born. Finally, Mom and Dad decided to move to California, where many other actors had migrated. Soon afterward, in 1934, my other brother, Russ, was born.

Unfortunately, things didn't get much better as far as Dad's career. He finally decided to learn a trade, eventually working as an electronics inspector at Hughes Aircraft.

On February 5, 1943, about eight-and-a-half years later, Lawrence Arnold Tamblyn was born in Inglewood, California. Also born that month was George Harrison of the Beatles (February 25th). World War II was still raging in Europe, and US General Dwight D. Eisenhower became the Supreme Allied Commander. It was also the year that the All-American Girls Professional League was created due to the shortage of male baseball players, many of whom were fighting in the war.

I was later told that after having two sons, my parents wanted a girl, and were going to name her Constance, Connie for short. Fortunately, after I was born, they decided not to return me, especially after winning a baby contest sponsored by the hospital.

My family life was quite normal – with a few exceptions. My brother Russ began to show an inclination for acting at an early age. Because of my dad's bad experience in entertainment, he had said, "No child of mine is going to be in show business." Of course, later on, Russ became the actor that my dad always wanted to be. Ironically, many years later Russ prematurely said the same thing about his daughter, Amber Tamblyn, who like her father was brimming with talent. Both had destinies to fulfill. For that matter, so did I. There was no way on God's earth you could stop any of us. Also, as fate would have it, my mother had the wisdom to encourage all of us to fulfill our destinies.

One of my earliest memories was blissfully sitting in a bathtub at the age of one with my two brothers watching me while I played with my rubber ducky. In a child's eyes, the small bathtub was seemingly the size of an Olympic swimming pool. Russ and Warren were not overly thrilled at the task of soaping up their bratty little brother, whose full attention was on his ducky as it exhibited its mysterious ability to emerge from the frothy water and float upright no matter how many times I pushed it under the water. Even at that age, I was vaguely aware that the country was at war with Germany and Japan. My grandfather, Thomas Triplett, and his second wife lived in Oceanside, in the vicinity of Camp Pendleton Marine Base. Often on our visits, I observed a lot of soldiers on leave and even saw a fistfight between two marines, probably over a woman. I also recall some military aerial maneuvers over the ocean. In 1945, Harry Truman became president; Hitler had committed suicide in April, and the European war ended on May 7, 1945. Nuclear bombs were detonated over the cities of Hiroshima and Nagasaki, and the Japanese surrendered later that year, on August 14th, V-J Day.

At that time, I was two years old. We lived in a very small rented home, located at 572 1/2 East Florence Avenue in Inglewood. I vaguely recall the crowds celebrating in the streets.

I also recollect Dad having a pet duck. Everyone loved our feathered pet – except my maternal grandmother. Every time that duck saw her, he would launch an attack, and mercilessly nip at her ankles while chasing her down the street. A terrorist duck! We also had a Rhode Island Red rooster, who was discovered by Russ' agent and was in a several movies. I was told that he was the rooster featured at the opening of the early movie newsreels, but

I have a hard time believing that. There are no IMDb listings for roosters. Dad had a thing about birds!

Much to my dad's ire, Russ was constantly doing crazy-ass things as a kid. As Mom once described it, if there was a tiny piece of glass in an empty lot, Russ would find a way to fall on it and cut himself. One time, Dad took us fishing. He went to cast his line, and as he swung the rod back the hook caught on Russ' hand. Of course, he had to be rushed to the hospital to have it removed. It followed suit that Russ took to gymnastics at an early age. He had no fear! He could do front and back flips, handstands, and like a simian do any number of maneuvers, leaping from one tree branch to another. He was always covered in cuts and bruises.

Then there was the time we went camping, and my father decided to take the three of us and our dog, Tuffy, out on a lake in a small rowboat. We were a short distance out when Russ stood up in the middle of the boat holding an anchor. Dad, who I liken to Jackie Gleason's character Ralph Kramden in *The Honeymooners*, reacted in his usual fashion.

"Put that down!" he barked.

Startled, Russ immediately let dropped the heavy anchor into the water. In doing so, it knocked some of the floorboards loose. As the boat began to take on water, Dad grabbed me. Everyone, including the dog, began to swim toward the shore – except for Russ, who was still in the middle of the sinking boat.

"I can't swim!" he cried out.

To his dying day, my father always jokingly claimed that he actually had to think twice about going back to save my brother.

Because of Warren's reoccurring bouts with bronchitis, the doctor recommended that he live in a drier climate. The San Fernando Valley seemed to fit the bill. We moved to our new home located at 6937 Ben Avenue in North Hollywood when I was about three years old. It was a small two-bedroom house, for which my parents paid $7,000. Today, the same home would probably be worth over a half-million dollars. Mom and Dad had one bedroom, and all of us boys had the other. We had a large yard with plenty of fruit trees.

Back then, neighbors were a lot more sociable than today. Everyone knew everyone. Coincidentally, our neighbors on either side were in show business. To our left, was Sunny Clapp who, in 1927, wrote the classic song "Girl of My Dreams." He lived all of his life collecting songwriter's royalties off of that one song. Sunny was an early inspiration for me, leading me to dream that perhaps I could write that one big hit song. On the other side was Martin Garralaga, a well-known film and TV actor who was featured in such movies as *The Gay Cavalier* (1946). It's fascinating how the meaning of the word "gay" has changed in my lifetime. Martin was perhaps best known for his portrayal of "Pancho" in the early *Cisco Kid* films. Our other neighbors were the Hayes and the Johansens. They both had daughters, Cookie Hayes and Linda Johansen, who became friends and playmates.

Early on, Mother became aware of Russ' innate talent and made sure that he took dancing lessons. He was also a natural acrobat. Willie Covan, the famed African-American actor and tap dancer, became his teacher. Willie, who was featured in the 1938 movie *The Duke is Tops*, integrated my brother's gymnastics into the dance routines. I still remember watching some of his lessons – Willie rhythmically pounding his cane on the hardwood studio dance floor, keeping perfect time to the pianist, shouting out the moves, while Russ did his routines. One thing I was convinced of at such a young age was that ol' Willie knew his stuff! [1]

There was a neighborhood movie theater, and on Saturday mornings Russ would do impromptu skits onstage in between movies, which the kids in the audience loved. On one particular day in 1947, a talent scout was in the audience and asked Russ to audition for a play. The show, *The Stone Jungle,* was being directed by Lloyd Bridges. Rusty Tamblyn, as he was known back then, landed the starring role, opposite Bridges. Lloyd's two sons, Jeff and Beau Bridges, were even younger than Russ, and both came to many of the performances. So impressed was Bridges by Russ' performance, he sent a letter to mom and dad telling them that he thought Russ was a great actor and would be a major star someday. His talent at such a young age landed him on the *Ed Sullivan Show.* This led to his first small role, a non-speaking part in the 1948 film *The Boy with the Green Hair,* starring Dean Stockwell. Dean would become Russ' lifelong friend, and years later, the godfather of his daughter Amber. After that, the rolls started coming in regularly. Russ was immediately launched into stardom with *The Kid from Cleveland* in 1949, and *Father of the Bride,* and its sequel, *Father's Little Dividend,* starring Spencer Tracy and a young Elizabeth Taylor.

My closest childhood friend was Anthony, who lived on Agnes Avenue, the street directly behind us. To visit each other

---

1   www.imdb.com - IMDb, *Willie Covan Biography*

we merely hopped over a few fences and walls. There was always something very different about Anthony, which of course I didn't recognize as a kid. He turned out to be a constant source of trouble and seemed to bring out the worst in me. But he and I were almost inseparable. Since he was one year older than me, he showed me a lot of things I never knew before but was absolutely the worst person to do so. For instance, he introduced me to the difference between boys and girls in the most shocking way.

One day when I was about four years old, Anthony came over in a state of alarm. He told me that doctors had removed all of the penises from girls. That's why they behaved differently than boys. Of course, I didn't believe him – until we went to another childhood friend's home. The girl lifted her dress, pulled down her ruffled panties, and revealed the area of the missing appendage. There was even what I observed to be an apparent gash where the penis used to be.

I was absolutely horrified. I ran home screaming and straight to my bedroom, not discussing the shocking discovery with my mom or dad. I had nightmares that evening, afraid that our family doctor would bring the scissors and do the same to me! I really didn't want to wear a dress or play with dolls. It bothered me to such an extent that I finally got the nerve to discuss it with Russ. He was always someone I could go to without judgment or repercussions. To my relief, I was told that girls were born that way; the difference was for a reason. The graphic explanation still left me puzzled for many years to come.

As I said, Anthony wasn't the best person to learn about matters of sexuality. Like the time we were walking in a nearby neighborhood street and I saw a man strutting in a very feminine manner. In asking Anthony about this, he told me that the man had stepped on a land mine in the war. For years after that, every gay man I came upon was perceived as a war hero. Today, I realize that perhaps some genuinely were.

I grew up watching TV shows like *Ozzie and Harriet* and *I Love Lucy*. However, my biggest influence was viewing old Laurel and Hardy, Three Stooges, and Marx Brothers movies and shorts, multiple times. There was something about slapstick comedy that stuck with me, perhaps because a lot of it originated on the Vaudeville stage where my father and mother met.

For me, life was full of adventures and discoveries. There was an empty lot up the street, filled with weeds and crabgrass. It was perfect for the neighborhood kids to play war, tossing dirt clods at one another, pretending they were grenades. It was also an opportune place for underground tunnels. We would dig gullies, cover them with wood, and then shovel dirt on top; complete stealth from unwanted visitors. Unfortunately, on one occasion our mailman decided to take a short cut across the lot and accidentally stumbled into our underground hideaway. In the process, he caused a massive cave-in. Fortunately, he wasn't hurt, and no one was in the tunnel at the time. When our parents found out, we were made to fill in all of the gullies, which stretched from one end of the lot to the other. We also had to apologize to the mail carrier who had to spend a great deal of time digging up and dusting off his mail. But Bob the mailman was a friendly sort. He realized that he was on our turf, and mostly laughed about his experience. Playing in the dirt is what kids did back in those days. Doctors now claim that being exposed to bacteria in dirt keeps children from allergies and asthma later on in life. But what the hell did we know? We were just kids being kids.

There were some other adventures of a different kind, like the time Anthony and I decided to investigate an old run-down shack nearby on an adjoining street. The only reason the shack was still standing was that the termites were holding hands. The entire structure had a pronounced tilt to it. We climbed in through a window and began to explore the interior. Rather than being barren, we found some boxes filled with old photographs, all dating back to the 1920s, one of which was a baseball team of that period.

While digging through the photos, I began to feel an eerie sensation and the hairs on my neck stood up. I slowly turned and was startled to discover an old man staring at us through the window. His pallor was ghostly white, and although he said not a word, he had a most menacing scowl on his face. I could have sworn I had seen his face on one of the photos.

The only way out was through the other window next to him. Anthony leaped out first, and I quickly followed, diving headfirst and rolling over on the outside dirt. As I jumped up and began to run, I turned to look back. The old man was nowhere to be seen. We both saw him, so I can't attribute this to childhood fantasies and imagination. However, I'll never really know if he was real or an apparition.

That wasn't the only supernatural experience I had.

I went through a period of having recurring nightmares. Each dream was always the same: A demented clown—definitely not the kind you saw at the circus — entered my bedroom from the closet. He crept up to my bed, spread his arms wide, and fiercely growled at me. Wide awake and terrified, I dove under the covers. After some time, I emerged to discover that the clown, like the old man outside the shack, had completely disappeared.

These serial episodes continued for several months.

Finally, one night I decided I'd had enough. Right on cue, the clown made his usual entrance from the closet, and his usual menacing walk up to my bed, and his usual hair-raising snarl. But this time I acted first; jumping up and spreading my arms in a most fearsome manner, I growled at him with everything I had. Surprised and shocked, the clown screamed in fear, turned around, and made a hasty retreat back into the closet. After that, I never saw him again. Years later when I read Stephen King's book *It*, I noticed the remarkable resemblance to Pennywise the clown. As a child, King must have had the same nightmares that I did. Paradoxically, years later King was known to have been an admirer of the Standells and mentioned us in at least one article.[2]

Recently I was invited to a lecture by author Stephen LeBerge, who along with Howard Rheingold wrote the book *Exploring the World of Lucid Dreaming*. LeBerge was addressing the issue of serial nightmares. Through his research at his Stanford University laboratory, he formulated the concept that you can significantly influence the outcome of your dreams by confronting whatever the demon is. Of course, as a child, I had no concept of *Lucid Dreaming*, but that's what I had unwittingly done when I

---

2   www.ew.com - *What Stephen King and "Fever Pitch" have in common* (2007)

had conquered the clown. Pretty damned brazen for a five-year-old.

Were the old man and the clown real? They were pretty damn real to me, but then again, imaginary monsters could easily exist in a child's eyes. My persistence in overcoming obstacles, supernatural or otherwise, would pay off much later in life. [3]

I was enrolled in Kindergarten at Victory Elementary School. I took to art almost immediately, painting on anything and everything. Unfortunately, I chose the school wall upon which to paint my most awesome masterpiece, a green sea monster. Back then, corporal punishment was used when an offense such as this occurred. The career of a budding graffiti artist came to an abrupt halt with a few swats from a two-foot paddle. OUCH!

My parents decided that I would get a much better education in a parochial environment, so I was placed in Laurel Hall Lutheran Elementary school. Part of our curriculum was Bible study, much of which was rather confusing, and brought out the skeptic in me. Like… how was Jonah able to be swallowed by a whale, when those animals were incapable of doing so? And… how did Shadrach, Meshach, and Abednego get thrown into the blazing furnace without getting burnt to a crisp? Of course, the standard answer was "God can do anything." There was a part of me that wanted to believe this since I'd always dreamed of sprouting wings and taking flight. One can always wish for the impossible. I attempted to do so on many occasions – with cardboard wings, I tried to sail off of the shed in our backyard, only to fall flat on my face. Saturday mornings we used to go to the morning

---

3   Ballantine Books, *Exploring the World of Lucid Dreaming* (1991)

matinees and watch the serials like *Superman* and *Rocket Man*. I tried emulating both with the same failed results.

My first-grade teacher was Miss Gooch. She had an uncanny resemblance to Margaret Hamilton, the Wicked Witch of the West in *The Wizard of Oz*. She had the meanest grimace I'd ever seen on a teacher. Gooch had a particular method for dealing with class clowns like me. She'd pick me up by my hair and hold on until I promised to behave, which was almost immediately. I always expected her to threaten me with, "I'll get you and your little dog too." I thought I had solved the punishment problem when I decided to get a buzz cut, but she then picked me up by the ears. DOUBLE OUCH!!

Laurel Hall was also where I met my first girlfriend, Pamela Stewart. Actually, she was the girlfriend of my best friend Buddy, but Pamela liked us both. Friends always shared, and at that age, girlfriends were just as sharable as toys and baseball cards. Eventually, Pamela dropped Buddy and we became exclusive. Pamela also had the distinction of being the first girl I ever kissed. I was invited to her home one day after school. Her mother went out to pick up the mail, and Pamela pushed me into a hall closet and laid a huge kiss on me. It was the sweetest, most precious gift I had ever received, and it gave me a tingling sensation from head to toe. It was an experience that shook me to my core, one that I remember to this day. After all these years, Pamela and I found each other on Facebook, and we often reminisce about that special moment.

Speaking of shaking, in 1952 I was sleeping alone in my bedroom when at about 4:00 in the morning, my bed started to violently shake, and then proceed to dance across the room. At first, I thought it was the clown coming to torment me again, but then I noticed that the entire house was shaking. Through the bedroom window, I could see the dark sky lit up by electrical sparks from downed power lines. I screamed and was relieved when the shaking finally stopped, and my family came rushing in to check on me. That was the 1952 Bakersfield earthquake, magnitude 7.7. I have since lived through three of them, and, quite frankly, would rather face a California shaker than a hurricane or a tornado. [4]

Anthony and I were still very close. However, I noticed he always came to my home to play; I never went to his. My mother regularly had him over for lunch or dinner. It wasn't until the day when he didn't show up that I got curious and climbed over several walls to visit his home. I found him in the backyard tool shed covered in bruises. His father, Salvatore, had beaten him, and had done so regularly for quite some time. I'd never noticed it before because the bruises were unseen. In those days, child abuse was rarely reported to authorities. I suppose that this was the cause of Anthony's constant knack for getting me into trouble, to try to equal the playing field.

When I finally met his father, Sal scared the shit out of me. A large, imposing man with a ruddy face, he had a foul mouth and obvious short fuse.

Anthony's mother, Rose, was equally strange, but in a different way. For instance, she professed to have received messages from God in the clouds and spoke of Martians living amongst us.

---

4   www.sjvgeology.org - San Joaquin Valley Geology, *The white Wolf Fault and the Bakesfield Earthquake of 1952*

She also babbled about "the Lady in White," which I attributed to her lunacy. One day, Rose finally went completely off her rocker, walking down the middle of the street, stripping off her clothes, and giggling like a child. After that, she disappeared for a while, and I later learned that she had been placed in the Camarillo State Mental Hospital. After an extensive stay, which included shock therapy, she finally returned home – still weird, but more subdued. I never again heard her talk about the Lady in White, but later learned that she wasn't so delusional after all.

One useful thing that Anthony had learned from his father was carpentry. He and I built a very elaborate tree house in an apricot tree on the side of my family's home. It had a shingled-roof with two kid-sized rooms and an attic. By running an extension cord out through the bathroom window, we had electricity – all the comforts of home. Anthony and I would spend many nights camping out in the tree house being gently rocked back and forth and listening to the lilting rustle of the leaves around us.

By then we better understood the difference between boys and girls, so the tree hut was the perfect place to explore those differences. We would often bring Linda and Cookie up there and play doctor with them, more out of curiosity than anything else. We also had ringside seats for the show in the window of Sunny Clapp's backyard rental cottage next door. The inhabitants were newlyweds and rarely closed their window shades. Anthony and I rather enjoyed the nightly performances. We were shameless voyeurs, but the show was worth it.

Having grown up in a show business family, I think it was in my genes to be a performer. At first, I wanted to be an actor like

Russ. At the age of seven, Russ got me a small part in an episode of the TV series *Big Town*. He was supposed to star in it, but because he was under contract with MGM, they wouldn't allow him to do it. The particular episode was called "Tough Guy." I think that was just the working title because I never could find it in the IMDb listing. In the scene, I said a few lines and shot my little brother with a squirt gun, which I enjoyed, especially since we had to do several takes to get it right.

Unfortunately, I never got to see the episode. On the date of the broadcast, my family and I were on a vacation which had been planned for quite some time. We were driving through Seattle when we decided to stop for the night. Back then, when you went to see a movie, they usually had some kind of intermission show. Such was the case when we went to catch a movie at a small theater. During the intermission, they asked for volunteers for a talent show, and wouldn't you know it, I raised my hand. As I confidently walked toward the stage, I noticed that both of my brothers shrank down in their chairs and my parents both sat with their mouths agape. Accompanied by a small band I sang the song "Four Leaf Clover," and a song I learned from my dad. Surprisingly, I took first place in the contest, perhaps more for my cuteness than anything. My prize was a $1.00 bill, and it was more money than I'd seen in my whole life! I ended up buying a toy sailboat with my fortune. This was actually my first paying gig as a singer – and perhaps the birth of my career.

Russ drove a cool maroon Mercury convertible, the rear-end lowered with fender skirts or "spats," as they used to call them. They were the rage back then but were the prime target of thieves.

My brother decided to stay one step ahead of them by attaching razor blades to the underside of the skirts.

Well, it didn't work out quite the way he thought it would. We all walked out to the street one morning to find blood spattered on the ground next to his car. The skirts were still there alright, but the rear side of his car was kicked in. I guess the razorblades were not such a *sharp* idea after all.

In addition to his acting, Russ was a natural at gymnastics in high school. He was able to compete in lots of competitions at sporting events and took the All-City championship. When he came home from school, he would walk up the driveway on his hands, open the front door, and go into our bedroom. Russ once accepted a dare to do something only a circus performer would attempt. He denies this ever took place, but along with other neighborhood kids I saw it with my own eyes. There he was, almost defying gravity, doing a handstand atop a telephone pole.

I did stupid and dangerous things myself. My family decided to purchase a new 1954 Buick Century. Dad learned he could save money by picking the car up at the factory in Flint, Michigan, right off the assembly line. We took the Santa Fe train to Flint, and checked into a hotel, in a room near the top floor of a twenty-five-story hotel. One morning, I snuck out of the room and took the stairs up to the roof. Slowly I walked to the ledge. But didn't stop there. I proceeded to climb it, and dangled the lower half of my body over the side. Nothing was stopping me from falling to the street below.

Why did I do this, you ask? Because I was a stupid kid, that's why. To this day I shudder at my lapse of common sense.

Yeah, that was me – always testing the limits. Like brother, like brother.

My mother played a very strong role in my upbringing. She was mostly the one to discipline me and set me straight. She also provided one of the most embarrassing moments in my life. Our house had only one bathroom. Without telling me, Mom had painted the toilet seat. After sitting on it, of course, I had a perfect white "O" emblazoned on my ass. Back then, we had only lead-based paint, so putting turpentine on my rear end was the only remedy – and not the most pleasant experience. For some time afterward, I was the *butt* of all the family jokes.

Mom was also responsible for teaching me how to stand up to bullies. Most every day I'd walk to and from school, which was about a mile-and-a-half. On the way back, a couple of kids began to harass me. Their strength was in their numbers since neither of them was bigger than me. On one particular day, Mom drove up on the scene. She quickly realized that the boys were ganging up on me and intervened. To my surprise and horror, she volunteered that I would be glad to take them on one-at-a-time, and then dared them to fight me. After a few moments' consideration, they both chickened out.

It was my mother who taught me not to allow my problems to gang up on me.

The neighborhood where I lived had a bully whose name was Doodie Miller, and he terrified all of us kids. He was pretty big for his age, always dressed as an Apache tribal warrior with war paint and carried an authentic-looking tomahawk. Even more menacing than that was the sound he made as he chased us:

SHHH shhhh shhhh shhhh, SHHH shhhh shhhh shhhh, rhythmically done as though he was beating a tom-tom drum while shaking turtle shell rattles. Although he never seemed to catch us, we truly believed that if he did, he would scalp us. These terrifying encounters with Doodie took place for several years. One day when I was alone, I was walking through an alley, completely unaware of the ominous presence behind me – until I heard the terrifying SHHH shhhh shhhh shhhh, which sent chills up my spine. I began to run as fast as I could, with Doodie in hot pursuit and gaining on me, the rhythmic SHHH shhhh shhhh shhhh increasing in speed and intensity. I knew my ass was grass because the alley ended with a high wall and no other means of escape. When I finally reached the wall, I attempted to climb it, but Doodie by now had caught up to me.

Oh God, this was it! I was doomed! My towhead locks were to become a permanent fixture on the handle of Doodie's tomahawk! What happened next is inexplicable, and uncharacteristic of me. I grabbed Doodie's outstretched hand and bit it as hard as I could. With a wretched, painful yowl Doodie dropped the tomahawk he had been holding with the other hand. But… there was no discernable clunk as the ax hit the ground. He quickly retracted his bleeding hand, gazing at it in disbelief, then tearfully screamed out the first actual words I ever heard him utter: "Why did you do that?"

To which I truthfully replied, "I didn't want to get scalped."

What he said next was something I didn't anticipate.

"I was only foolin'!" he bellowed, as he picked up the rubber tomahawk with his good hand. Then he turned and ran in the opposite direction, howling like a wounded dog all the way down the alley and around the corner.

I don't think I or any of the other kids saw much of Doodie after that, but we did hear rumors that he had a rather large bandage on his hand for quite some time.

Doodie was another phantom I had conquered, perhaps out of desperation, or by reenacting the confrontation with the clown. Or maybe it was simply taking to task my mother's words of wisdom, "The bigger they are, the harder they fall."

There would be many more Doodies to confront in my life.

CHAPTER 2

In 1955, Rosa Parks was arrested for civil disobedience, simply because she refused to sit in the back of the bus. It's also the year that the Vietnam conflict began, and the Mickey Mouse Club debuted on ABC TV.

That was also the year I entered the seventh grade at Sun Valley Junior High School. I was eleven years old. It was quite a change for me, going from a small, private parochial school to a public one with a lot more kids and no compulsory religion classes.

It was also where Anthony was enrolled. He almost got me into trouble on the first welcome night at the school. Fortunately, we didn't get caught, but I was with him when he cut the cord to the flagpole.

It was also at Sun Valley where I attended school dances and was introduced to the rock 'n' roll music that would influence me for the rest of my life: Chuck Berry, Little Richard, Buddy Holly and the Crickets, Elvis Presley, Fats Domino, Bill Haley and His Comets, and many more.

At Sun Valley, I took up the clarinet and played in the school marching band. However, my life took a dramatic change during a school sock hop in the gymnasium. For entertainment, there was a small combo who had just taken a break. I walked up on stage and picked up a guitar. I didn't know how to play it, but that didn't stop me from doing an Elvis Presley impersonation. I impressed the hell out of my friends, but the school staff wasn't too thrilled about my impromptu gyrations, not to mention my fooling around with someone else's property. I was sent home from school and received a severe tongue-lashing from my parents.

After this incident, I became strongly interested in playing the guitar. However, after receiving numerous guitar lessons, my instructor gave up on me. He said I wasn't learning anything from him. He was right. I had begun to pick up guitar riffs from 45 records. I quickly discovered that you could play almost any song with a combination of four chords. I remember one of the first songs I learned to perform was Link Wray's "Rumble."

The misadventures with Anthony continued. Like Ralphie in *A Christmas Story*, I received a BB gun for my Christmas present. I don't think it was a Red Rider, but it was pretty damned authentic in appearance – and a dream come true. It was my twelfth birthday. Other than the time I missed a target and shot out the window of a neighbor's home, the weapon didn't do much harm.

Until one day.

Anthony and I were fooling around with the gun and I playfully pointed it at him.

"How would you like it if I pointed it at you?" he snapped angrily.

I wasn't about to back down from his dare, so I puffed up my chest and replied, "Go ahead."

He took the gun from me, cocked it, and aimed it at my chest. I still didn't budge. Then Anthony aimed it at my face, point-blank. I was determined not to chicken out, so I didn't flinch. Little did I realize that he had his finger on the trigger. It suddenly went off, hitting me directly in my right eye. Blood came spurting out.

I was rushed by ambulance to the Adventist hospital in Glendale. My parents finally arrived, and everyone was panicked, perhaps even more than me. At first, the doctors couldn't tell how serious it was, or even if I would lose my eye. They had to run X-rays to see where the BB was lodged. It wasn't until the following day that we learned the results. Miraculously, the BB had bounced off of my eyelid. During that fraction of a second, I happened to blink – and that saved my eye. It was one of many close calls in my life.

All were happy and relieved at the good news, especially Anthony – whom I'm sure was beaten to a pulp by his father for doing such a stupid thing.

I was left with a severe eye contusion; the injured eye was considerably swollen. This had to be treated at the hospital, so my stay at Adventist turned into two weeks. Both eyes were bandaged so as not to cause extra strain on the good one. This had its positive side because I was forced to live like a blind person. In just that short period, my hearing and other senses compensated for the loss of vision. I could identify people by their footsteps and scents. This might have led to my fondness of sounds and music. It inspired me years later to write a children's song emphasizing the importance of sound in our lives.

Listen if you can to a singing bird
And you will suddenly understand

There can be beauty in sound
But it has to be found
And you can find it anywhere in the land.
Listen if you can to the falling rain
And you will suddenly realize
That everywhere you look is a wide-open book
Which you can read without using your eyes.

There were many ups and downs during my hospital stay. On the upside, one of the nurses at the hospital got flirty with me – maybe it was just to cheer me up, but in my mind's eye she was a hot blond who was coming on to me. Needless to say, I looked forward to her visits. The downside was that I had to eat hospital food. Being a Seventh Day Adventist hospital, it only provided vegetarian food, considerably blander than today's meatless meals.

When the bandages were finally removed, I had considerable difficulty in focusing on anything. I was finally able to see some of the staff I had been communicating with, and I must say that the imagined appearances did not match the actual – the blond bombshell nurse turned out to be a rotund brunette with a very painted face.

When I was finally discharged, I had to wear sunglasses any time I went out in the sun. Of course, this caused considerable teasing at school. Back then, only the tough dudes wore shades. I was just a skinny punk kid.

Sun Valley Junior High was a long walk for me down a road that ran parallel to the railroad tracks. Anthony convinced me to catch slow-moving freight trains and jump off when we got to the school. We did this successfully on many occasions, which considerably cut the travel time to school. We also met lots of hobos camped along the railroad tracks. Almost all of them were pretty cool people who enjoyed their lifestyles, and they had lots of interesting stories to share. Like us, but on a much grander scale, they hopped onto a passing train, but then rode in boxcars from city to city.

This mode of transportation began to turn sour for me one morning when the train we hopped gathered too much speed for us to be able to jump off when the time came. We had to ride it all the way to Burbank and then hitchhike back to school. On another occasion, the train was going too fast for Anthony, so I decided to do him one better. In running alongside a boxcar, I reached up to catch hold of the ladder. Unfortunately, my feet tripped on the gravel, and I let go of the ladder, falling and rolling toward the imposing wheels. I narrowly avoided catastrophe. Anthony couldn't believe his eyes. To this day, I cringe when I think of how close I was to amputation by the train's wheels.

Yeah, that was me; like my brother, I was always testing the limits.

Sun Valley Junior High had its share of students who would later become famous. One of my school friends was Linda Evans who starred in such TV series as *The Big Valley* and *Dynasty*. I ran into her years later when she came to see us at PJ's nightclub in Hollywood. I almost asked her, "Why didn't you mention who you were back when I knew you?" She was the sweet girl who sat next to me in homeroom long before she became famous. Also, my friend Paul Peterson of the *Donna Reed Show* and Mouseketeer Karen Pendleton went to our school. As I later worked with Cubby O'Brian and with Dick Dodd, I seemed to have close ties to the Mickey Mouse Club.

The boys and girls in middle school had an unusual way of bonding – they would go steady. The guy would provide a bulky ring, and the girl would wear it on a chain around her neck. You would never directly ask a girl to go steady. If you found some-body attractive, you would ask a friend to intercede on your behalf – almost like a second. That was the extent of the relation-ship. In many cases, you rarely communicated with the object of your affection. I can't remember how many girls I went steady with, but my skull and crossbones ring got lots of wear. I wonder why in the hell I never approached Linda Evans.

I would be remiss if I didn't mention our English teacher, Ms. Caruthers, who was an ex-stripper. Some of the hormonally-rich boys in her class failed English because they were too preoccupied drooling over her shapely figure. Boys just couldn't get enough of her tight skirts and low-cut blouses. I heard that she later retired from teaching and went to back into stripping full-time. She must have decided that Burlesque was far more lucrative. At least that way she got paid for having her body swooned over.

In April 1956, my brother Russ struck up a relationship with Elvis Presley. Elvis had just finished his second movie, *Loving You*, and wanted a place for him and his buddies to hole up so he asked Russ if he could rent his beach house in Malibu for a few weeks. So Russ came back home and stayed with us.

I was a big fan of Elvis, especially his records like "Don't Be Cruel," "Hound Dog," and "Heartbreak Hotel." Like Carl Perkins, and Gene Vincent and the Blue Caps, there was something raw and untamed about these early rockabilly songs that spoke to me and influenced my music writing.

I returned home from school one day, and Russ was talking on the phone.

"Hey Larry!" he said, beckoning me over, "there's someone who wants to talk with you."

Curious, I walked over, and Russ handed me the phone. In a deep Southern drawl, I heard, "Well, hello, Larry."

I paused for a moment, then shyly responded, "Hi, who's this?"

He chuckled and said, "Your biggest fan, Elvis."

I almost fainted on the spot. Russ had told him about my rock 'n' roll aspirations. Elvis finished the conversation with "Keep pickin' away at that guitar, buddy."

I was sworn to secrecy by Russ not to give anyone his phone number, which now temporarily belonged to Elvis, but made the mistake of telling Anthony, who then told another friend. Soon word got out in school that I had Elvis' phone number. Kids were doing everything to extrapolate the information from me, including quite a few interesting propositions from some of the girls. However, I kept my mouth and pants zipped, and never revealed the sacred number. Elvis would have been proud.

Russ later served as an uncredited choreographer for Elvis in the movie *Jailhouse Rock*. [5]

As mentioned, Dad had a fondness for birds. One day he brought home a Mexican Red Headed Parrot that he'd purchased

---

5   www.fromthevaults-boppinbob.blogspot.com - *Russ Tamblyn, From the Vaults*

from a pet store. In honor of our next-door neighbor, he named the bird Pancho.

Pancho soon became an important member of the family. When Dad came home from work, he would immediately grab Pancho and play with him, rarely acknowledging anyone else. Placing Pancho on his lap, he would turn the bird over on its back and then scratch his head. Pancho would always respond with a very contented "Ahh-h-h-h-h." I really believed that Pancho was human, because not only did he repeat words, but he was also able to understand them and, in some cases, string them together into sentences. My family by then had converted to Mormonism, and my oldest brother Warren, a staunch Mormon, taught Pancho to say "Joseph Smith." At the same time, Anthony was teaching Pancho a few swear words. Much to Warren's chagrin, Pancho came up with the phrase "Go to hell, Joseph Smith."

Pancho was also able to identify different members of the household. I was over at Anthony's house one day, and I heard my mother calling "La-r-r-r-y!" I ran home only to discover that it wasn't Mom who was calling me, but Pancho. He had perfected the timbre of Mom's voice. He even laughed at me as I walked into the house. The bird could also identify the cat. He used to call out, "Here kitty, kitty, kitty." When the cat showed up, he would get laughed at as well. If you asked him "How does the eagle go?" he would spread his wings and turn his head to the side. Parrots worship eagles.

I might have been a little jealous of all of the attention Pancho received. One day, just before Dad was to arrive home from work, I took Pancho out of his cage and put him in my room. Then, I mischievously placed our fat cat inside the birdcage and spread some of Pancho's feathers around. When Dad arrived home, like clockwork he went straight to the birdcage. I can still hear the agonizing scream. When I could no longer hold back, I let loose with a sinister chuckle and admitted the prank, assuring Dad that the bird was perfectly unharmed.

Unfortunately, the prank didn't get the results that I was hoping for. Instead of giving me some much-needed attention, Dad didn't talk to me for a week.

Much like me, that parrot had gallows humor. By then, our dog, Tuffy, was getting very old and would soundly snooze on the hardwood floor. Dad would let Pancho loose, and he would roam around on the floor, playfully dragging his beak on the flooring. He would eventually sneak up behind the dog, and then bite him on the tail. Poor Tuffy was always startled awake, only to see that damned bird who would let loose with his maniacal laugh. Unfortunately, the poor dog spent his last days suffering surprise attacks from the mischievous redhead. I do believe that when he finally passed, he was indeed at peace.

I put my first rock 'n' roll band together when I was just 13 years old. We used to rehearse at my home. The neighbors all enjoyed the music, and many, including Sunny Clapp from next door, would drop by to listen. The band pooled money together to make our first recording at a local recording studio. I still have the acetate of "Rocking Joanie" by Larry Tamblyn and the Blackjacks. The song was very much influenced by "Be-Bop-A-Lula." Besides Bill Haley and His Comets, Gene Vincent and the Blue Caps was one of the first rock groups that inspired me.

My family seemed to get a kick out of our band practices, including Pancho. When my dad would put him on the floor, the bird's eyes would dilate (meaning he was grooving to the music), and he would dance around, singing, "Du-de-du-de-du." In fact, it got so the band didn't have to play for Pancho to perform. All we'd have to do was clap our hands in rhythm, and Pancho would do his song and dance. He was a natural. Pancho the rock star!

Anthony continued to have a knack for getting me into trouble. He began to shoplift at a local market and dared me to join him. I hesitantly accepted the challenge and heisted a few little things. Well, wouldn't you know it, Anthony managed to get caught and squealed on me. When my mother learned of this, she marched me over to the store where I had to face the manager, and first apologize to him and then reimburse the money from the stolen merchandise, which amounted to a few dollars. I never shoplifted again.

Anthony later chose to play a sick joke on the owner of a neighborhood liquor store. Old man Balzer was nice to all of the local kids, and his store on Van Owen Street was one of our hangouts. In the trashcan behind the store, Anthony found an empty beer bottle and filled it up with his urine. He then screwed the cap back on and snuck it into the store, placing the bottle on the shelf next to the other spirits. The amber color perfectly matched the other Schlitz beers. We then returned home.

But then, I began thinking about Anthony's horrible prank; God forbid, what if someone would purchase that bottle, and worse yet…take a swig. Ewwww!

I hurried back to the store, and stealthily removed the bottle. Balzer was never the wiser. He would have been pissed.

Anthony always seemed to avoid scrapes while managing to get me into them. One day he called up the leader of a local gang of thugs and challenged him to a fight. Of course, he had no intention of following through. However, since I was Anthony's friend, I reaped the results of his prank. It was a day when my mother happened to be taking Dad to the doctor's office, so I was home alone. The gang showed up at my door, pushed their way in, and when I wouldn't hand over Anthony's address, they beat the shit out of me, leaving me with a black eye and a swollen jaw.

The gang was finally caught when someone squealed on them. I think one of them had to do time in juvenile hall. They were pretty big, ugly-looking dudes. At least they didn't use guns back then. What one goes through for a friend!

I used to sleep in the enclosed patio in the rear of the house during the summer. I had a girlfriend named Marsha, who lived nearby, and she invited me to come to her house late at night when her parents were asleep. She would sneak me in through the back door, and into her bedroom. Then we would slip under the covers. We never went further than kissing, nor did I have the necessary skills or experience. But it was exciting and, yes, very dangerous.

Marsha and I continued these rendezvous throughout the summer, until one night when things went awry.

As usual, we made out, but on this particular night we were both tired and fell asleep. We were awakened in the morning by a knock on her bedroom door. It was her father. He wanted to say goodbye before he went to work!

I quickly gathered up my things and rushed into the closet. Once inside, I realized I'd made a huge oversight. Marsha unlocked her door, and her dad stepped forward to kiss her, tripping over my shoes, which had been left right in the middle of the room! Watching this through a crack in the closet door, I was absolutely petrified. I was dead for sure! Fortunately, he hadn't noticed what he'd stumbled over, said goodbye to her, and exited the room. An extremely close call, and one that could have proven to be deadly for me! We both laughed about it, but I was still shaking from the experience when I walked back home.

Marsha was a very sweet, pretty girl. Our romance fizzled out by the end of the summer, after my mother caught me after sneaking out one night. Poncho had squealed on me. During the night, he had called out "La-r-r-r-y!"

In hopes of setting me on the straight on the narrow, my mother talked me into joining the DeMolays, a fraternal organization for boys aged twelve and up. My mother thought that joining them might help me elevate my morals. In fact, it had the opposite effect. Our hip DeMolay group leader decided to take us on a field trip to Tijuana. After all, what better place for a group of boys to experience high ideals than a nightclub filled with hookers? Once there I was approached by one well-endowed woman, but fortunately I had neither the money nor the dexterities to follow through.

At one of the DeMolay meetings, though, I met Scott Engel, a terrific guitarist and singer with whom I was very impressed.

Scott would later partner up with Standells drummer Gary Leeds and John Maus to form the Walker Brothers. Another older adviser was a good friend of the famous singing cowboy Roy Rogers and his singing wife Dale Evans. One day he took me to their home. I found them both to be very down-to-earth and genuinely nice people. I also met their daughter, Linda. That evening, Linda and I were sitting on the sofa necking while the others were in a different room. I was just barely getting to first base when Dale Evans came walking by. To my astonishment, she didn't say a word. I would later learn that Dale had quite a rough life before meeting Roy. Linda and I remained friends but eventually fell out of touch. To this day, I don't really know if Dale Evans saw me getting fresh with her daughter.

It was during this period that I began to see changes in my dad. He seemed to be very distant. He would yell at me for the slightest reason. One time, I was playing out on the street, and a car came speeding by, running over and killing my new pet dog. I was in tears, and inconsolable. It didn't help matters when Dad came out of the house, and instead of offering comfort, screamed at me for being irresponsible. He later apologized, explaining that he wasn't feeling well. But as a kid, I didn't fully understand, and refused to forgive him.

I began to hate him for his bursts of anger.

I hadn't realized it, but along with the change in behavior, my father had been sleeping quite a lot. He was taken to the doctor, who then referred him to an oncologist. The news wasn't good. Dad had a brain tumor. He was operated on, and the tumor removed. It was malignant. We were told that he had six months to live.

The family chose not to tell him. I always questioned that decision but kept my end of the promise and never mentioned it to Dad. We spent those last months enjoying his company, going on vacations, and visiting with relatives. We tried to make the best of it, sharing jokes with Dad, laughing, singing, but it was never quite the same knowing that the end was coming.

In removing the tumor from the left side of his brain, the frontal lobe, which dealt with speech, was affected. Dad's condition worsened. It was very difficult for him to communicate. There were many things that I wanted to discuss with him, like telling him that I finally understood and forgave him for his abusive behavior, but because of his condition, I was unable.

The dreaded day finally came, much sooner than I had expected, and I wasn't ready to deal with it. His funeral was especially difficult for me. So many things left unsaid. I never had a chance to say goodbye.

I can remember Russ crying when they played my dad's favorite song "Pennies from Heaven." I was devastated too, but I masked my emotions, and never revealed how angry and betrayed I felt. After six months of knowing his life was coming to an end, it was almost a relief for me when he finally died.

It wasn't until much later that I realized the major effect he had on me, both in talent and who I am as a person. I also had no idea that he would, on several occasions throughout my life, make his presence known to me.

This was also about the time I left the LDS Church. There was a wild side to me that I hadn't yet explored.

Pancho took Dad's death as badly as we did. He began to scream uncontrollably from sunup to sundown. We tried everything to console him. I even scratched his head, but to him it wasn't the same as Dad. My mother was in mourning, so the bird, as a constant, vocal reminder of my Dad's absence, wasn't much help. We were forced to give Pancho to a pet shop.

Instead of selling him, though, the pet shop owner chose to keep him – even after the store caught on fire and the bird laughed throughout the entire evacuation. The pet shop was eventually re-built, and Pancho stayed with them for over forty-five years. The owner grew very close to the bird and eventually took Pancho home to live with him. I guess the kindly old gentleman had successfully replaced the loss of my dad. If I only had the same luck!

It didn't help that my mother remarried almost immediately after Dad's death, a man she hardly knew. By then, Russ and Warren no longer lived at home. Russ had married actress and model Venetia Stevenson. Warren lived with his Mormon friends from Brigham Young University. So, I had to deal directly with my stepfather. Mom later admitted that it was a terrible mistake.

Pat was a window washer from New York whom she had met while vacationing. He was pretty decent at first, but that was just his cover. Eventually, he became abusive toward both Mom and me. Pat constantly told me that I was good for nothing and that I'd never amount to shit. None of us had known that he was an alcoholic. A certain amount of that type of emotional abuse stays with you for a long time. I guess that if I followed in his footsteps washing windows, I would have been considered successful.

One thing that was wonderful about my friend Anthony is that he loved my mother and felt protective of her. It was because of this that a near catastrophe occurred. One day, Pat was on a drunken rage and began pushing my mother around. After he left, Anthony and I arrived to discover that she had some bruises. She told us what had happened, and we took her to Anthony's home. His parents were away for a few days. Soon, Pat arrived in a drunken rage and demanded to see her. Anthony and I refused to let him in. Anthony went out the back way and returned around the side of the house with his father's gun, confronting Pat on the front lawn. However, even after Anthony threatened him with the gun, Pat refused to leave.

Anthony and triggers. I don't know if he intended it or not, but the gun went off, miraculously missing Pat. To keep the peace, Mom came out and agreed to return home with Pat.

Soon the police arrived, and Anthony was arrested for firing the gun. We tried to explain that he was only trying to protect my mother who had been beaten by Pat. But surprisingly, the detective said, "It's every man's right to beat his wife, and you had no cause to fire the gun."

Anthony was taken to the police station, but Pat, feigning benevolence, refused to file charges, and Anthony was set free. After that, Pat promised to reform, and later even joined the Mormon Church in order to prove that he was actually willing to change. Yeah, right.

In September 1957, I attended North Hollywood High School, where both of my brothers once were students. All of the buildings were old and decrepit. I found it to be very depressing, and I only lasted one semester there before transferring to John Francis Polytechnic High School in Sun Valley, which had recently been built.

One of the most positive influences on my life as a kid was my brother, Russ. Nine years my senior, I looked up to him. He did his best to fill in for the loss of our dad. Russ was always in my corner. I was a lot closer to him than my other brother Warren, who had absolutely no interest in the entertainment industry, and with whom I never seemed to bond with.

Russ, by then, was considered a movie star, but he always included me in his life. He was under contract at MGM, so I spent quite a few days with him on the movie sets, including those from *Retreat Hell* with Richard Carlson and Frank Lovejoy, *Hit the Deck* with Debbie Reynolds, and the musical *Seven Brides for Seven Brothers* with Howard Keel and Jane Powell. On some days, I would go into the small theater on the studio lot and watch Tom and Jerry cartoons. It was not uncommon for Russ to bring stars like Debbie Reynolds to our home to visit.

In 1958, Russ starred in a movie called *High School Confidential*, playing an undercover narc that comes to a new high school and muscles his way into the drug scene. Directed by Jack Arnold, the co-stars were Jan Sterling, John Drew Barrymore, and one of my favorite bombshells, Mamie Van Doren who is today a Facebook friend. I was even given an autographed photo of her. Va-va-voom!

More importantly, the film featured one of my rock 'n' roll heroes, Jerry Lee Lewis, who performed the movie's explosive title song. Jerry Lee was also influential in changing the direction of my music career. Up until then I had been a guitarist, but after seeing Jerry Lee in action I began to take an interest in the keyboards. Jerry Lee Lewis was way ahead of his time. He, along with my other idol Little Richard, made it possible for a singer/ keyboardist to take center stage. He sat behind the keyboard and sang rockabilly, the likes of which I'd never heard before. With his long, blond hair drooping over his face, he was all over the keyboard, an amazing showman who did things to the piano I'd never imagined, like climbing on top of it! After seeing the movie, my musical perspective changed forever. Along with feeding my interest in the entertainment business, Russ was also instrumental in me losing my virginity at the ripe old age of fifteen.

I was spending the weekend at his beach house. He had several friends over, including actor Nick Adams. One of Russ' friends was a very sexy young woman, the ex-girlfriend of a well-known actor. On this particular evening, she had gotten pretty drunk and passed out in the bedroom. In front of the others, Russ said, "Larry, it's time for you to get laid, and I want to make sure you do it right." He added that the girl in the other room was a willing participant. The others laughed and egged me on. I don't know if it was from being put on the spot or from raging hormones, but I braved going into the bedroom, took off my clothes and slipped under the covers next to the groggy girl. Everything seemed to… well, fall into place.

Somewhere in the fog, though, she began to mumble "Oh Russ…Rusty." Then, in a moment of passion, she reached up and ran her fingers through my hair. Suddenly they came to a screeching halt, as if "where are the curly locks?" Her fingers then slid down to feel my face – the jig was up! I got slugged, and I deserved it.

Later on, she laughed about it, so I guess it wasn't all that bad. This impromptu rendezvous started me on a quest that would last a good part of my younger years. Anything in a skirt was fair game.

My second sexual liaison was implemented unknowingly by my other brother, Warren. I traveled with him and several Mormon women to Salt Lake City. One night, he went to see a few of his college friends, leaving me alone with a twenty-one-year-old married woman whom I'd known years before when I attended church. Her husband was away on a mission. I'd always thought that she was a nice, wholesome girl… until that night, when she attacked me on the bed.

The first part was rather awkward because she had to remove her temple garments. They're like Long Johns, given only to members who are worthy of going into the temple. They're supposed to protect you, I guess— just not from yourself. After removing them, the rest was, well, pretty much no holds barred!

Warren was never the wiser; he would have killed me. But, hey, she started it, and Warren contributed – unknowingly – to my continuing delinquency.

CHAPTER 3

1958 was the year Khrushchev became Premier of the Soviet Union, the US Supreme Court ruled unanimously that Little Rock, Arkansas schools must integrate, Ricky Nelson's "Poor Little Fool" was number one on the Billboard charts, and Elvis Presley was inducted into the US Army. Memorable films of that year included *Cat on a Hot Tin Roof* and Alfred Hitchcock's *Vertigo*.

In January of that year, I began attending Polytechnic High School. Ironically, the school mascot was – you guessed it – a parrot. The school had a Driver's Education program, which I happened to have completed during the summer. Back then, you could get a driver's license with the completion of the program. As it turned out, I was only fifteen-and-a-half when I passed my license exam. I was perhaps one of the youngest drivers that year to get a license.

There was a great story floating around the high school in those days about some guys who had tied a chain between a telephone pole and the rear axle of a police car, then sped by the cops in their hotrod. When the cops took off to chase after them, the chain ripped off their axle, leaving them sitting motionless in the middle of the street with their siren blazing and lights flashing. George Lucas must have heard the same story because he included it in his early masterpiece *American Graffiti*, when a group of greasers named the Pharaohs talked Richard Dreyfus' character Curt into doing the same thing. Back then, if you had a lowered '56 or '57 Chevy, custom metallic blue paint job, Spinner hub caps on your wheels, fuzzy dice hanging from your mirror, custom tuck and roll upholstery from Tijuana, and a car club plaque in the rear window... man, you were the bee's knees.

It was also in high school that I formed my first rock band, the Emeralds. Members included Frank Fayed, Ron Montenegro, Wayne Edwards, and Darron Stanky. Most of them later went on to successful music careers.

North Hollywood and Sun Valley were heavily populated with Hispanics, some of whom were close high school friends of mine. My first serious girlfriend was a Latina named Nancy Garcia, who lived in a Sun Valley barrio. Our relationship was strictly platonic, but I sincerely thought I was in love with her. When I found out she was cheating on me, it broke my heart. As it turned out, years later I took Nancy out on a date, and I couldn't for the life of me figure out what I originally saw in her. Love sure as hell is blind.

I think the breakup with Nancy caused me to do some pretty stupid things in those days. In high school, a very curvilinear blond sat behind me in science class. One day, I was leaning back against her desk, and she grabbed my hand, guiding it slowly up her dress. Other male friends around me quickly caught on and closed in so no one would see this brazen act. It became an almost daily ritual in the class. It was extremely difficult to pretend to pay attention to the teacher as he gave a lecture on human anatomy while my mind was on just one particular part of the anatomy. Today I still cringe about this.

One day, my friends Judy and Patricia approached me on the way to class. Judy asked, "Hey Larry, we heard some rumors about you in science class. Are they true?"

I feigned ignorance. "What rumors?"

Judy's face then got red, "You know, sticking your hand up a girl's... dress."

My face displayed mock outrage. After taking a deep breath for dramatic purposes, I uttered, "How long have you known me, Judy?"

"Well, ever since Sun Valley Junior High," she shyly admitted, with Patricia nodding in agreement.

"And have you ever known me to do something as crazy as that, especially in front of a teacher?"

The complete absurdity of their accusations slowly set in. Both girls' faces turned a bright shade of red and they embarrassedly shook their heads no. They finally apologized for believing such a wild story.

It wasn't long afterward that I finally took the blond from my science class out on a date in my stepdad's beat-up Studebaker, in which he had left some of his window washing equipment. We went to a drive-in theater, where most of my trysts would take place. Quite honestly, I don't know if anyone ever went there to see a movie. We jumped in the back seat, took off our clothes and were about to make love when she stuck her foot in a cold bucket of water on the floor. I silently cursed Pat. Talk about a turn-off! But eventually, things warmed back up. From there on, my sexual proclivities became rather routine.

With the help of my parents, I purchased my first car, a 1952 Ford Mainline two-door sedan. To pay for it, I got a summertime job in a lamp factory. My job was to stick the lamp bases in a vat full of varnish. Working over a tub full of this stuff all day during the summer, with no air conditioning, left me pretty high by the end of my shift. Today, this would not come close to being acceptable standards by OCEA rules. I stuck it out until the fall when I returned to school.

I was a junior in high school when my music career began to show some promise. My band had finally started to earn money, playing for many wedding receptions and quinceañeras. Aside from the happiness and celebration of these events, a few of the receptions turned out to be quite combative. In many instances, after heavily consuming cervezas relatives of the groom would get into fistfights with the relatives of the bride. The fighting would continue to escalate until we played the crowd favorite "Corrido Rock," at which point all of the guests would cease fighting, make amends, and unite in dance.

We also played at a lot of school hops, both assemblies, and nighttime dances. I remember one night at a school dance, Russ brought in actress Tuesday Weld a big star at the time, to see me perform. The kids went wild when they saw both of them. My brother always supported my music in any way he could.

Fortunately, I had a car in which I could travel to the gigs; unfortunately, it was the cause of a painful memory. On the afternoon of a gig at the local Masonic Lodge, I was in a rush to run a few errands beforehand. In the process, I slammed the car door on my left middle finger. Holy shit, did it hurt! I rushed home, and my mother wrapped the swollen finger as best she could. That evening, I could only use four fingers on the guitar frets.

Every so often, I forgot and used my middle finger. The pain was unbearable. Maybe it was karmic payback for some of my sexual misdeeds. However, the show must go on, so somehow, I managed to get through the rest of the evening. I'm pretty sure I broke the tip of my finger, but it was never put in a cast. As a reminder, it's still slightly crooked today.

It also seemed that the police always singled me out as a possible drug offender. When the cop would shine a flashlight into my eyes, they wouldn't dilate properly. The doctor referred to it as "impaired pupillary light reflex," and didn't perceive it as anything serious. More than likely, it was the result of my earlier eye injury. This was perhaps why I shied away from drugs throughout much of my younger years.

In school, I belonged to a car club called the Innocents. They were anything but. They were more like the Pharaohs in *American Graffiti*.

I had a club party at my house, and it turned out to be quite a drunken affair. In fact, without anyone knowing it, one beefy member passed out in Sunny Clapp's yard. My mother and stepfather didn't hear about it until the following day, and I caught hell. So much for my membership in the Innocents. However, I remained good friends with several members, who were also great singers: Darron Stankey, Jim West, and Al Candelaria. We had a lot of talent in our high school. At the time, a friend of my brother's named Speed Copp acted as my manager. He set up an audition with Andex Records, a small label owned by Herb Alpert. We were introduced as Larry Tamblyn and the Echoes. At the audition, we played some songs that I wrote as well as some of the Echoes' material, in which Herb was much more impressed. Without my consent, Speed told Herb we were a package deal. I was completely embarrassed when the group told Herb that I wasn't part of their songs.

So, the label signed my three friends without me. The group soon left Andex to sign with Indigo Records, where they changed their name to the Innocents, after the car club. In 1960, they recorded the hit song "Honest I Do," produced by Gary Paxton and Kim Fowley. The record hit #28 on Billboard magazine charts. It was followed up by "Gee Whiz," which also reached #28 on Billboard. Then they backed up Kathy Young who recorded "A Thousand Stars" which reached #6 on the Billboard charts. [6][7] Being so close and yet so far from fame was a tough pill for me to swallow, and in the back of my mind I was constantly reminded of my stepdad's contention that I was destined for failure. But I refused to give up. Music was my mistress; she'd seen me through a lot of trials and tribulations, and I wasn't about to give up on her.

My band did lots of local shows, but there was another rock 'n' roll performer that we always seemed to be competing with for the same gigs. I was told that he was especially good. I didn't realize to what extent until the evening I was introduced to him at a high school hop in San Fernando. Ritchie Valens, who was several years older than me, gave me a welcoming embrace before his performance. He wasn't the greatest-looking guy in the world, but his wide smile and genuine warmth, plus amazing talent,

---

6   www.wikipedia.org - *The Innocents (US band)*
7   www.history-of-rock.com *Kathy Young and the Innocents*

more than made up for it. When he performed, he weaved his magic. Ritchie sang and played the guitar with such wizardry that I almost wanted to quit my musical career before it had barely started. He was the embodiment of everything that I wanted to be.

It wasn't long before Ritchie went on to considerable fame. His first record, "Come On, Let's Go" was an instant hit, followed up by "La Bamba" and "Donna." Ritchie Valens became a major star and a pioneer of early Chicano Rock. Of course, there was considerable envy on my part. I wanted to be up there with Ritchie in the limelight. But all of my dreams, hopes, and aspirations, pinned to the success of Ritchie Valens, were shattered on February 3, 1959 – two days before my sixteenth birthday – when he perished in a plane crash near Clear Lake, Iowa, along with Buddy Holly and J.P. "The Big Bopper" Richardson.

After that, I found it very difficult to pick up a guitar and play again. That is when I began to seriously make the switch to the piano.

In retrospect, I don't think that the movie *La Bamba,* made some 30 years later, did Ritchie justice. As good of an actor as Lou Diamond Philips was on screen, in my opinion he didn't have anywhere near the charisma that Ritchie had. The story itself was deeply flawed. The romance between Ritchie and Donna was pure fiction. The real Donna treated him like shit and could care less for him. Anyone who has ever listened to the lyrics would agree; "Donna" was a torch song.

The year after Ritchie's death, I was surprised to receive a call from *the* Donna. She sounded very confident and informed me

that she was going to record a song. She asked if I would be interested in being in her band. I wasn't sure, but out of loyalty to
Ritchie I agreed and met with her at her parents' home. Right
away, I knew this was something I didn't want to be involved in.
She didn't have much of a voice and was obviously just trying to
capitalize on Ritchie's fame, as well as, of course, her name. Donna's song was titled "Lost Without You." Like I had predicted, it
went nowhere.

This incident made me even more determined to follow in
Ritchie's footsteps. If Donna could do it, I sure as hell could.

At an alumni get-together years later, my high school friend,
Ken Lowry, reminded me of one of the most embarrassing days
in my life. He and a few friends joined me in auditioning for
Ritchie's label Del-Fi Records, which was owned by Bob Keane.
At that time the record company was located at 1610 N. Argyle, in
Hollywood. We went there totally unannounced and without an
appointment. The record company refused to meet with us. So,
we did the next best thing – we set up in the men's bathroom and
began to perform our repertoire. We weren't going to budge until
we met face-to-face with the head of the record company. Finally,
they gave in – I'm sure purely because of the complaints of the
other tenants in the building who wanted to use the restroom
without all of the racket.

The following day, Bob Keane invited us to a small recording
studio to lay down our audition tape. He was not present in the
studio when we recorded. However, I brought in my lyrics for
him to see. A little while later, he finally arrived at the studio to
listen to us. The first song was probably not the most appropriate

for winning the hearts of a recording company who'd just lost their major act in such a tragic manner.

"Rockin' at the Cemetery", written by yours truly.

Well all them cats are rockin' at the cemetery
I said all them cats are great big mean and hairy
Come on and jump and jive and don't look alive
Rockin' at the cemetery.

Keane only listened to the first verse before he violently threw the lyric sheets up in the air, yelled some obscenities, and stomped out of the studio. I never heard from him again, and I can't say that I blame him. Not my most stellar moment. Attribute it to the unhinged ambitiousness of a teenage rock star wannabe.

I finally got my shot at the music business in the latter part of 1959 when Speed Copp introduced me to the owner of Faro and Rampart Records, Eddie Davis. Eddie signed me to a record contract, and we also formed a publishing company called Tamcoda Music, made up of the first syllables of our last names. At that time, Eddie's labels were small operations. To finance his recordings, he worked as a fry cook in a small diner. Speed Copp kind of drifted off, and I never heard from him again. But Eddie would go on to become a major force in the birth to Chicano Rock, and it was through him that I later became involved in that music.

Eddie was also my mentor and manager. I don't think I fully appreciated the help, encouragement, and guidance he gave to me in those early days. My first recordings with Faro were my original songs "Dearest," a doo-wop ballad, and the rockabilly flipside, "Patty Ann."

For some reason, which I've never been able to figure out, I am listed on the Rockabilly Hall of Fame. [8]

I had the pleasure of working with a couple of great musicians on that session. One was the renowned sax player Plas Johnson, who is perhaps better known for his slinky solo in "The Pink Panther Theme." The other was guitarist Tommy Tedesco, who went on to become part of the Wrecking Crew – Hollywood session musicians who backed up almost every artist in the business.

The following year, 1960, we recorded two more of my originals "This is the Night" and "Destiny." "This Is the Night" was a regional hit in several markets including Philadelphia, where it reached #1. Eddie also sent me out on a small tour to promote the record. I had a chaperone, Allen, who took me to various venues and parties. It was a culture shock for me because at one of these events I was hit on by several pedophiles who invited me to join them in their hotel rooms. Even though I was repulsed by their offers, I turned down them down as gracefully as I could. Allen seemed to think nothing of the offers. Back in those days, I knew of several young up-and-coming singers who accepted those kinds of propositions – anything to advance their careers.

---

8   www.rockabillyhall.com – The Rockabilly Hall of Fame Legends List, *Larry Tamblyn, The Rockabilly Hall of Fame*

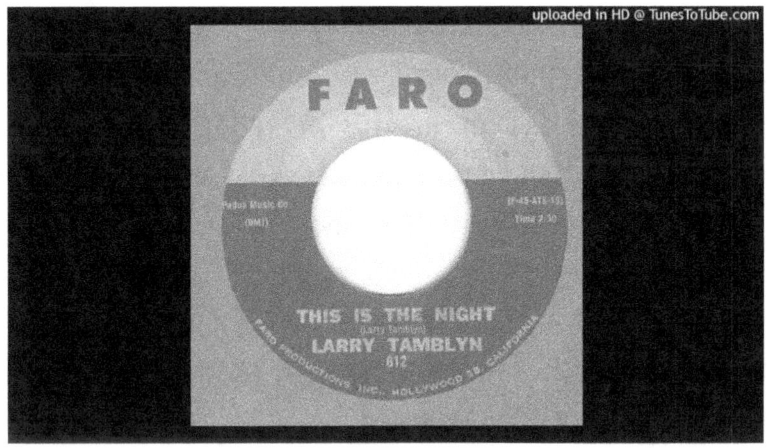

This is the Night record label

That same year, Eddie booked me on my first TV appearance, the original *Lloyd Thaxton Show*, on local channel 13 KCOP in Hollywood. Lloyd sat behind a desk, spinning records and lip-syncing to them. Unusually, the studio had no ceiling, using natural sunlight instead. Rainy weather played hell on some broadcast days. Lloyd played a few records before interviewing me. I can remember one of them was an instrumental by a group I'd never heard of, Paul Revere and the Raiders, with whom I would one day tour.

I also had the good fortune to do a show with one of my idols, and the number-one selling female vocalist, Connie Francis, who recorded such hits as, "Who's Sorry Now," and "Lipstick on Your Collar." This was the very first major concert I ever performed, and I will always cherish the memory. We were performing in San Francisco. At the airport beforehand, Connie asked me to go with her to get a soda. Leaving her entourage behind, we had only walked a short distance around the corner when suddenly the exhausted singer fainted. Like in a romantic movie, I caught her in my arms. What young hormonally-charged teenager wouldn't have dreamed of this scenario – his dream girl in his arms? Fortunately, Connie was a very petite five foot one, and I was able to carry her to a sofa and revive her, before going back for help. She later graciously thanked me and autographed a photo: "To Larry my hero – Follow your star."

Thanks, Connie – I think I did follow my star.

Several years later, Connie and I crossed paths again.

In 1960, I experienced another of the biggest thrills in my life: being on the set of *West Side Story*. I got to meet many of the stars of the film. One whom I'll never forget was Natalie Wood. I had such a huge crush on her in *Rebel Without a Cause*. Such a beautiful face – with the mouth of a sailor! I mean, I thought I knew all of the dirty words, but Natalie taught me a few more. And Rita Moreno was as vivacious in person as she was on screen.

I was taken to the gymnasium set, where they were about to film what would be become one of the most famous dance scenes. Some of the actors from the Sharks were standing around. One of them was flipping a knife. They were some pretty gnarly-looking dudes. Then they began their *Tendu* and *Plié* ballet exercises, and it suddenly brought everything into perspective. Academy Award winner George Chakiris became a lifelong friend of Russ, and eventually me. Unlike his character in the film, George has always been a kind and generous soul.

The highlight of the day was being invited to the sound stage when part of the musical score was being recorded. I'd never heard music like that in my life. Johnny Green conducted the orchestra doing the composition of Leonard Bernstein. They were recording the fight scene between Russ and George. Unlike regular motion pictures where the music is written and recorded in post-production, most of the scores for musicals are done first. They brought in Russ and George to go through their scene. Unknown to many was the fact that this was a choreographed dance routine. They needed to make certain that everything worked – and it did, flawlessly.

Nineteen sixty was also the year I graduated from high school. In addition to making my own music, I listened to favorite radio stations like KRLA and KFWB and developed an interest in becoming a disc jockey. Sometimes I would practice in my bedroom with a record player and a microphone, pretending I was actually on the air. Then Pat entered the room one day and began to give me criticism. Of course, he considered himself to be an expert at most everything, so I was given direction in diction and personality – this coming from a window washer.

Finally, I enrolled in the Don Martin School of Radio and Television Arts. Many of the top radio personalities, including Bob Eubanks of KRLA had graduated from the school. However, it wasn't quite what I thought it would be.

At that time, to begin as a radio broadcaster one had to become a combo-man, which meant one also had to run the transmitter, and to do so required a First-Class Radio Telephone license. So, I had to take courses in algebra and geometry, subjects normally associated with electronics engineering. We were then told that we had to pass Third, Second and finally First-Class license tests. But no problem, the school had the answers to the tests. As it turned out, during the time I attended the school all of the test questions were altered. But I managed to get a Third-Class Radio Telephone license. After graduating, I had a chance to work at a small station for less than minimum wage. All of a sudden, my music career started to look a lot more promising.

Eddie Davis had put a lot of faith in me by promoting many of the concert events I played at. Along with Russ, who was not always available, it was Eddie who I always went to when I needed personal help or advice. For example, the time I thought I had gotten a girl pregnant. I told Eddie of my predicament, and without question he offered to take care of any medical bills or pay for an abortion (which was illegal at that time). To my ultimate relief, the girl eventually informed me that she'd had her menstrual.

I'll never forget Eddie's words of wisdom: "A stiff prick has no brains." He was absolutely correct, but unfortunately, I didn't take his words to heart (or I should say a certain part of me didn't). I don't think that I ever thanked him enough for his advice and mentorship.

By 1961 and into 1962, I was involved with monthly concerts at the Rainbow Gardens in Pomona. I was the coordinator/arranger for the house band, the Mixtures, comprised of several of my old bandmates, including Wayne Edwards. The group also recorded for Eddie Davis. It was my job to learn the hits of the guest artists, like the Beach Boys (back then they were primarily a vocal group), Shirelles, Conway Twitty and Ral Donner, and then, before the concerts, teach them to the band. Then we would back the performers up during the show.

I was also playing gigs with various other bands, including one with Mouseketeer drummer Cubby O'Brien. Like Dick Dodd, another Mouseketeer drummer who was later part of the Standells, he was an incredible drummer. I made solo appearances at record hops promoting my record. I even had a very good female friend who I brought along with me as a sort of covert cheerleader. When I got on stage, she would begin to scream, soon joined in by other girls.

I also made guest appearances in concerts and local California TV shows, promoting my single records. I don't understand how, but I was also was booked at an all-black concert in San Francisco. At first, I thought nothing of it, until the star of the show, Lou Rawls, jokingly referred to me during the soundcheck and rehearsals as "white boy." Then I got it! I knew what it had been like for many black entertainers during those perilous years when the color of your skin was a hindrance. Pat Boone had covered Little Richard's songs like "Tutti Frutti," "Long Tall Sally," and "Lucille," and Fats Domino's "Ain't That a Shame." Unbelievably, the white media helped turn them into bigger sellers than the original versions. Boone later said in an interview that he thought he did those performers a favor, and that they were glad that he made those records. My answer to Pat: No, you didn't. You did them an injustice. The original performers only collected minimal fees, and he took away record sales from them.

I was one of those "white kids" who loved the original artists. I saw right through Pat Boone's feeble attempt to cover those great songs. Little Richard and Fats Domino were my heroes. I grew up listening to R&B artists. I spent many nights listening to my brother Russ' old R&B 78s. I was familiar with the works of John Lee Hooker, Jimmy Reed, Screamin' Jay Hawkins, Memphis Slim, Percy Mayfield, Otis Blackwell, and many more. They were all great influences on me. And the perversity of squeaky-white Pat Boone making a feeble effort to do "soul" was about as absurd as Larry Tamblyn being booked on an all-black show. Today, I often joke about this during my concerts. [9] [10]

My recordings didn't reach a national audience, and I was beginning to feel that I would never make any further headway in the record business. I began to have doubts about my singing and music writing abilities, that I could ever come close to matching the success of my friends Ritchie Valens or the Innocents. That all changed one day when I heard the song "Angel Baby" by Rosie and the Originals. Written by Rosie Hamlin, the San Diego teenager who fronted the group, the song was #1 on the radio charts and sounded as though it was made by a bunch of kids who had picked up their instruments for the very first time. It had the same four chords that I first learned when picking up the guitar: E, C# minor, A and B, monotonously repeated over and over. Rosie's nasal voice didn't add much to the song. If that wasn't bad enough, it featured an abysmal screechy sax solo, and the drummer got lost somewhere in the middle; instead of playing the snare on the two and four beats, he somehow ended up on one and three. I think he eventually found his groove near the end. This could have been the instrumental backing

---

9   www.okayplayer.com - *Hound Dog And 9 More Times White Artists Covered Black Musicians' Songs.*
10   *Chuck Berry, Hail Hail Rock "n" Roll* (1987)

for hundreds of old doo-wop songs, many of which I used to play at high school dances. I thought, geez, if Rosie and the Originals could pool their pennies together, go into a recording studio, and have a hit record with such an awful unoriginal song, I still had a chance.

Later, as if to tell me that my taste sucks, *Rolling Stone Magazine* quoted John Lennon as saying that "Angel Baby" was one of his favorite songs. Was he on acid when he heard it?

Rest in peace, Rosie Mendez Hamlin, who passed away in 2014 at the age of seventy-one. [11]

Even though I wasn't making a whole lot of money from the concerts and shows, I loved doing them. On many of these gigs, I played the keyboard since there were so many more guitarists than keyboardists around. One day, my stepdad was lambasting me with his usual diatribe, "You'll never amount to anything, you're a loser."

This time he was joined by my brother Warren. "Look, the chances of you making it in this business are a million to one."

"Your music is a pipe dream," sneered Pat. "You ain't got shit going on."

"You need to go back to college and learn a career, like I did," Warren suggested.

I finally resolved to stand up for myself. I looked both of them squarely in the eyes and said: "I'll tell you what, in six months I will be making a damn good living with my music!"

"Sure, right," Pat snorted. "A big star like Russ, huh?"

---

11 www.rollingstone.com - *Rosie Hamlin, Rosie and the Originals 'Angel Baby' Singer, Dead at 71* (2017)

At that point, Mom intervened. "Leave him alone, both of you. He's got the talent and he's happy at what he's doing. That's what's important."

They both guffawed as I stomped out of the room.

As it turned out, within six months I proved them wrong. I was not only earning a good living, but also making more money than both of them combined!

CHAPTER 4

In 1962, John F. Kennedy was president, and he was faced with the Cuban Missile Crisis. The world was on the brink of nuclear war, John Glenn became the first American to orbit the Earth, and the first Beatles' single, "Love Me Do," was released.

In late 1961, Eddie introduced me to a band called the Starlighters who were looking for a lead singer and keyboardist (no relation to Joey Dee and the Starlighters of "Peppermint Twist" fame). Since I was mostly playing the keyboards by then, it wasn't a difficult switch for me. However, the group leader had other plans, and the band fell apart after a few gigs. The remaining members, guitarist Tony Valentino, bassist Jody Rich, and me as lead singer and keyboardist, decided to form a new group. A young drummer, Benny King, was added in 1962.

I came up with the name Standels (initially with one l). Later on, during a Dick Clark interview on *American Bandstand* when I was asked how the name came about, I answered that it was because of us *standing* around in booking agents' offices." From then on, we all stuck to that story.

During one of these agency visits, we were asked to step into their small recording studio to record a demo. With the music track already pre-recorded, "I'm Walking in the Night" would become our first known recording, and years later, after it was long forgotten about, the demo disc was presented to me as a gift by my friend Bob Irwin of Sundazed Music. What a gem!

Eventually, we signed with the McConkey Artists Agency, located in a rundown building in Hollywood. The booking agency was run by husband and wife Mack and Gail McConkey. One of our first bookings was at a small club in Santa Barbara. Unfortunately, by the time it came to perform the McConkeys had a nasty marital split. As a form of retribution, Mack called the club and told them that a few of us were underage. When we got there, our IDs were checked, and we had to return to our homes. What a bummer.

Gail more than made up for this with our second gig. She booked us at the Oasis Club in Hawaii. Brother and sister act John and Judy Maus were just finishing up there, and the next act had canceled. The Standels were booked instead.

Here I was, 19 years old, my first extended time away from home, the lead singer/keyboardist of a rock group – performing in paradise! As fate would have it, I had been reading James Michener's *Hawaii* before learning about the gig. Little did I know that I'd finish reading the book in Hawaii while performing there.

Our bass player and self-appointed leader, Jody Rich, bore a strong resemblance to an impish troll with his pointed nose and matching chin. He turned out to be quite a punctilious taskmaster and a major asshole. Claiming to be an ex-Marine (which I still to this day doubt-because of the height requirement), he demanded that we obsequiously follow his orders as though we were in boot camp. Whenever we went out in public, we all had to dress in our stage attire. We were made to keep all of our clothes in spotless condition, pressed and ironed every day, and our shoes spit-shined to military perfection.

After several months of performing at the Oasis Club, Jody evolved from drill sergeant to monster, so much so that we nicknamed him "Napoleon," who he also strongly resembled, both in appearance and stature. Why did all the major dickwads seem to be short guys? He began to take amphetamines to stay awake at night. One day, he was so hyped up he was speaking rapid-fire. He came up with a plethora of songs and demanded that we learn them immediately so we could perform them *that evening*! But he didn't sing lead – I did! He insisted that, from then on, we would rehearse every day, all day long. On off nights, he imposed a curfew. To make matters worse, he gave us an edict that no girls were allowed in our rooms – *the curse of Fred*. In reality, the real reason for this was that Jody was married and, like Fred, jealous of the chicks we were picking up on Waikiki beach.

Jody also began to tell us macabre stories, which, true or not, caused Tony and me to question his sanity and try to keep a safe distance from him. For example, he confided that at one time he worked as a paramedic and had sex with dead bodies. Whether true or not, this was beyond appalling!

Jody continued to pop the pills like candy. By then, he was almost psychotic. He would fly into a rage at the slightest provocation. He was most harsh on Benny, who was just fifteen years old at the time (I didn't know his true age until years later), picking on him constantly. After a few months, the poor kid could take no more. He called his parents, and they brought him back home. As a replacement, we were forced to use the drummer from the Oasis House band. He wasn't bad, but because of his girth had a tough time fitting into Benny's uniform jacket.

By then, we'd had our fill of Jody. Finally, one day in defiance we refused to listen to anything he had to say, and when he ordered us to spit-shine our shoes, I told him, "Fuck off!"

"Vaffanculo!" Tony added for good measure.

Jody, at first stood there with his mouth open, then retaliated, "You can't tell me to fuck off, you pieces of shit."

"We just did," I responded.

"Eat sheet!" Tony added.

Jody's face turned a dark shade of red. "Both of you assholes are fired!" he roared. "Get out!"

We both turned and stomped out of the room.

After coming down from his high, Jody realized he didn't have a band or a lead singer any longer. He'd essentially fired himself. He came to our apartment, and said meekly, "Listen, you guys, I don't know what came over me."

"Could it be all of the pills you've been popping?" I suggested.

Out of necessity, we made a truce, with the understanding that Jody would lay off. Well, he did and didn't; I mean, he completely stopped turning the screws – because he started screwing. Yup, Jody had finally found something else to occupy his mind – a young woman with whom I'd had a brief fling. I couldn't care less so long as he was out of our hair.

My unquenchable thirst for women continued. The club had a strict non-fraternization policy with the Japanese performers. But we used to sneak some of the chorus girls out late at night and bring them to our room. Mizuki, Aiko, and Kiyomi, among others, became regulars in our beds. Many of the girls called each of us "Butterfly," an affectionate name meaning someone who flitters from one girl to another. I also had a torrid affair with the stripper Miki Moto. At the same time, I met the former Miss Kyoto of Japan on Waikiki Beach. She invited me to dinner, and to her hotel room. So, I was doing double duty with both, a dream come true for a nineteen-year-old kid in paradise.

Then there was Tori, the Polynesian girl I also met on the beach. She was beautiful, intelligent and statuesque. We spent many evenings together on the beach around campfires, sometimes in luaus joined by locals with their ukuleles. "Rari," the song that Ed Cobb wrote years later and the flip side of "Dirty Water," could have been written about Tori. I thought I was really in love with her. The romance continued until she left for college on the mainland. I kept in touch with her, but several months later I received a Dear John letter. She had fallen for some college dude. Looking back, it was perhaps the best choice she could have made.

After six months, the gig in Honolulu came to an end and so did our relationship with Jody. We returned home and went our separate ways. I got in touch with Gary Leeds, a drummer with whom I had worked briefly with another group, the Biscaynes. He in turn recommended his friend Gary McMillan, who had played bass in the same group. For band purposes, Gary changed his last name to Lane. Gary was a shy person, and I guess he enjoyed his privacy. Both Garys joined Tony and me, becoming the Standells second line up.

*Standells Early 1962, Left to right: Benny King,
Larry Tamblyn, Jody Rich, Tony Valentino*

*Standells Late 1962, Left to right: Tony Valentino,
Gary Lane, Larry Tamblyn, Gary Leeds*

Gary Leeds was a likable guy with an infectious personality and a wicked sense of humor. He loved to play extravagant practical jokes on people, gallows humor of the worst kind, which I happened to appreciate. Before I ever knew him, he was one of the perpetrators of one of the most notorious pranks in the Los Angeles area. Tujunga is located in a canyon east of the San Fernando Valley. Out of sheer boredom, he and his friends decided they would use a legendary monster to terrorize the area. At night, mostly during the weekends, one of them would put on a werewolf costume, sneak up on unwary victims and scare the shit out of them. Of course, reports of this bloodthirsty creature lurking about were reported to the police. It made front-page headlines in the LA *Herald-Examiner*: "Werewolf terrorizes Sunland Tujunga."

Gary and his friends were eventually caught and brought to justice. Since no damage was done, with the exception of some soiled undies, the boys weren't charged with any crime. I had read about the court proceedings before knowing Gary, and the boys testified that the creature really did exist! Since I greatly admired this brazen act, I later asked Gary about this episode. He claimed he was sworn to silence and wouldn't reveal anything. Damn! However, he would later inspire us to play the vilest practical jokes on each other.

The band altered its name to Larry Tamblyn and the Standels, mostly to take advantage of my last name. At that time, my brother Russ was a major Hollywood star. Our next booking from McConkey was in a small club in Fresno. Going from paradise to this dive was a complete letdown. To make matters worse, the location was rather depressing, right across from the railroad tracks, and it was during their foggy season. We performed for maybe six people each night. They were trying to build their business back up, but I don't think we were helping much.

I remember one evening a 300-pound inebriated woman passed out on the stage. No one bothered to move her, nor could they. So, we stepped over her for most of the night, until she finally sobered up, rolled off the stage, and staggered out of the club.

While playing there, Tony and I were picked up on by a couple of women in their forties. Back then, twenty-year-olds considered women that age to be ancient. I was rather hesitant, but after entering into our small rundown apartment, Tony whispered to me in his thick Italian accent, "Old Cheeken makes good soup."

In late 1962, we were booked at a small nightclub in Ridgecrest, California, another bland spot on the map in the high desert northeast of Los Angeles. We played there three nights per week and would travel back home during the other days. We had larger crowds there, but our luck wasn't getting much better. It seemed that one of the local boys thought Gary Leeds was making eyes at his girlfriend, so he walked up to Gary outside and sucker punched him, knocking him out cold. Gary Lane tried to intervene, and the guy's friends jumped him. Soon we were all involved in the brawl. However, Leeds had received the worst of the injuries. His front teeth were knocked out. It took him a week to recover.

The following week, I had one of my strange visions or spiritual manifestations. All of us were sleeping in the same motel room. I was awakened by an inebriated man, who opened the door, staggered into our room, and then fell between two of the beds. I jumped up and ran to the spot where he had fallen – but he wasn't there! Everyone else was asleep.

To this day, I don't know if I actually dreamed it or if it was an apparition! According to several locals, there was lore about a man who had died in that motel.

If that wasn't alarming enough, several days later I happened to turn on the TV news to learn that a large cargo plane had just crashed in the vicinity of my home in North Hollywood, causing multiple deaths and injuries. I was horrified – our family house was on the landing path to Burbank airport, known at that time as the Lockheed Air Terminal. I called home immediately, got no answer, and rushed home. It was a harrowing return trip that evening. After a two-hour drive, I turned into the neighborhood on Hart Street off of Lankershim Boulevard, only to be stopped by a police barricade. When I explained that I lived there, I was permitted in. I finally arrived at the scene on the corner of Ben Avenue and Hart Street and was aghast to see that it was the same lot in which we used to play.

The AP story of December 14, 1962, described it this way:

HORROR HITS N. HOLLYWOOD –
DEATH RAINED FROM SKY.
North Hollywood (AP) – Civil Aeronautics Board Investi-gators dug through charred wreckage Saturday, trying to learn why a four-propeller cargo airliner crashed in flames in a San Fernando Valley residential industrial area Friday

*night. Nine persons died. The Flying Tiger Line Super Con-
stellation, arriving after a regular daily flight from Boston
and Chicago, tore down crackling power lines and smashed
or burned nine houses and two industrial plants. Two
houses were destroyed. The liner, flying eastward, crashed
at 10:10 p.m., about a mile short of its goal – Lockheed Air
terminal. Its gas tanks exploded, flames engulfing a house.
One engine hit a truck. The fuselage ground ahead for about
500 feet, battering into a home where a couple – unhurt –
watched television.* [12]

The wreckage rested on a concrete wall, which miraculously saved
the couple inside. I looked down Ben Avenue and was relieved
to see that our home, only fifty yards away, was untouched. I
hurried up to the driveway and rushed inside the house. There
I was met by my mother who told me about the event. Pat had
staggered home about an hour after I arrived, having spent the
evening at a bar. By then he had conveniently left Mormonism
to return to his old habits. I could see the totality of the carnage
the following morning. I hadn't noticed that many of the homes
to the west of the crash on Hart Street and Bose Avenue were
completely destroyed. Going further west, I could see the first
ominous signs of the carnage. Directly across from Hart Street
on Laurel Canyon Boulevard was a large billboard for Carpeteria.
During its descent, the aircraft's engine rotors had chewed up the
top of the billboard, an eerie sight indeed.

---

12 www.gendisasters.com – *North Hollywood, CA Cargo Airline Crashes
    into homes* (1962)

It was a real circus-like atmosphere in our neighborhood. Crowds of people came to see the wreckage of the plane, unaware that this lot had provided so much pleasure to the neighborhood kids. There were even hot dog vendors. Some of the band members came over to witness this bizarre scene for themselves.

I don't know if it was the airplane crash or Pat's drunken rampages that finally convinced Mom she'd had it with Pat. She came to her senses and divorced him. She then sold the house, and she and I moved to a small apartment in Van Nuys

CHAPTER 5

1963 was a tumultuous year. John F. Kennedy was assassinated, the KKK dynamited a Baptist church in Birmingham, Alabama, and Martin Luther King delivered his historic "I have a dream" speech. Beatlemania was sweeping England, and although it would not reach our shores until early the following year, some of us were already picking up its signals.

We were booked at the Esquire Club in Eureka in January of 1963. At that time, we had learned about the Standel amplifier and decided we might be sued for using its trademark. So we decided to alter the name again, this time to "Larry Tamblyn and the Standells," adding an extra "l."

The Esquire was a noticeable improvement after our last gig; we drew fairly good crowds there. We were told that there was one group who were the top draw in that area: The Legends. Whenever and wherever they played, the Legends sold out the place. No other band came close. The clientele in Eureka was mostly lumberjacks, along with an assortment of local women. I'll never forget the night we went to a party, and a rather burly dude challenged me to a drinking contest. I was not a big drinker, but after spending so much time playing in clubs, I was able to mix up my drinks pretty well. This guy only drank beer. We started with a couple of Buds, and then switched to mixed drinks, followed by straight shots of tequila. It was not one of my proudest accomplishments, but I put Pete under the table that night. After such a distinction, I was well-respected by all of the men in the club, and evidently it was a special turn-on for the local women. I had been working on one particular divorcee for some time. With my reputation of putting Pete on the floor, she easily succumbed to my wishes.

We had performed at the club for about a month when we received the worst possible news; the Legends were performing at a competing club in nearby Arcata. Sure enough, our crowds vanished the next night. It was heartbreaking. On our off night, we decided to go check out the competition. Yes, they were a polished act, not only musically but with choreography and comedy – a real lounge act. I introduced myself to the group in a friendly way, telling them about our band. But the Legends seemed a bit caught up in their Northern California fame, saying but a few words to me. Ah, what notoriety can do to your ego! Legends in their own minds.

Back at the Esquire Club, things went from bad to worse. We tried to implement similar dance steps and comedy bits, but our lame attempts were met with indifference. At the end of the week, we were sent back home with our tails between our legs.

Back in LA, we went into the studio with Eddie Davis. As Larry Tamblyn and the Standells we recorded two of my songs, "The Girl in My Heart" and "You'll Be Mine Someday," and these were paired as our first single, released on Eddie's Linda label later that year.

In May, McConkey booked us into a small club in West Hollywood called the Royal Room. It was another roach-infested dive with nightly fistfights, but at least we were close to home. We were paid under-scale, which was more than many bands make today, and worked four nights per week. Everything went pretty smoothly until the evening when an undercover cop approached us for our ID's. To say that I was scared shitless would be an understatement. I was terrified of the repercussions of being caught underage in a nightclub. Responding to his demand to see my ID, I told him that I hadn't brought it.

"If you're not 21," he replied sternly, "it'll go a lot easier for you if you tell the truth."

With all of the chutzpah I could muster, I looked him squarely in the eyes, and bleated out, "Of course, I'm telling the truth".

It must have been convincing enough, because he said, "I'll be back tomorrow night, and you'd sure as hell better have it."

During our remaining sets that evening I was quite literally shaking, all the while thinking *what have I gotten myself into*? As we were packing up later, I discussed the matter with Tony. He assured me that we would take care of it. That was the good thing about my Pisano back then; I could count on him, as he could me.

Early the next morning, Tony and I headed south of the border to Tijuana, where you could get anything for a price. We began to ask around. I don't know how, but Tony was able to communicate in Spanish. Eventually we were led to the right person who had a fake draft card, which he sold us. Tony and I then hurried back to LA, where I used his mother's typewriter to fill out the card. It was as simple as that to fix. Only afterwards did I realize that I didn't capitalize California on my address. To make it appear more authentic, I rubbed the card in the dirt until it looked like I'd had it for a few years.

Sure enough, as we were about to perform that evening, the cop showed up and demanded to see the ID I'd promised to show him. I uneasily pulled out my wallet and presented him with the fake draft card, hoping he would miss the typo. He took a quick look at it and said, "I knew you were old enough. Nobody would bluff like that to a cop."

It was another close call.

For several weeks in August, we performed at Tykes in Pasadena. The following month, I met a girl named Carla, whom I casually invited to come and see us at our next gig, the Trophy Room up in Sacramento. Even though it was about a six-hour drive from my home in North Hollywood, she said it wasn't very far for her to go.

The Trophy Room was an upscale venue, and we developed a good following there, mostly people in their early twenties. Again, the main act was our old rivals the Legends who were the big draw there like everywhere else.

Shortly after receiving a telephone call from Carla, she showed up; not at the club, but at my motel room. We had a wild night together, and she returned to LA first thing the next morning.

Gary Leeds got into some trouble at the Trophy Room. For some time, he had been carrying on with two women, and it so happened that both of them showed up at the club on the same night. As fate would have it, they ended up standing next to each other and began to converse. Eventually, the talk got around to boyfriends, and they were both amazed at the similarities.

Sandra: "You're here to see your boyfriend? So am I."

Jamie: "Really, where is he?"

Sandra: "On the stage, the drummer!"

One of the first rules of being a musician is that you never have two girlfriends in the same venue. Evidently, Gary liked to live dangerously. On our break, Sandra, an airline attendant from Alaska Airlines, cornered him and made as if to kiss him, but instead gave him a well-deserved right cross to his chin.

However, of the two women, Sandra was the girlfriend Gary liked better. Later that night, he tried to make amends with her while we were all together at a movie theater. During the movie, to get back at Gary, Sandra began making passes at me. She wasn't very subtle about it either; she persisted in rubbing my crotch. Even though she got more and more aggressive, I spurned her advances. She later praised me for rejecting her, saying I was a loyal friend to Gary.

My own love life wasn't any less complicated. The next day I received a disturbing call from Carla, the girl I had slept with the month before. "Larry, I'm pregnant, and you're the father."

Not exactly the words I wanted to hear. After picking myself up off the floor, it took me a few moments to collect my thoughts.

"So, you're telling me that just one time, four weeks ago, and you're pregnant?"

"Yeah", she responded. "It was quite a surprise to me. I was just tested today"

I should have further checked into the pregnancy cycle of a woman. Had I done so, I would have learned that pregnancy is usually discovered after five to six weeks, at least one month after her last period. Her timing for the pregnancy test was decidedly suspicious. I later concluded that she was already pregnant when I was with her, and that the guy who had knocked her up had refused to take responsibility. Furthermore, she might not have been pregnant, at all, and was scamming me. So, she decided to pin it on the musician; he can afford it! Back then abortion wasn't legal, and I paid $500.00 for the procedure. Regardless, it was worth it at the time. Eddie Davis' admonition, "a stiff prick has no brains" came to mind.

At least I learned an important lesson from this: always wear a condom.

Later in September, we returned to Tykes in Pasadena, and began to build quite a following. But it was a small place, the pay wasn't all that good, and we only played four nights per week, so we started looking for other gigs in town. Through several friends, I heard that a much more popular and higher profile venue was looking for a house band.

The Peppermint West Lounge on N. Cahuenga Boulevard in Hollywood was an offshoot of the famous Peppermint Lounge in New York City. The New York club's house band was Joey Dee and the Starlighters, whose hit "The Peppermint Twist" had topped the charts in 1961. The Peppermint West was Hollywood's answer to the famous Twist club. It was one of the hippest places in the city.

In November I took it upon myself to set up an audition there. We impressed the club so much that we were chosen on the spot as their house band and given a long-term contract.

Eccentric costume and wardrobe designer Marusia owned the club. Her TV credits included *The Loretta Young Show*, *The Dinah Shore Chevy Show*, and *The Rosemary Clooney Show*. Hungarian-born, she spoke with an exotic accent much like Eva Gabor. [13]

____

13 www.imdb.com - *Marusia*

The manager of the lounge was Mario, a transvestite who had performed at the famous Finocchio Club in San Francisco. First opened in the early 1930s, Finocchio was one of the first clubs to feature female impersonators. As I later learned, Mario also had another talent. [14]

The Peppermint West had professional male and female dancers. Most of the guys were gay, making it easier for me to score on the girls. One of the few straight male dancers, Manny Garcia, has remained a good friend over the years. One night each week was designated "Celebrity Night", so-called because various known Hollywood actors would attend. Mario would announce the visiting celebrities, such as Robert Conrad, June Allison, and Diana Dors, from the stage. The audience would turn and enthusiastically applaud in the direction Mario indicated. Personally, coming from a show business family, I couldn't fathom why any A-list actor would go to a nightclub to ask to be spotlighted. That probably explains why, on some Celebrity Nights, Mario would point to the very darkest areas of the club, where mysteriously even people supposedly standing right next to the stars couldn't see them.

Marusia could only be described as an aging diva. She wore long flowing dresses and veils, and pranced around the floor like she was the star of the show. Her make-up was so thick that she had a ghostly pallor. It wasn't long before we were subjected to Marusia's eccentric behavior. She interrupted us right in the middle of a song, and said, "I vant you to play Tvist."

So, we played 'Ooh Poo Pah Doo,' a song that you could twist to.

---

14 www.sfgate.com/news - SF Gate, *What a Drag: Finnocchio's to Close / Cross-dressers have entertained at club for 63 years*, 1999

"NO, NO, NO, NO Ooh Poopy Do! I VANT TVIST!" she screamed, as one fake eyelash began to slide down her cheek, and the caked make-up cracked around her frown.

So, we launched into Chubby Checker's "Let's Twist Again." This seemed to satisfy Marusia, and she strutted off the victor. Like the famous Peppermint Lounge, the club liked to maintain the Twist image; however, Twist on demand was a total pain in the ass. From then on, to avoid future confrontations, whenever we saw Marusia we would automatically break into a Twist song.

We had only been performing at the Peppermint West for a few weeks when I met the stunningly beautiful Miss USA and Miss World contestant, Amedee Chabot. The blonde-haired beauty queen was exceptionally alluring, and needless to say I was very attracted to her. We started dating and were soon seeing a lot of each other. I was even invited up to her parents' ranch, where we often rode horses up and around the Griffith Park trails. It seemed to me that the relationship was getting serious. Then one day, things took a sudden about-face. We were riding near the top of the canyon when she pulled back on the reins and came to a stop.

She turned to face me. "Larry, I really like you," she said, "and I love being with you."

I thought, *wow, she wants the relationship to get a lot more serious.* I was prepared to gallantly dismount the horse to wind up in an emotional embrace there, atop the hill, a picturesque view of the San Fernando Valley below us. However, I wasn't ready for what came next.

She motioned to herself and proclaimed, "You know, being a beauty queen and contestant, we have to be single,"

That's logical, I concluded. *She feels she wants to keep our romance a secret. I can handle it.* Then she pulled the carpet out from under me.

"I recently got married."

I was in shock. After a long pause to catch my breath, I gasped, "When?"

If I wasn't already stunned, her response almost knocked me off the horse, "Actually, it was before I met you."

I was completely dumbfounded at what I was hearing. It took a moment to process this new information. I stuttered, "I-if that's the case, why were you dating me?"

Her answer still puzzles me to this day. "Well, I thought that if I dated others, I wouldn't be discovered and have my crown removed."

By then, my shock had turned to rage, and I lashed out, "That's so fucking decent of you to tell me!"

She tried her best to soothe me. "I'm so sorry I hurt you, Larry. You've been very special to me."

But I wasn't having any of it. "I'm so fucking glad that I could be of service." I yelled, then turned the horse around and galloped back down the hill to the stable. Jumping off the horse, I ran to my car and drove off.

I never saw Amedee again. That's the way life is: sometimes it embraces you, and in other times it kicks your ass.

As Walt Disney once said, "You may not realize it when it happens, but a kick in the teeth may be the best thing in the world for you." [15]

---

15 www.imdb.com – *Amadee Chabot*

The Standells were performing at the Peppermint West when President Kennedy was assassinated on November 22, 1963. Like the rest of the world, we were in a state of disbelief, and we were sickened by the thought of having to perform that evening. Fortunately, the club decided to close, and the next evening was an off night. I was in mourning for several days after that.

When we returned, Gary Leeds brought in a European magazine, and showed us an article about the Beatles. We guessed correctly that it was only a matter of time before their popularity spread to the United States. They were already beginning to see some airplay in the States with "Please Please Me" and "From Me to You." We totally dug their mop-top hairstyles and began to adopt the same look, making us the first American group have long hair. We also made appearances at several schools and began to create a following with teenagers. Admittedly it was because of our Beatle mop top appearance rather than being a lounge act.

Standells late 1963 with long hair

Walking around with lengthy locks was quite a unique experience. Everywhere I went, people would point and stare. One evening before performing, the group entered a noisy, crowded restaurant in Hollywood. It suddenly got very quiet, followed by a few uncomfortable chuckles, then mock kissing sounds. In the show business capital, where people had already begun to accept blacks and gays, lads with long hair were still just a bit too much for them to tolerate.

Mario decided to take advantage of the buzz surrounding the Beatles by hanging a huge banner in front of the club. No longer was the Peppermint West a Twist Club, it was now a "Beatlemania" Lounge. The craze caught on fast, and soon people were jamming the Peppermint West to see the Beatle phenomenon. *Tiger Beat* Magazine came in to do a special article on us. It was at this point that I allowed Tony and the others to talk me into shortening the name to the Standells, even though I did all of the lead singing. They convinced me that this was the only way we could become famous like the Beatles. Of course, the Dave Clark Five found success, and Dave wasn't even the lead singer!

We began to put on more of a show than we used to, of course adding a lot of Beatles songs to our repertoire. We also included jokes and choreographed dance routines. At one point, I stepped out in front of the group to sing the Isley Brothers' "Shout," a wild song, which caused everyone to get up on the dance floor. While singing the phrase "Just a little bit softer now," the band began to play more quietly, and I began to crouch until I was completely bent over on my back and the band was at its softest. Then, I would sing, "Just a little bit louder now," as the band began to raise the volume, and slowly rise off my back until we were all screaming the "shout!" finale to the song, jumping up and down along with the audience. It was a definite crowd-pleaser.

During this time, we also appeared in a few high school concerts, including one with a doo-wop group called the Bluejays. We had to go on stage right after them. On their exit, one of the members left an eye-watering gaseous cloud on stage, in which we were forced to perform. It was deemed by Tony that from then on whenever anyone would pass gas it was called a "Bluejay," which he pronounced "Boo-jay." He was usually the worst offender.

We also developed many other code words:

Senos: Italian for breasts.

Fa Puzza: Italian for bad breath.

Bus Stop: Seeing a girl's thighs while wearing a mini skirt, derived from noticing such young women sitting on bus stop benches.

Pallamini: Anything noteworthy or unusual.

Ponza: Italian for fat belly.

These code words were very handy because they could be used in public without anyone being the wiser.

In October of 1963, we were booked to appear on *That Regis Philbin Show*, the follow-up to the *New Steve Allen Show*. Unfortunately, Regis simply did not have the comedic ability to replace Allen. Many of the famous skits, like "Man on the Street," were missing. Regis' genuine warmth and openness more than made up for it, however. The show was syndicated nationally, and shown locally in Los Angeles on KTLA, Channel 5. It was taped at the Vine Street Theater. It was an old building. We had to walk up and down the stairs to get anywhere, sometimes getting lost in the process. The studio was on the main floor. One of the songs we were asked to do was the Beatles' "I Want to Hold Your Hand." It wasn't the last time we were asked to perform the song or work with Regis. The show was broadcast on New Year's Eve, 1963. [16]

---

16 www.wikipedia.org – Wikipedia, *The Steve Allen Playhouse*

CHAPTER 6

1964 saw quite a few milestones in the nation's history. After three civil rights workers were murdered in Mississippi, the Civil Rights Act of 1964 was passed, but it did not stop the continuing racial violence across the country, and the 24th Amendment to the Constitution was ratified. It was the year the Surgeon General announced that smoking may lead to lung cancer. The Beatles held the Top Five positions in the Top 40 singles chart in America.

One evening during a break at the Peppermint West, a short, balding man with large frog-eyed glasses approached us. He introduced himself as Burt Jacobs and said he had a lot of connections in the record business.

He surprised us with his next comment: "If I can get you a record contract with Liberty Records, will you let me be your manager?"

Of course, we agreed. Sure enough, on February 6, the day after my birthday, Burt was able to sign us with Liberty Records, sight unseen. It was a feat that seemed next to impossible – until we learned about the unusual pull that Burt had with the record company. Burt was a bookie, and many of the people at Liberty Records were into him for bets!

Born in Brooklyn, New York, a cigar-smoker and loud dresser with a bad toupee, Burt was the stereotype of what Hollywood would cast as a high-pressure agent. Phil Silvers could have played him to a tee. He was known to associate with some pretty shady characters. One day, we were in his office and began talking with a very kindly old gentleman. We found out later that he was the Godfather of the West Coast. With this type of reputation, one would think that in signing with Burt, you would constantly fear for your life. However, the opposite was true. Burt loved the Standells and would do anything for us.

Liberty assigned us to songwriter and record producer Dick Glasser, who had previously produced Vic Dana and the Ventures. Glasser was not a good fit for the Standells; he didn't seem to have the feel for our type of brash rock 'n' roll. For example, our first recording for Liberty was a song I wrote and sang called "The Shake." It was supposed to be a loud, screaming rocker, but Glasser instead turned it into a pop song with almost a polka beat, and doo-wop singers in the background, cooing "Ooh-wee-ooh." Adding to the ruination of my song, he put a very out-of-place Melodica lick throughout and an odd instrumental break and modulation in the middle. The flip side, another song I wrote and sang titled "Peppermint Beatle," was almost as bad. However, I did not complain because I was told that the producer was always right.

We had members of the Wrecking Crew on this session, including guitarist Glen Campbell, who at that time was strictly a session musician. I remember the first time I met him. We walked into the recording studio, and he was sleeping on the sofa in the lobby. The engineer came out of the control room, spotted Glen, woke him up, and jokingly asked if he ever went home. Glen explained that after the session the previous evening it was so late that he just decided to crash on the sofa. He was such a down-to-earth guy; he seemed to be out of place in Hollywood.

As if the long-hair look was just a stepping-stone, Gary Leeds began to have even more bizarre ideas for the Standells. For starters, he wanted us to change the name of our band. He had recently seen the movie *Village of the Damned*. In the film, aliens impregnate all of the women of a remote English village. The result: They gave birth to children with supernatural powers, so much so that they became a threat to the village. The children all had blond hair. Gary thought it would be cool to change the band name to The Children and bleach our hair blond. I nixed that idea immediately. We had put in too much effort as the Standells and had already signed with Liberty Records. I wasn't about to throw it all away for a dumb gimmick. After that, Gary began to sour on the group.

It was also right about that time that I met an attractive young woman who I would eventually marry, airline stewardess Linda Mason. After my experience with Amedee, you'd think I'd be shy about meeting a love interest in a nightclub. I was still only twenty years old and wasn't ready for any type of serious relationship.

There were warning signs from the start of our relationship. Late one evening, I was sitting with Linda on her sofa with my arm around her shoulder When I was suddenly stunned by a blinding flash of light and an apparition, which appeared for a fleeting instant, causing me to jolt upright. Its message was simple and direct: "This isn't right."

Only I experienced this, and Linda was none the wiser. For that matter, neither was I. Instead of taking this extraordinary vision to heart, I quickly wrote it off, trying to explain it away. I decided that my mind was playing tricks on me. "This isn't right" could mean anything. But somewhere deep down inside, I knew exactly what it meant. I just refused to listen. The apparition, although momentary, seemed to be someone very close to me, but I didn't fully realize who it was until years later.

Soon after that, I had what can only be described as a bizarre encounter with Mario. As I was walking by him, he stopped me and said, "Larry, there's something I have to tell you." I thought *Oh shit, he's hitting on me.* Instead, he told me something that shook me to my core.

"Sometimes I get visits late at night," he began to explain. I was about to say, "Tell me something I don't know," but Mario stopped me cold when he added, "spiritual visits." He continued, "I don't ask for these visitations, but last night your father came to me."

At that point, my mouth was agape in astonishment. *How did Mario know my father was dead?*

He went on to tell me about my dad having regrets that he left me so young and that he was in my corner, my guardian angel. Oh boy! Mario went on to say that there was soon going to be a huge shift in my life; things were going to change for the better. So, this was Mario's other talent – a transvestite medium. This could only happen in Hollywood.

As it turned out, Mario's prognostication was spot-on. Burt received an offer for Standells to headline at the Thunderbird Casino in Las Vegas, beginning in March.

It was a huge leap from the Peppermint West. The timing of this was uncanny. This had to have been my father's intervention. In later years, I would realize that my father must also have been the apparition who appeared to me when I was with Linda. I never discussed this with Linda, but the message would come back to haunt me many times to come. I never was able to pay gratitude to the man through whom my father spoke such words of comfort. Thanks, Mario, wherever you are. Sorry I misjudged you – you are indeed an angel. And to you, Dad, I apologize for being such a fool in not listening to you!

The gig at the Thunderbird was not landed solely because of our successful run at the Peppermint West; it was largely because of our long locks. The news release stated, *U.S. Answer to the Beatles Pauses for T-Bird Stand. With the Beatle craze now in full swing the Standells—long hair and all—are out to prove they can top the British group.*

Really? What were we going to do when we arrived at Heathrow Airport in London, wave our fists at the cameras and challenge the Beatles to a battle of the bands? In reality, they would have kicked our asses. P.T. Barnum himself couldn't have come up with a bigger pile of bullshit.

Our one-week run in Vegas was successful, but not without incident. We had brought a couple of the Peppermint West dancers along with us, Jerry and Suzanne, and they danced behind us onstage while we performed. According to the hotel, when housekeeping knocked on his door, Jerry answered the door in drag. Although Jerry denied this, it caused quite a stir. In those days, being gay was one thing, but dressing in drag was quite another – in in Las Vegas. WHOA NELLIE! However, Burt was able to straighten things out with the Casino. He had a lot of friends in high places in Vegas, after all.

Of all the possible misadventures in Las Vegas, one incident proved to be potentially destructive to our run: I became very sick with a high fever. I had to call a doctor to my room, and he was able to bring the fever down with some antibiotics. However, I had also developed what is commonly known as VT, or Vegas Throat. Most singers who perform in Vegas know about this condition. Due to the dryness of the climate, the combination of no humidity, high heat, dust, and pollen, singers like me begin to lose their voices. Jon Bon Jovi and George Jones complained about Vegas Throat, and after a serious romp with VT, Bono of U2 stated that he would never again work in Las Vegas.

I take partial blame because I don't think I properly hydrated myself. The end result is that "Shout" was becoming more of a whisper. I tried everything to cure myself, but nothing seemed to work. Finally, by chance, I ran into Mizuki, one of the chorus girls from Hawaii that used to sneak up to my apartment who by then was working as a dancer in Vegas. She told me of a cure that a lot of singers used: a mixture of apple cider vinegar and honey. She explained that the vinegar ate away at the mucus and killed the bacteria while the honey coated the throat.

The thought of taking this concoction was revolting. Nevertheless, I went to the market and returned to my room with the two items. I mixed the potion, held my nose, and then gargled it. On several occasions throughout the night, I came close to gagging. Sure enough, though, almost overnight my voice returned. Sometimes old home recipes genuinely work, especially ones from a chorus girl named Mizuki! It wasn't the last time I saw Mizuki. She seemed to appear in my life every time I needed her.

No, we did not go to London to challenge the Beatles, instead later that month we were booked into P.J.s nightclub on Santa Monica Boulevard in West Hollywood. Originally known as the First Discotheque, P.J.s was owned by Bill Doherty, Paul Raffles, and Phil Tanzini. My friend Trini Lopez had just finished his run there, after recording his successful live album *Trini Lopez at P.J.s.*

Once again, we were offered a long-term contract, but with one condition: to be the house band we had to get rid of our long hair. The club had a conservative image and mop top hair just didn't *cut it*. Okay, bad pun.

We had just begun to perform at P.J.s when Liberty came up with the idea of recording a live album. It was at this most inopportune time that Gary Leeds, disheartened with having to cut off his long hair and being turned down in changing the band name, announced that he was quitting the group. He made up a cockamamie story about being drafted into the army, but I knew that it was something else. As it turned out, Gary joined with colleagues John Maus and Scott Engel who had a band called the Walker Brothers. The Walker Brothers then made what I thought to be one of the most brazen moves ever by a rock group. In February 1965 they moved to London, with advance publicity – *they were there to reverse the British Invasion* – and made a huge splash in the UK press. It didn't take long before the Walker Brothers had their first hit record, "Make it Easy on Yourself," followed by

"The Sun Ain't Gonna Shine Anymore," which hit the UK #1 slot, and #16 in America. However, other than that one Top 20 hit, the Walker Brothers never saw their huge UK success duplicated in America, and all three remained in England. [17]

This didn't help my self-worth at all – added to the Innocents, and Ritchie Valens were three more friends and acquaintances who had gone on to stardom, passing me by! Once again, I heard my stepfather's words that I'd never amount to anything. I eventually came to realize, however, that Gary and the others had their own paths to follow, as I did mine. Wild Gary certainly did make his mark. Over the years, we have maintained our friendship across the pond. During the Standells' 2010 tour in Europe, he introduced us at the UK concert. It was a reminder at how small the world is, and how one should never allow distance to destroy friendships.

Gary's departure from the Standells left us in a bind, especially with an album recording just a few weeks away. We auditioned a few drummers, but none of them felt right. Then in walked young, handsome and self-assured Dick Dodd. Being half Hispanic and half Irish, Dick also seemed to have a real *punk* attitude, like he could kick anybody's ass who tried to mess with him. My immediate thought was, *This guy is sure full of himself. If he's half as good as he thinks he is, we've really got something here.*

When we learned that he was an ex-Mouseketeer and friend of Cubby O'Brien with whom I had once played, the ribbing began.

"So, can you seeng the Meeky Mouse song?" snorted Tony.

---

17 www.wikipedia.org - Wikipedia, *The Walker Brothers*

Without hesitation and with a straight face, Dick responded, "Maybe, if you give me a blow job. I got a little tired of the ones Minnie gave me."

Gary and I doubled over laughing, but Tony couldn't quite see the humor. I thought, *Wow, this dude has some balls.*

I then asked how he heard about us, and he said, "Jackie DeShannon told me that you need a drummer, and thought I would be a good fit." Jackie had recently had a Top 10 hit with "What the World Needs Now". "I was in her band for a while," Dick added.

"Cool," I responded. "Anyone else?

"Eddie and the Showmen," he said.

I'd heard of them. They were a surf band who had released several popular records, including "Mr. Moto" and "Squad Car."

"They're a pretty popular group, why did you leave them?" I asked.

"Surf music wasn't my thing. I'm more into R&B and rock, the kind of stuff you guys do."

Being able to walk away from a group like that was even more impressive. However, I should have seen this as a forewarning of his tendency to be disloyal.

There was already a set of drums on the stage, so I invited Dick to sit in. I'd never seen someone more confidently slide onto a drum stool.

Tony, still smarting over Dick's earlier remark, said, "What kinda stuff you do?"

Dick grinned, "Whatever you want, Paison," then proceeded to go into an impressive series of rolls on the snare and toms, ending with the crash cymbal.

Is this guy for real? I wondered. And I was about to find out. "How about 'I'll Go Crazy'?" I suggested.

Dick performed the James Brown song impeccably, including the stylized breaks and ending. It was as though he'd always been our drummer, and with even a bit more pizzazz than Gary, twirling the drumsticks to boot! When we were done, all of us, including a begrudging Tony, stood there with our mouths open. I knew that Dick provided the solid backbeat I was looking for. Not too shabby for a surf drummer.

Then to my astonishment, Dick reached for a nearby mic stand, adjusted the boom, and pulled the mic up to his mouth. "Hey, do you mind if I sing one?"

If I was not already impressed by his drumming, I was blown away when he belted out "Help Yourself." My dream was realized; we had found our drummer – and another lead singer! Little did I know that Dick would eventually sing the lead on our biggest hit record.

The live recording of the album, *The Standells in Person at P.J.s*, went off without a hitch. Recording genius Wally Heider set up in his portable studio behind P.J.s, with cables running into the club. I sang most of the songs, with Dick singing lead on three. The only problem with the album was the producer, Dick Glasser. How can you ruin a live recording? Glasser found a way. He decided to speed up the tape to make it "more exciting." Unlike today with digital recording, back then you could not speed up a tape recording without increasing the pitch. With apologies to my Mouseketeer friends, I ended up sounding like Mickey Mouse!

The Standells in Person a P.J.s

We drew in such a large crowd while at P.J.s that they had to double the size of the room. It went from a two hundred capacity to seven hundred and fifty. The Bobby Fuller Four was added to the bill, and they rotated sets with us. I remember having a few conversations with Bobby. Being from El Paso, Texas, he was an unusually well-mannered guy, extremely talented, and very self-assured. Coincidentally, he had hooked up with Bob Keane, the owner of Del-Fi Records who had passed on me earlier in my career. It was with Keane's Mustang label that Fuller had the Top 10 hit "I Fought the Law" two years later.

Many have said that P.J.s was owned by the mob, and I did see some pretty mean-looking gumbas go in and out of offices there. I do know that the club was purchased in late 1971 by organized crime figures Eddie Nash and Dominic Lucci, along with Hal Glickman, and the club name changed to Starwood, where many rock legends like Van Halen, the Go-Go's, and Mötley Crüe began their careers. [18]

Also rumored to be mob-related was the mysterious death of Bobby Fuller. On July 18, 1966, Bobby's dead body was discovered by his mother in her blue Oldsmobile in the parking lot of his Hollywood apartment. The police ruled it a suicide. Inside the car, they had discovered in Bobby's hands a plastic hose that led to a gasoline can. The car had been in the lot for thirty minutes. Sloppy police work was evident. They failed to dust for fingerprints, even though his body showed signs of advanced rigor mortis, suggesting that Bobby had died elsewhere. Whether or not this was even remotely connected to PJ's is anyone's guess. I do know that Bobby had everything to live for, and when he left his mother to run an errand, he said he'd return shortly. Besides, taking one's own life by consuming gasoline is practically impossible.

During our performances at PJ's, many celebrities came to see us. On numerous occasions, Russ and my friend George Chakiris from *West Side Story* visited me, and we had drinks together. Also, I was thrilled to strike up a conversation with one of my all-time favorite actors, the great Edward G. Robinson. Like George, he was not at all like his tough-guy image but was instead a kind and generous person. One night, the Rolling Stones came into see us. Everyone thought they were outrageous looking.

---

18 www.wikipedia.org - Wikipedia, *Starwood (nightclub)*

June Wilkinson in an impromptu performance at the live recording session
by the Standells at P.J.'s in Hollywood
last week. Liberty's Dick Glasser recorded the act. Bottom right Lennie

Standells at P.J.s with June Wilkinson

On November 21, 1964, we had our first taste of stardom when we were included in a Dave Clark Five concert at the Long Beach Arena, along with Joey Paige, and the Vibrants. When we were entering the concert hall, a crowd of teenage girls saw us and began a hot pursuit. Gary Lane tripped and fell. The girls caught up to us and began pulling our hair and trying to tear off our clothes.

We met the DC5, and they seemed like rather nice chaps, very clean cut compared to the Beatles and Rolling Stones. Of course, they were different in other respects. Dave Clark owned the name, and the others were employees with no ownership rights whatsoever. Regardless, they put on a great show, and we were thrilled to be part of it.

Meanwhile, my on-again-off-again relationship with Linda proved to be even more daunting at PJ's. She always managed to let me know that I wasn't good enough for her, which added to my lack of self-esteem. Much to my anger, she began to meet other men at the club while I performed; some of them were Hollywood bigwigs. It pissed me off, having my girlfriend being scored on while I performed on stage. On the positive side, it inspired me to write my song, "Mr. Nobody," later recorded and released on Tower Records. You can feel the seething anger in my lyrics.

Try so very hard to take my baby
Try so very hard to take my love
Mr. Nobody you see
You can't creep up on me
And take away the girl that I'm to marry.
Take away my house and all my money
But never try to take my love from me
So, Mr. Nobody you've lost
With her I am the boss
You're not the one with whom she has an interest.
You can thank your lucky stars that I have told you
You'd better realize that this boy ain't no fool
So, you can take your fancy car and drive away real far
The world is full of nobodies like you are.

Okay, I was young and stupid. I looked at Linda's behavior as challenging, even after I received an anonymous letter, obviously from mutual friends informing me that Linda spoke of me in demeaning terms. I chose to ignore it.

But my foolhardiness didn't end there. It was right about this time that I also received my draft notice. I just couldn't go in. The other guys depended on me, and we were very close to seeing the end-results of all of our efforts. Besides, I considered the war in Vietnam to be immoral. When I was due to report for my physical, I tried staying up all night, going there in dirty clothes – and to show that I was mentally deranged, during my interview I talked about looking forward to killing "gooks." This may have worked for others, but not for me. I passed with flying colors. Shit!

At PJ's, I met a young Greek actress named Aspa Nakapoulou, who had been in several movies, *Aliki* (1963) and *Casablan* (1964). She revealed to me that her US visa was about to expire and that she wanted to stay in the country. I told her about my situation. I don't know who came up with the idea, but we decided that a business marriage would help us both out. The Standells' attorney, Sy Cohen, arranged the deal. The following week, we flew to Las Vegas and were married. Aspa was a very sweet young woman, and by all intents should have been a love interest, but I was still blindly hung up on Linda.

As it turned out, I needn't have gone through with this marriage. Because of the constant worrying about Linda and going into the service, I developed an ulcer. It alone was enough to keep me out of the military. A year later, I had the marriage annulled, and haven't heard from Aspa since. However, she later worked in the movie *B.O.R.N.* (1988), where she met my brother Russ, who also acted in it. She completely confounded him when she mentioned our secret marriage. I'd only told my mother about this. I was so ashamed I didn't tell anyone else, including band members.

Several songs from the PJ's album were released as singles, including "I'll Go Crazy," "So Fine," "Linda Lou," and "Help Yourself." The latter, sung by Dick, got some airplay on local radio station KFWB and rose up the local charts in Los Angeles. On January 28, 1965, we appeared on Dick Clark's *American Bandstand. We* were introduced by Dick as: "One of the hottest records in the country. Four very handsome gentlemen. Ladies and gentlemen, the Standells."

After performing "Help Yourself," Clark interviewed us. During the interview, he asked me how we derived the name, and, in an off-the-cuff response I told him it was "From standing around." That was the story that the group stuck to from then on.

Clark then asked me, "How long has this music been going on?"

I couldn't miss a smart-ass comeback: "I'd say at least a couple hundred years."

I also excitedly told him about our upcoming tour to Nicaragua, not knowing yet that it would turn out to be a complete disaster!

Several weeks earlier, a group of wealthy coffee plantation owners from that country happened to see us performing at PJ's. They made Burt Jacobs an offer he couldn't refuse: "Come to our wonderful country and perform." The deal was sealed, and it was agreed that the Standells would perform at various 'venues' for three weeks in Nicaragua. Our good friend, KFWB and KRLA radio personality Reb Foster, decided to accompany us.

None of us could have known what we were about to get ourselves into. We were under the impression that Nicaragua was an exotic tourist destination. In reality, it was exactly the opposite. Not only did American tourists avoid Nicaragua, but also the country had never been visited by any kind of musical act from abroad. Thus, the Standells were billed as "Los Standells, Los Beatles Norteamericano," meaning "The Standells, the North American Beatles"!

Nicaraguan Poster for Standells

The flights to Nicaragua should have given us a clue to the primitive conditions that lay ahead. Going from LAX to Guatemala was unremarkable, but the connecting flight from there to Nicaragua was quite nerve-racking. We boarded an old plane, which can only be described as a Ford Tri-Motor. This did not sit well with Tony. Like Gary, he hated flying.

"Thees thing ees not going to fly," he said. "I geet off."

But I held him down. "Come on, Tony, this is a real adventure."

As it turned out, Tony was damned near right. It seemed to us that as the plane lifted into the air, it barely cleared the trees and mountains. Also on the flight was a group of nuns, saying their rosaries throughout its duration, along with a few goats and chickens in the rear cargo area. After a few hours, the plane began to descend, but all we could see were the treetops of the rain forest.

Tony's face turned an ashen white. "Sheet, we gonna crash!"

I tried to calm him as much as possible by shaming him. "Look at the nuns, they're not afraid, and neither are the goats."

Okay, I admit I was *pulling the wool* over his eyes.

Finally, the plane found its way to a clearing, which turned out to be the Managua airport.

When we arrived in the city of Managua, we thought we were in the slums. I asked the cab driver how long it would be before we were in the city.

"Thees is it, señor," he replied.

At first, we thought he was trying to put one on us. But when he dropped us off at the hotel, we realized just how serious he was. A Class "A" hotel in Nicaragua was the equivalent of a tenement building in Los Angeles.

The timing of our arrival didn't help much. It was their Independence Day, celebrating the defeat of American Imperialists during the Banana Wars, 1898 -1934. [19]

---

19 www.wikipedia.org – Wikipedia, *United States Occupation of Nicaragua*

Since the sweltering hotel room had no air conditioning, I watched the celebrations from my balcony window. Unlike American parades, the festivities took place over a wide area, with marching bands going every which way. We had been invited to the American Embassy, where I met a very nice young woman and asked her for a date. We went to a decent restaurant up in the hills. On the way back, our cab drove right through the town square where the main festivities were taking place.

As we inched along, a few people noticed me inside the cab and gathered curiously around. More and more people joined them until it became a huge mob. Evidently, my being a gringo on the very day they were commemorating their hatred of Americans caused them to curse me, the "Yankee Imperialist." They started to jeer and shout threats at us, calling my date "*la puta*." Then the raging mob began to shake the cab, jostling us around inside. The cab driver wasn't about to see his car get damaged – forget about the gringo. He pulled out a gun and waved it at the crowd, which caused them to scatter, allowing the car to finally get through the crowd. I quickly discovered the difference in the way we were perceived among the wealthy and the peons. We were loved by one and despised by the other. From then on, when we weren't performing, I stayed inside the hotel.

Remaining in the hotel didn't provide much in the way of enjoyment, however. I had invited my date up to my hotel room, which she readily accepted. However, the hotel had a non-fraternization policy. As we were about to enter my room, a short-statured bell boy interceded.

Shaking his finger at me, he firmly said, "No permitir, el permiso en la habitacion."

Damn little munchkin! No doubt it applied especially to Yankees. On the other hand, Managua had an abundance of whorehouses which were far less discriminatory, and which seemed to be the only source of recreation in that city.

For the concerts, we had a group of people who were assigned to transport and set-up our instruments. After our first performance, one of them asked Dick what he could do to help. Dick told him to tear-down his drum set, and then stepped away to attend to another task. Dick returned later to discover the guy had taken his assignment to heart. Every element of the drums had been completely disassembled – the skins, stands, foot pedal, all of the metal pieces, down to the nuts and bolts. The man smiled and said, "I deed what you asked, señor."

We quickly learned that we had to be very specific in expressing anything to these well-meaning people.

The "events" pretty much amounted to performing at movie theaters and soccer stadiums. Doing two or three shows per day, including a daily live performance at the radio station, much of our time was devoted to driving between events on dirt roads and through rainforests. I later learned that there were cannibal tribes who dwelled around Lake Managua, some of which we probably came uncomfortably close to. The hot tropical weather was stifling, especially tough when having to perform in it. We went through at least two to three changes of clothes each day. They were soaking wet from perspiration after each performance.

Only the "haves" could afford to attend our concerts, leaving the "have-nots" angry at being excluded as well as the perceived opulence we represented. The people who attended loved the Standells, but for the wrong reasons. Being billed as the North American Beatles was the same to them as the real thing. During our concerts, teenage girls screamed out "John!" "Paul!" "George! "Ringo!" We didn't help matters any by autographing photos under those names. I even signed one as "George Lennon." They didn't seem to know the difference.

The last stadium concert was the most memorable, and at the same time most terrifying. In addition to our regular crew, we were provided with a military escort armed with automatic weapons. At one point during the concert, we played a Beatles song, and the crowd went wild and began to rush the stage. In America this behavior would have been considered normal, but not so in Nicaragua. One of the military guards abruptly fired his Uzi into the air. If that weren't scary enough, he then waved it in the Standells' direction, sending the crowd and us scattering!

This was the deciding factor in our hasty decision to cut the tour short and return to the USA post haste. We concluded that Nicaragua wasn't ready for the Standells or rock 'n' roll!

However, we quickly discovered that leaving Nicaragua wasn't nearly as easy as entering it. At the airport, our luggage was already checked in and on the plane when a potbellied military Capitán with an intimidating demeanor and a large, bushy mustache halted us.

"You no can go!" He informed us.

With shock and dismay, we watched as the plane took off with our luggage – and without us! We learned that while we were touring Nicaragua, the powers that be conveniently decided to form a musicians' union. Our group was assessed a rather hefty sum of money for "traveling dues," which oddly enough, amounted to everything we had made and then some. We were told we would be thrown in jail if we didn't pay up. As Burt argued with El Capitán, we were certain he would be shot right there on the spot!

The Nicaraguans had latched onto capitalism and the musicians' union terminology very quickly and conveniently. It took two days in an oppressively torrid climate without a change of clothes for Burt to begrudgingly settle the matter.

When we finally landed in Los Angeles, we were exhausted and unarguably malodorous. We exited the airliner, walked down the stairway, and upon reaching the tarmac knelt down and kissed the ground!

After several weeks rest, we were booked at the Peppertree Lounge, located in the famous North Beach area of San Francisco. It had a cool atmosphere, with a young crowd and a nice sized dance floor. The audience was receptive to the Standells. Late at night, we used to walk to an after-hours club nearby. Going down the stairs to the entrance, we'd always step over a few inebriated winos along the way. As serving drinks after 2:00 AM was illegal, the club had a unique way of getting around the law. Drinks were served in coffee cups. Whenever a cop was spotted on his way to the entrance, a bell would sound, and all of the customers would quickly sober up. Any liquor bottles behind the bar were immediately stashed.

During our off nights, we also caught some of the other clubs like the Hungry i, where we happened to catch one of the rare performances of Lenny Bruce. He was under investigation by the FBI at the time for "lewdness," so I was disappointed to see a rather tame Bruce. After all, he had a reputation of doing the most unexpected things. His entire routine was done sitting by a tape machine, playing back different bizarre sounds, and making inane comments. But that was Lenny!

Also, in North Beach was the Condor Club. It had quite a reputation. For instance, one night after closing a bouncer named Jimmy and his girlfriend Theresa decided to have mad sex on top of the grand piano, which was on a hydraulic lift. Apparently, the couple was going at it so passionately they didn't notice that the lift had somehow been activated. Tragically, Jimmy died of asphyxiation. They weren't discovered until three hours later, still sandwiched together. Too bad, but what a way to go!

As with many of these types of clubs, the Condor drew an interesting variety of customers, including delegates from the 1964 Republican National Convention, which nominated Senator Barry Goldwater for president. One of the biggest requests at the convention was for reservations to see the legendary stripper Carol Doda, the very first topless dancer who performed at the club. Through silicone injections, she'd gone from a size 34B to 44DD. Silicone at that time was a new technique. [20]

I was quite surprised one evening when a well-endowed blond sauntered into the Peppertree Lounge and plopped down next to

______

20 www.sfgate.com - *Legendary S.F. Stripper Carol Doda dies at 78* (2015)

me at the bar. Even more astonishingly, she turned to me, smiled and said, "Hi there."

Not knowing what to think, I returned the smile and said, "Hi" in return.

"My name's Carol Doda. What's yours?"

My wide-open mouth must have revealed my total shock at meeting the legendary stripper. "Larry Tamblyn of the Standells. It's very nice to meet you!"

None of the usual pickup dialog followed like "You're cute" or "Can I buy you a drink?" Carol simply asked, "Would you like to go to my pad and have sex?"

I was stunned. How could I refuse a direct proposition from such a sexually attractive woman? We strolled to her apartment above the Condor. I can't imagine that I was the first such conquest of Carol's; I was more than likely an addition to quite a distinguished list. Do I feel cheap? Nah!

Manny Garcia, my friend from the Peppermint West, would often come to visit us wherever we played. Manny taught me how to skateboard way before it was ever popular. He also did a really neat thing with Levi jackets, he dyed them different colors. We went out to eat one night in San Francisco, both of us wearing his Levi jacket creations. By then our hair had grown out a little. At a table next to us sat three intimidating rednecks who'd had a bit much to drink. The greasiest one of the trio began with the little jabs.

"Well, don't they look pretty?"

The other two laughed with him and soon joined in the heckling: "I like the cute one in the purple jacket" – meaning me – "I wonder if she puts out."

It got so bad that everyone in the restaurant stopped talking and looked at us in dismay.

I tried to lighten up the situation.

"Look, guys, we're musicians and this is the way we dress."

But that didn't stop the three from getting rowdier. The larger one with the crew cut and pockmarked face wasn't going to back down. "So, let me get this straight, she needs to make an excuse for the way she looks. But there ain't no excuse for faggots."

The others joined in with more insults.

Finally, I'd had enough and blurted out, "I guess there's nothing we can do that will satisfy Larry, Moe, and Curly here."

Me and my big fucking mouth!

The three didn't take kindly to being likened to the Three Stooges. They began to mumble things like, "Let's get 'em outside," and "Yeah, the fuckin' fags deserve to get their asses kicked."

At this point, Manny and I were terrified for our lives. We put down money to pay the bill, and then slowly rose to leave. Knowing we were most likely about to get the shit kicked out of us if I didn't do something, an idea came to me.

"I'm sure going to enjoy the Kung-Fu class tomorrow," I remarked to Manny.

He caught on immediately. "Yeah, we need some practice for the black belt competition next week."

On the spur of the moment, Manny and I did a few jabs. The three goons looked at each other questioningly, like *maybe these guys are for real?*

It was perhaps for this reason that we miraculously escaped unscathed from the diner. We had pulled it off; one of the greatest snow jobs ever, and another close call for me!

Manny and I are still friends, and we often joke about this. Today, he's an exclusive hairdresser in Beverly Hills.

Tony had almost the same thing happen in another restaurant, but with completely different results. He had been dating an Italian girl from San Francisco pretty regularly. Eventually, he learned that her dad was a major figure in the Mob there. One evening, Tony, his girlfriend and her father, Joseph Miasano, were having dinner in the Fior d'Italia on North Beach. Much like with Manny and me, there was a table of miscreants sitting next to them. Likewise, they had imbibed a bit too much beer and began to make rude comments about Tony's appearance. Finally, Mr. Miasano calmly but sternly spoke to the three: "It would not be wise for you to continue."

The four took this as a joke and kept up their rancor, augmented by more beer. Before leaving the restaurant, Miasano asked to use the restaurant's telephone and made a quick call.

Later that night, the four were found in an alley behind the restaurant, beaten within an inch of their lives. The following day, Tony showed me a news clipping about the beating, told me what had happened, and said that Miasano had never said another word about the affair.

Back in those days, you could stumble across almost anything in San Francisco. One night at the Peppertree, a man to whom I took an immediate dislike approached me. You know when you get those perspicacious gut feelings about someone? My intuition turned out to be quite accurate. He was handing out literature to some of the customers and attempted to hand a packet to me. I took one look at the Nazi symbol on the brochure and told him, "You know, I was born when Hitler was still running amok. Go fuck yourself."

He very calmly did an about-face. Maybe it was my imagination, but I could have sworn that he goose-stepped while making his exit. I have never lost my disgust of those who openly display this symbol of hatred.

I later called and told the FBI about him. They took my name but didn't seem to be a bit concerned about him. I guess their attention was more focused on Lenny Bruce. Apparently, lewdness was far worse than Nazism.

Tony had always complained to me about Dick. In fact, they both complained to me about each other. So, I thought I'd pay Tony back with perhaps a fitting prank. He was the perfect patsy for this because he was so gullible. After the gig, one evening, Tony was excitedly called into Gary's room. There, Dick's body was sprawled on the floor.

Tony cried out in alarm, "Whaaaaaat, what happeneed?"

Gary, with a straight face, said, "Dick is dead."

"NO!" Tony screamed, "We gotta do someting." He kneeled next to Dick. "Deek, Deek, you can't do thees!"

As though he though Dick had a choice.

We all gathered around Tony and Dick.

"We're going to have to cancel doing gigs for a while until we can find a replacement," I said.

"Yeah, I think we're going to have to call Dewey back," Gary added.

Tony disliked Dewey even more than Gary did.

"NO!" Tony screamed again. "Deek, you can't ruin my life like thees!"

Dick then grabbed Tony and kissed him on the cheek, and said, "Okay, I won't."

Tony's reaction was worth all of the scheming. At first, he sat there with his mouth open. After the initial shock and relief set in, he broke into a wide grin and began laughing along with the rest of us. That was the wonderful thing about Tony back then; he was a perfect foil and had the ability to laugh at his own expense.

But this is about the time I began to notice a change in his demeanor. He seemed to inflate his role in the group. Not much, but enough for me to take notice.

A lot happened during those few weeks at the Peppertree Lounge. We were quite thrilled when Burt called to tell us that we were signed to appear in the motion picture *Get Yourself A College Girl*.

Standells Get Yourself a College Girl

Sam Katzman produced the film. It was directed by Sidney Miller, and featured newcomer Mary Ann Mobley, along with Nancy Sinatra, and Chad Everett. Besides the Standells, other performers included the Dave Clark Five, the Animals, and the Jimmy Smith Trio. Not having a hit record, it was very unlikely for a group such as the Standells to get a movie role, even though Sam Katzman, a noted "B" film producer, was involved with it. It wouldn't be our last film with him.

We had to fly back and forth from San Francisco to Los Angeles each day to film the movie, getting no sleep in the process. In the film, I sang our song from the PJ's album, "Bony Maronie," and also performed an altered version of "The Shake." The lyrics were slightly re-written, a new vocal was recorded, and the song was renamed "The Swim."

After meeting Chad Everett and Nancy Sinatra, my biggest thrill was in conversing with Jimmy Smith, the famous jazz organist. Jimmy was one of my idols. I'm proud to say that I used his same Hammond B-3 organ during our performance in the movie. The portions with the Dave Clark Five and the Animals were filmed in London and edited to appear as though they were in the same party scene.

On the set there was a problem with an actor who was cast as the emcee, and who simply had one line to say, "Ladies and gentlemen, the Standells." For some reason, he just could not get the line right. Perhaps he'd chosen the wrong profession. After a series of wasted takes, director Sidney Miller fired him on the spot and brought in Donnie Brooks as the emcee. Donnie, of course, was the singer of the 1960 hit, "Mission Bell." He would appear with the Standells later in *Shivaree* and became a good friend until his death in 2007.

I happened to notice that during our performance in the movie, I was mostly hidden behind some balloons and a female dancer's feathered hat, so it was difficult to even see me, let alone reveal that I was the lead singer. Added to this was Tony's position at the center of the group. Unbeknownst to me, he lip-synced along with me in this and other appearances, making it appear as though he was singing the lead. This was pointed out to me later by a fan who had assumed that Tony was the lead singer in the group. It marked the beginning of what I deemed to be petty jealousy on his part. I believe that it was a further example of him trying to boost his profile in the group while lessening mine, probably because of his own insecurities.

It took several days to complete the movie, which was released on December 18, 1964. [21]

We wrapped up the gig at the Peppertree, and the night before returning to LA, I happened to catch the next performers after us. To this day, there are very few experiences that blew me away as much as seeing and listening to the Byrds for the first time. The almost-hypnotic and overpowering Rickenbacker 12-string guitar, plus Jim McGuinn's solid vocals were what made them so unique. I was transfixed throughout their entire set. In my opinion, they were groundbreaking as the first group to bridge folk and rock, influencing many other groups, including the Beatles with their folk-rock songs like "Norwegian Wood" and "You've Got to Hide Your Love Away." Although they managed only a

---

21 MGM Pictures, *Get Yourself a College Girl* (1964)

short period of success, today most music experts rightly consider the Byrds to be as influential as the Beatles, the Beach Boys, and the Rolling Stones.

After returning home, no sooner had I purchased a new Farfisa organ than we received a request to do the theme song for the Ivan Tors film, *Zebra in the Kitchen*, featuring *Dennis the Menace* star Jay North. We had the honor of being produced by noted composer/arranger Perry Botkin Jr. and were given the task of performing a song written by North's father, singer/actor Hal Hopper. This turned out to be quite a chore because it was originally intended as a jazz song to be performed by the likes of Frank Sinatra.

I was given the latitude of changing the song any way I saw fit, so I completely rewrote the chords and the melody. I sang it, but I received no writing credits. The song was released on MGM Records. The flip side was a Beatleish song that I sang called "Someday You'll Cry", which I had written one year previously. Another ode to Linda's promiscuousness which had been rejected by producer Dick Glasser. I don't remember the reason, but I imagine it was because the song was something he couldn't ruin. Over the years, "Someday You'll Cry" has become a fan favorite.

In late 1964, I was quite thrilled when we were asked to guest star on *The Bing Crosby Show*, along with Beverly Garland, Frank McHugh, and Gary Morton. The name of the segment was "Bugged by the Love Bugs," and we played the part of a fictional rock 'n' roll group by that name. Bing Crosby had been a favorite singer of my dad's. I think Dad had every one of his records. I

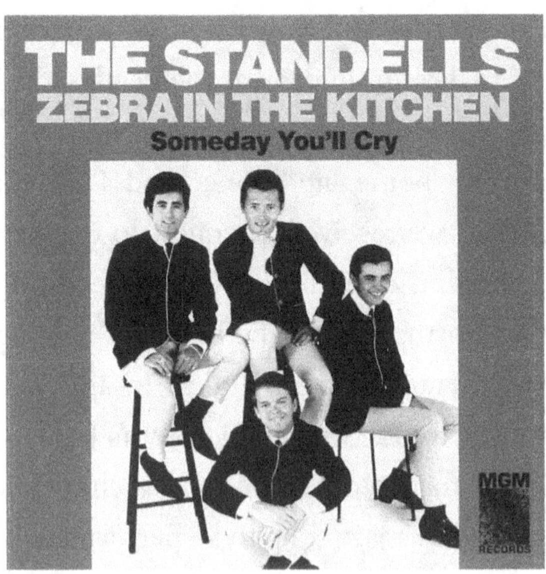

Standells Zebra in the Kitchen

was convinced that us being on the show must have been some of his doing. In the show, positioned behind the Farfisa, I sang "Someday You'll Cry" and "Come Here," which was also written by me. This was yet another show in which I later noticed that Tony inexplicably lip-synced to some of these songs along with Dick and me, even though he did none of the lead singing.

The biggest thrill was when we backed up Bing Crosby, singing "Kansas City." Right before filming the scene, I jokingly started to sing "White Christmas." Everyone on the set roared with laughter – except for Bing. He turned to me, rolled his eyes and said, "You're putting me on." Surprisingly, Bing completely overcame his crooner image by really rocking the song. The show was a complete thrill for all of us. I could envision my dad smiling.

The Bing Crosby Show episode with our appearance was broadcast on January 18, 1965.

In December of 1964, Burt could see that we were not a good fit with Liberty and found a way for us to get out of our contract with them. In hindsight, Liberty was essentially a very good label, what he should have done was get us another producer. VeeJay Records had just moved their headquarters from Chicago to Hollywood and seemed to be the perfect record label. They had a very strong R&B history with icons like Jimmy Reed and John Lee Hooker, whom I idolized, as well as popular acts like the Four Seasons, Dee Clark and Gene Chandler. Most impressively, however, was that they'd released hit singles by the Beatles, before they signed to Capitol, as well as their first US album *Introducing the Beatles*.

However, once again, we were placed with a producer who wasn't right for the Standells – Sonny Bono. At that time Sonny and Cher were just beginning to gain notoriety with not only their music but also their outlandish clothing.

Our first recording for VeeJay, "The Boy Next Door," was written by Sonny Bono with one of his managers, Charles Greene, and would have been a better fit for a blue-eyed soul act, in my opinion. Bill Medley of the Righteous Brothers might have been able to do it justice, but not me, And I think even Medley would have refused to do the corny narration in the middle. Sonny was a protégé of Phil Spector and emulated the Wall of Sound for which Spector was famous. Our four-guys hard-rock sound was replaced with a dozen musicians, including many from the Wrecking Crew. Cher and I, along with several others, sang background. Reciting the banal narration for TV show performances was a total embarrassment for me.

The follow-up, "Don't Say Goodbye," while better, was released unfinished. The flip side, "Big Boss Man," sung by Dick Dodd, was much closer to our sound.

Soon after the release of these recordings, VeeJay Records went bankrupt and closed their doors.

During this period, we were called into an ADR studio to record a music track for Connie Francis' film, *Follow the Boys*. ADR (Automated or Additional Dialogue Replacement) is a process that involves overdubbing dialogue or music onto existing film footage. We had to follow along and play music for a dance scene, which, as was typical, was done in several takes to accommodate, long shots, close-ups, and so on. Rhythmically, it was completely screwed up, because in some scenes they were dancing faster than others. So, we had to have a conductor to guide us through the tempo changes.

We then appeared as a bar band in the *Ben Casey* episode "Three Li'l Lambs." The episode guest-starred Marlo Thomas and my old acquaintance Nick Adams, who, as you may remember, was in the next room when I lost my virginity. I didn't even recognize Nick until I saw the TV show. By then, he'd become a well-known actor, starring in the TV series *The Rebel*.

CHAPTER 7

1965 was the year that Martin Luther King Jr. led the Civil Rights March from Selma to Montgomery, Alabama, The Voting Rights Act guaranteeing African Americans the right to vote was passed, and race riots broke out in Watts, California. As part of this unrest, an increase in anti-Vietnam war protests was seen, including 35,000 people marching on Washington DC.

Nineteen sixty five was also a pivotal year for the Standells. It was the year I ditched the Farfisa and purchased my first Vox Continental organ, a model that had just arrived in America. On January 2nd, along with Dobie Gray, Donna Loren, and the Olympics, we appeared on *Sam Riddle's Hollywood A-Go-Go*, performing "The Boy Next Door" and "The Shake." It was taped at KHJ TV and regionally syndicated. Also that week, we appeared on *Shindig*, performing the Animals' "Don't Let Me Be Misunderstood," and Dave Clark Five's "Come Home." Joining us on the show were the Blossoms, Glen Campbell, Dick and Dee Dee, Bobbie Sherman and Bobby Goldsboro. Bobby was quite a character; being a country boy, he did a mean cricket sound, which was so authentic the crew mistakenly thought one was loose on set! Bobby would appear with us again on *Shivaree*. He was really a fun guy to be around. *Shindig* was broadcast on March 25, 1965.

The following week, we appeared on the *Lloyd Thaxton Show*. By now, he had a much superior indoor set. Lloyd remembered me from the first time we met, and after our performance we had a great visit. I kept in touch with Lloyd after that and remained good friends until his death in 2008. I still remember him today, sitting behind that console at the old KCOP outdoor studio, lip-syncing to all of the hits. Lloyd truly loved rock 'n' roll. [22]

In late January, we landed guest-starring roles on the *crème de la crème* of sitcoms, *The Munsters*. The show aired on CBS at 7:30 PM on Thursdays – prime time – and was one of the top-rated comedies at the time. It was my favorite TV series which ran on CBS at 7:30 every Thursday, and I watched it faithfully every week. Appearing on the show was one of the highlights of my life. We played ourselves, not only performing music but acting as well. Wow!

What made Munsters sitcom so unique was that it turned situation comedy on its heels. Most sitcoms, like *My Three Sons* and *Green Acres*, involved average families in their day-to-day activities, sometimes caught up in unusual circumstances. The Munsters were also an average family – at least they thought so. The only difference was their frightening appearance to others, resulting in some of the most hilarious skits on TV. Like other TV dads, Herman Munster went off to work each day with his lunch box. His place of work, though, was a funeral home called Gateman, Goodbury and Graves. Occasionally, he was picked up by "the company car," a hearse. He was a good-natured, clumsy yet lovable buffoon, unaware of his super strengths, which played a prominent role in many of the show's gags. Aside from his childish temper tantrums, he was a compassionate and caring father

---

22 www.lloydthaxton.blogspot.com - *Why Lloyd Thaxton Disappeared*

to his son Eddie and daughter Marilyn, and devoted husband to his wife Lily.

I can remember arriving for our first day at Universal Studios and seeing the exterior of the Munsters' home at 1313 Mockingbird Lane for the first time. One must understand that the filming of the exterior and interior of the home was done at two different locations on the Universal lot. The Victorian house, located on the Universal back lot, was actually the exterior for many films, such as *So Goes My Love* (1946), as a backdrop for the '50s TV series *Leave It to Beaver*, and the 1964 series *The Kraft Suspense Theater*.

In1964, the Munsters' home was set in the fictional neighborhood of Mockingbird Heights. Its make-over included the mansard roof and four windows which were altered into the famous covered "widow's walk" with a tented roof. A crooked vampire bat weathervane was added, along with darker paint which made the home appear more sinister. Adding to the effect was a scattering of creepy-looking shrubbery which was constantly being swayed by a wind machine, accompanied by faux lightning and thunder.

Like other studio lot exteriors, 1313 Mockingbird Lane was actually a façade. Beyond the facing, there was little more than a small entry space, with a supportive frame behind it. All of the interior filming was done at Stage 30 where the individual sets were located. I was absolutely blown away when I entered the set for the Munsters' living room. It was made to look filthy with dust and cobwebs, which again played into many of the show's gags, including the Standells episode "Far Out Munsters." During one of the opening scenes, upon entering the Munster's living room, I uttered, "This calls for a party," then pounded on the sofa, which emitted a billowing cloud of dust.

Of course, the greatest thrill for me was meeting the cast: Fred Gwynne, who played Herman Munster, the Frankenstein monster-like family patriarch, Yvonne De Carlo, his vampire wife Lily, Al Lewis, the wise-cracking vampire grandfather, Butch Patrick, who played Herman and Lily's son Eddie, a pint-sized vampire, and Marilyn, their daughter, played by Pat Priest who was the sole 'normal' character in the family and thus the 'black sheep'! All were seasoned pros. Back in those days, the makeup procedure was far more arduous than today, using chemicals and compounds which had much greater toxicity than those presently used. It required several hours in the makeup chair for Gwynn, DeCarlo, and Patrick. Because of this, the actors would sometimes work sixteen hours a day.

Performing as an actor was no problem for me, but I had one challenging scene in which I was talking to our manager. My line was, "When those Munsters find out what we're willing to pay, they'll practically fall over dead." I was eating a banana during the scene and just couldn't get the eye-hand coordination correct. It took about twenty takes and half a dozen bananas to get it right, and after we finished I sure as hell felt like I was going to fall over dead! Butch Patrick and I still joke about this scene today.

Who could forget Eddie Munster turning on the phonograph, and loudly playing Standells music, causing Lily to throw the cat in the air, popcorn popping in Herman's hands, and smoke blowing out Grandpa's ears? Of course, etched in stone – at least for Standells and Munsters fans – is Eddie uttering the immortal words, "Hey, Pop, those neat guys are the Standells!"

During the show, we performed an original song "Come on and Ringo," written for this episode by acquaintances Pat and Lolly Vegas. We also performed the Beatles song "I Want to Hold Your Hand." Many have asked why we did a cover song rather than an original. This was almost two years before we had our first hit single, so we were not in a position to make demands. We did what they told us to do. The recordings were done primitively on the Universal sound stage, then lip-synced during the filming. Television crews weren't adept at recording rock groups back then, so there were only two mics. One was for the instruments and the other for the vocals. Again, without noticing, Tony lip-synced along with Dick and me in both songs. Since Dick was in the background behind the drums, it appeared as though Tony was one-half of the dual lead. Many fans have spoken highly of our performance of "I Want to Hold Your Hand," but out of respect for the Beatles I still cringe when I hear it.

One of the most difficult acting challenges came not during my speaking lines, but the satirical poetry reading by a beatnik with bongo drums. It became especially difficult to keep a straight face when Herman Munster was asked to contribute his talent, winging it with an ad-libbed poem. I have no words to describe how painful it was for me to keep my contemplative, serious-faced demeanor while sitting through Fred Gwynne's recitation, "Ibbidy bibbidy sibbidy sam, Ibbidy bibbidy canal boat."

On the other hand, Lily Munster's performance of "He's Gone Away" was quite the opposite. She had incredible pipes. If not for the setting, makeup and laughter track, Yvonne De Carlo could have been singing the song on Broadway. In addition to her role of Moses' wife in Cecil B. Demille's landmark film, *The Ten Commandments* in 1956, Yvonne had an impressive career on stage with the Steven Sondheim Broadway musical, *Follies* in 1971-2.

Originally broadcast on March 18, 1965, and countless times afterwards in syndication the "Far Out Munsters" episode has become a classic, viewed by millions of people around the world. Many associate the Standells solely with our appearance this show, not realizing that we went on to have several chart records. Most of the cast as since passed away, but Butch Patrick has remained a good friend of mine ever since.

The dialog at the end of the show, when we're saying goodbye to the Munsters is my favorite:

Herman Munster: "If your act ever dies, give me a call at the parlor."

Me: "We really dig you people."

Grandpa Munster: "And someday we'll return the favor."

Herman (*As we exit*): "You know, Lily, I'm going to sleep a lot better knowing that the future of America is in the hands of boys like these."

If he only knew how many fans would go on to quote those priceless lines verbatim. [23] [24]

---

23 "Far Out Munsters" episode of *The Munsters* (1964)
24 www.imdb.com - IMDb, *Far Out Munsters*

```
NOTE: ALL PERSONNEL DUE TO FIRE HAZARD PLEASE WATCH YOUR SMOKING & USE BUTT CANS

PROD. #24832                    UNIVERSAL TV         THURSDAY, FEBRUARY 11, 1965
"FAR OUT MUNSTER"                                    SHOOTING CALL: 8:00A
DIR: JOSEPH PEVNEY                  "D" UNIT         LOCATION: STAGE #16
ASST DIR: DOLPH ZIMMER/POSTER H. PHINNEY                      STAGE #17
ART DIR: HENRY LARRECQ
SET DECO: JIM REDD              THE MUNSTERS
PROP: EDDIE KEYES                                    2ND DAY OF SHOOTING
DESCRIPTION                                          D/N        SCS        POS

INT. MUNSTER'S LIVINGROOM                            D           1          1
Sc. 32 (LARRY,GARY,TONY,DICK)

INT. ENTRY HALL                                      N           1          3/8
Sc. 34 (LARRY,GARY,TONY,DICK,BEARD,GIRL,HERMIT,ATMOSPHERE)

INT. LIVINGROOM                                      N          18        4 3/8
Sce. 40 thru 57 (HERMAN,LILY,EDDIE,GRANDPA,BEARD,GIRL,LARRY,GARY,TONY,
                 DICK,HERMIT,MARILYN,ATMOSPHERE)

EXT. PORCH                                           N           1          3/8
Sc. 38 (LILY,HERMAN,EDDIE,GRANDPA,BEARD,GIRL)

INT. ENTRY HALL                                      N           1          3/8
Sc. 39 (HERMAN,LILY,GRANDPA,EDDIE,GIRL,BEARD)

INT. ENTRY HALL                                      N           1          1
Sc. 58 (LILY,HERMAN,GRANDPA,LARRY,GARY,EMILO,DICK)

        COMPANY MOVE TO STAGE #17 APPROXIMATELY 5:00P

INT. THEATRICAL OFFICE                               D           1          1
Sc. 10 (MURDOCK,LARRY,GARY,TONY,DICK)

                              CAST CALL
ARTIST                       CHARACTER             MAKEUP          ON SET
LARRY TAMBLYN                 LARRY                 7:30A           8:00A
GARY MCMILLAN                 GARY                  7:30A           8:00A
TONY VALENTINO               TONY                  7:30A           8:00A
DICK DODD                    DICK                  7:30A           8:00A
ZALMON KING          (NEW)   THE BEARD             8:00A           8:30A
                     (NEW)   GIRL (SC. 39)         7:00A           8:30A
KELTON GARWOOD       (NEW)   HERMIT                8:00A           8:30A
FRED GWYNNE                  HERMAN                7:00A           9:00A
YVONNE DE CARLO              LILY                  7:00A           9:00A
BUTCH PATRICK                EDDIE   (MINOR)       8:00A           9:00A
AL LEWIS                     GRANDPA               7:30A           9:00A
PAT PRIEST                   MARILYN               7:30A           9:00A
ALEX GERRY                   MURDOCK (LOOP 3:00P)  4:00P           4:30P
FRANK KILLMOND               BELLHOP               CARRY

MUSIC DEPARTMENT:
GIRL WITH GUITAR                                   7:30A           8:30A
MAN WITH BONGOS                                    8:00A           8:30A

ATMOSPHERE:                        REPORT TO STAGE #16
4 STANDINS                   7:30A
1 STANDIN                    8:30A
7 WOMEN                      8:15A
4 MEN                        8:15A
1 WELFARE WORKER             8:00A
                              CREW CALL
CAMERAMAN                    7:30A       RECORDER             7:30A
CAMERA OPERATOR              7:42A       CABLEMAN             7:30A
CAMERA ASSISTANT             7:18A       SCRIPT SUPERVISOR    7:42A
GRIPS                        7:30A       WARDROBE MAN         7:30A
```

Standells Munsters

In April, we appeared at Harvey's Gold Street Club in Garden Grove, California, where we were asked to back up one of my idols, Chuck Berry. We rehearsed for a short time with Chuck before doing the show. He told us, "Now if you fuck up, we're going to stop the song right there, and start over again."

I don't know what musician worth their salt could have screwed up "Johnny B. Goode" or "Sweet Little Sixteen," but I guess Chuck had performed with a few.

Also, that month we were booked at the Tiger-A-Go-Go room at the Hilton in San Francisco. Capitalizing on our TV appearances, we drew large crowds there. The club had their version of the Playboy Bunnies, called the Tiger Kittens, scantily dressed in tiger bustiers and tails no less. Me-ow! Staying at the hotel made it convenient for us to cajole some of them to our rooms.

Later, on May 28th, we were booked at Garden Grove's Alamitos Intermediate School "Swing into Summer" assembly. During this timeframe, Tony became more-and-more discouraging and critical of my singing, expressing this to other members of the group, and further adding to my lack of self-esteem.

We continued to make guest appearances television. On March 20th, we performed "The Boy Next Door" and "Big Boss Man" on Dick Clark's *American Bandstand*. And on April 10th, we appeared on *Shivaree* with Bobby Goldsboro again, as well as my old friend Donnie Brooks. Sonny and Cher were also featured on the show. All three were shown clapping to the beat during our performance of "The Shake." Once again, I was placed on the side of the stage behind Tony, and anyone watching at home could not tell that I was singing the lead vocal. This was further proof of my lack of self-assertiveness in not insisting that I be in the center. But again, I hadn't noticed this until someone pointed this out years later. We also were guests on the early *Glen Campbell Show* (before the *Glen Campbell Happy Hour*). Much later, when I first heard "Gentle on my Mind," I couldn't believe it was Glen Campbell. I never knew that he could sing! On July 12th, we appeared on the *Hollywood Discotheque* TV show, hosted by our friend Reb Foster. We continued to regularly perform on the show whenever we were in town.

In late 1965, we were introduced to Greengrass Productions and producer Ed Cobb, who was also a member of the successful vocal group the Four Preps. The company, part of Attarack Corp, included Senior A& R Director Ray Harris, and Seymour Heller Management Company. Heller was Liberace's manager. We were signed directly to Greengrass who in turn had a production deal with Tower Records. Our manager Burt Jacobs also joined them.

"Dirty Water" was written by Ed Cobb and presented to us as a potential song to record. The inspiration for the song was said to have come to Cobb during a visit to Boston while on tour with the Four Preps. As the story goes, while there he was mugged along the banks of the Charles river. Also, rumor had it that Ed had dated a girl there, and she had to be back home before midnight.

Ed's demo recording didn't do the song much justice. His *basso profundo* voice, a key ingredient to Four Preps vocal stylings, didn't exactly exude a rock 'n' roll persona. Quite frankly, we weren't impressed with the song at all. "Dirty Water" was written as a 32-bar standard blues song, using the same chord structure as "Big Boss Man." So "Dirty Water" could be sung to the music track of "Big Boss Man." The harmonica solo is in precisely in the same spot and sounds almost identical.

I told Cobb, "We'll do the song if we can arrange it."

Ed agreed, "Sure, why don't you guys work with it until you're happy, then we'll get together in the studio." He also made an excellent choice in suggesting that Dick sing the song. One of the things I originally admired about Cobb was his easiness to collaborate with. Unlike other producers, he genuinely listened to our ideas. Over the years, that relationship would sour.

The following week, the band got together to learn the song. When listening to the tape, Tony came up with the famous riff: Dum-dum-dum…dump-da-dum. It was catchy. Tony may not have been the greatest guitarist, but he had a knack for coming up with the simplest most endearing guitar riffs. Thus the famous guitar riff eventually became the first thing many beginning guitarists learned. That was Tony's genius. He had previously created the guitar lick from the '60s song "Let's Go." Before joining the Standells, Tony and a friend named Lanny Duncan co-wrote the song, but Tony was never credited when it was recorded by the Routers which included Lanny, but not Tony, as well as future Walker Brother Scott Engel on bass guitar. "Let's Go" became a Top 40 hit in 1963.

Dick, who was a life-long fan of the Boston Red Sox , looked at the lyric sheet, and said, "You know, this really needs to sound like I'm telling a story about Boston. It needs some kind of introduction." So he wrote, "I'm going to tell you a story, it's all about my town. I'm going to tell you a big fat story, baby. It's all about my town."

We loved it; it started the song off with a bang, expressing the grittiness along with the love of Boston. Dick then created fill-ins, like "Aw, that's what's happening, baby," and "You're the number one place." We all laughed when he took the phrase "Along with lovers, muggers and thieves," and added, "Aw, but they're cool people." Later, for even more grittiness, he added, "Have heard about the Strangler? I'm the man, I'm the man," a reference to the notorious serial killer who had terrorized the city between 1962 and 1964. It was perfect. Talk about low-life, you couldn't get any lower than that!

Gary, solid as always, added the bass line, perfectly tying it directly to the bass drum pattern.

My contributions were subtler. I altered the chord structure. After playing an E, then A/E, most musicians would have played a standard E 7th, which I changed it to an E extended 7th. But this was part of what made the song unique and different from other standard R&B songs like "Memphis Tennessee" – or "Big Boss Man." When we played "Dirty Water" together for the first time, we knew we had something special. In November 1965, we finally went into the recording studio with an arrangement we were happy with.

Being labeled as "Garage Rock" is very fitting for the Standells. "Dirty Water" was recorded in a converted garage studio in Westwood, owned by recording engineer Armin Steiner. It was done on an Ampex 350-3, a three-track tape recorder. The control room was in a bedroom over the garage studio. The walls were all stuffed with fiberglass, and during the summer with no air conditioning, it smelled like a gymnasium. I've always considered Armin to be a genius. Besides "Dirty Water," he helped create many other hits in that small studio.

Back then, Tony hadn't yet acquired a fuzz pedal for his guitar, but the original Vox AC-30 made in the UK provided us with a way in which we could distort the sound. The amps came with a variable voltage regulator, which could be set according to any country's voltage. In this case, we changed the 110 setting to 220, thereby cutting the amplifier voltage supply in half, providing the perfect distortion. This seemed to be a much simpler process than the Kinks' Dave Davies, who cut a slit on the cone of his Elpico amplifier to get desired similar kind of distortion on their 1964 hit "You Really Got Me." [25]

All of the instruments were recorded on one track, then ping-ponged to a second track, meaning the recorded track was re-recorded on a second track, along with new instruments. This time a tambourine and bass drum played with a mallet were added, almost doubling the bass line. The latter provided a much heavier bass drum and rhythmic pattern, previously unheard of in rock music tracks. The background vocals were then added on the second track, and the lead vocal on the third. The song was recorded in mono, the only possible way it could have been done.

The finished version of "Dirty Water" bore little resemblance to the original version on Cobb's demo. However, none of us were given writer's credits – or even musical arrangement credits. Those were given instead to Ed Cobb's close friend Lincoln

25 www.wikipedia.org - Wikipedia, *Dave Davies*

Mayorga – someone who never actually set foot in the recording studio. I greatly admire him as a composer and arranger, but in truth, he had absolutely nothing to do with the creation of "Dirty Water." Lincoln readily admits this. One of Ed's quirks was his loyalty to his friends and doing special favors for them.

The flip side, "Rari," was also recorded in Armin's studio. The song featured an incredible vocal performance by Dick, with intricate vocal harmonies by group members. One of Ed's major strengths was his ability to bring out the most dynamic performances from Dick, which in my opinion were never duplicated anywhere else, even in live performances. Like "Dirty Water," the instruments were ping ponged. Added were Dick's thundering toms throughout the song.

References to a stereo version of "Dirty Water" "taken from the original master" are unadulterated bullshit. The supposed stereo version was, I believe, created sometime in the mid-eighties. I can assure you that it is *not* true stereo but simulated. Also, the claims on YouTube of "original album version," inferring that there was another version, are pure fiction. The 45 RPM and album versions are one and the same.

After the recording was finished, we completely forgot both songs. As much as we liked it, never in our wildest imaginations did we dream that "Dirty Water" would become an iconic rock song.

With the recording session over, we got back to work. We were booked at the Pussycat A Go-Go in Las Vegas in November, for four weeks. We alternated with another band, spread over an eight-hour timeframe. Our apartment there had aluminum foil in the windows, so the light was filtered out. I don't think I ever saw daylight while I was there. By then, I had grown tired of dealing with Linda's adventurous behavior and had broken off our relationship. If only I had stayed that smart.

In December, we returned to the Tiger-A-Go-Go where we were billed as "The Return of the Wild Standells." By then, we were fairly well-known and drew record crowds. Since the Vox amps were new, we were astonished one evening to suddenly hear a loud radio call coming over Tony's amp. "Car three, pick up party of four at United terminal."

Tony turned around and exclaimed, "Whathefuck ees thees?"

Come to find out, the radio dispatch call was coming from inside the Hilton. The problem, as I learned, was not from the amp, but from his new Vox Tonebender. Those in the know claim the problem results from improperly shielded electronic equipment.

A short time later, along with Paul Revere and the Raiders, the Standells became one of the first American rock groups to pick up a sponsorship from Vox. The company had been taken over by Thomas Organ Company. Vox originally had some of the best tube amplifiers until Thomas redesigned them into transistor-powered amps. We were also provided with their guitars and basses which the guys thought were junk. Now they are very much desired by musicians. Ah, nostalgia.

CHAPTER 8

In 1966, the Miranda Rights warning came into effect, up to 200,000 protestors attended anti-Vietnam War protests throughout the world, the mini skirt came into fashion among the younger generation, and *Star Trek* and *The Monkees* both debuted on NBC.

I had actually been called by someone from Screen Gems to audition for *The Monkees*. However, at that time the Standells were beginning to gain popularity and I was fiercely loyal to the other band members, so I decided to pass. I wonder to this day what would have happened if I had taken the plunge. Having already appeared and acted on *The Munsters*, I might have had a chance!

But I was destined to be a Standell not a Monkee, and 1966 was also the year the Standells gained national prominence.

In January, we returned to Los Angeles and our regular gig at PJ's for the very last time. It was here that I had my first altercation with Dick. During the break, I walked out to the front of PJ's, and there standing on the sidewalk was Dick with Ray Harris and Ed Cobb. As I approached them, Dick expressing a great deal of concern that he had received his draft notice.

Joining the trio, I tried to empathize with him by saying, "Shit, Dick, I'm so sorry you got this."

"Easy for you to say," he lashed out. "You weren't the one who got the notice."

I responded, perhaps in a less empathetic manner than I should have. "That's not true, I did receive one and…"

"You're full of shit," he interrupted. "You're fucking lying like you always do."

"Wait a minute," I angrily responded. "That really was uncalled for."

He reached out and grabbed me by the collar and said, "Fuck you, you're nothing. Everyone knows that I'm the star of the group. You're jealous of me and want me to go into the army so you can go back to getting the glory."

I pushed his hand off and was about to let loose with a punch when Ray and Ed separated us both.

"Come on, you two," Ray pleaded. "This is total bullshit. Knock it off, both of you!"

Ed's and Ray's interference was a good thing, allowing us to both cool down. After collecting ourselves, we both apologized to each other.

I realized that Dick's erratic behavior was done more out of fear than anything, but it also sent up a red flag. Who had put this idea into his head that he was the star of the group? Years later, I came to realize that Ed and Ray more than likely had originated this, and it was their intention to eventually pull him away from the group. Convenient, also was the fact that, although Burt came to the club that evening, he was not outside with his partners Ed and Ray.

Later, Dick was able to avoid the draft due to a medical condition. But sure enough, when our gig ended at PJ's, Dick suddenly announced that he was quitting – the first of four times he left the

Standells. He sought his fortunes elsewhere and joined a group called the Ravens.

Tony didn't waste any time in railing against Dick. "Dat fuckeen Mexican ruined my life!" One of the countless times he said this. However, Tony had helped create this situation since he'd openly expressed that he preferred Dick's singing over mine, which had no doubt added to Dick's self- aggrandizement. Dick found a new group where he would be more prominently featured.

Future gigs were delayed until we found a new drummer. Consequently, things got really tight with money. I was broke and depressed. With nothing better to do, Tony and I drove to Las Vegas to stay at his friend Kevin's home. It was there that I happened to run into my dear sweet friend Mizuki who was still a chorus girl working in one of the shows at a casino. We hopped into bed for old time's sake, and later she generously gave me a few hundred dollars. It was the first time I'd ever taken money from a woman, and I thanked her profusely. We now had enough gas money to return to LA. I've often wondered what became of her. I am eternally grateful for her giving me a boost when I needed it.

We finally found Dick's replacement, a Canadian guy called Dewey Martin, who'd been working mostly in the Pacific Northwest with a group called Sir Raleigh and the Coupons, who had also made a single for Tower as Sir Walter Raleigh. I liked Dewey He was a good drummer and a great vocalist, but the others didn't care for him. Granted, he was a bit eccentric, but that to me was part of his charm.

Dewey did some recording with us. He played drums and sang the lead vocal on "Why Did You Hurt Me," a song written by Dick and Tony. His vocal track was later erased and re-recorded by Dick. I think it was perhaps one of our best songs.

One of Dewey's eccentricities was that he had a pet ocelot, which he took with him to our gigs. The big cat stayed in the motel rooms with us. One morning, Tony awoke screaming with the creature sucking on his toes. Dewey, like me, had a very wry sense of humor which neither Tony nor Gary understood. His wisecrack didn't go over too well with Tony: "Sucks, doesn't it?"

On another night, a maid entered the room and the cat approached her. She screamed holy hell, and we were forced to find another place to stay. The guys weren't too happy about that. It didn't matter that Tony had a nasty dog that he would bring to some of the gigs. You'd be petting him one minute, and he would viciously attack you the next. I kept my distance from Tony's dog from then on. I would much rather have dealt with Dewey's ocelot.

We played a several gigs with Dewey, finally ending up in February at the Troll A-Go-Go in San Jose. This gig lasted for a couple of months. The club was a notorious hangout for the Hell's Angels. Almost every night, there was a fight. On one particular evening, I made friends with one of the Angels when I warned him that the guy behind him was about to clobber him over the head with a beer bottle. He dodged the guy's blow and then decked him. Afterward, he came up and thanked me, then presented me with his business card. His name: "Fuck Up," president of the San Jose chapter of the Hells Angels. He told me that if I was ever in a jam with bikers to show this to them. I stuck the card in my wallet and nearly forgot about it. I never knew that it would be my "Get Out of Jail Free" card.

Years later, while waiting in a dark alley to get into a recording studio near a ghetto in Los Angeles, I was approached by a couple of large, intimidating biker chicks. They began to hassle me, and I had the strong impression that I was about to be mugged. Then I remembered the card, which was still in my wallet. In an act of desperation, I pulled it out and showed it to them. "Hey, have you ever heard of this guy?"

When they looked at the inscription on the Hells Angels business card, they were both stunned.

"You know *Fuck Up*?" the burly blond said, her scowl changing into a look of awe.

Relieved, I boasted, "Yeah, he's a buddy of mine."

Both women then practically bowed down to me. I was told that Fuck Up was considered a god in the biker world. The girls became instant friends, and I realized I had gotten out of another huge jam.

Meanwhile, in San Jose in March 1966, the big news arrived in the form of a phone call from Burt. He was very excited.

"Your record is a fuckin' hit!" he said.

At first, I was in shock. "Which record?"

"'Dirty Water,' of course."

Bill Vermillion, program director for WLOF in Orlando, had chosen to add "Dirty Water" to his playlist, and it had risen to number one there – a breakout hit. Bill was solely responsible for its success. [26]

---

26 www.savagelost.com - *WLOF & Bill Vermillion: Florida Top 40 Legends* (2016)

Dick Dodd must have heard the same news because it wasn't too long afterwards that we heard from him. He wanted to re-join the group. I was against it for the simple reason that I questioned his loyalty, which seemed to be a re-occurring problem with him. Tony, however, conveniently forgot his animosity towards Dick and said, "I don't like that fuckeen ocelot! I want Deek back."

Suddenly the "fuckeen Mexican' was back in favor. His opinion was backed up by Gary, who said that we needed Dick because he sang the lead on "Dirty Water." Thus, I was overruled. I was really sad to lose Dewey but when told of the situation, he understood. Things worked out OK for him. A few months later he joined a new group called the Buffalo Springfield.

Dick traveled up to San Jose the following day and fit right back in like he'd never left. We had more or less forgotten "Dirty Water," so we decided we had better re-learn it.

We continued playing clubs up and down California, once again playing at the Trophy Room in Sacramento. We performed at other venues, finally ending up in Seattle at the Esquire Club.

At that point Attarack decided that we desperately needed an album, so Ed Cobb flew up to Seattle. We had already recorded a few songs, including the title song, plus "Rari," and "Why Did You Hurt Me." Ed gathered together some more material, and we put together – or should I say, *threw together*? – an album. Ed decided we would record it at Kearney Barton's Audio Recording Studio. Barton is now credited as having helped create the "original Northwest Sound," with such records as the Kingsmen's "Louie Louie" and the Sonics' "Psycho." His studio was perfect for the Standells. Like in Armin Steiner's studio, the recording was done on an Ampex

350-3, a three-track tape recorder. It took us two days to record the *Dirty Water* album. In addition to "Dirty Water" and "Sometimes Good Guys Don't Wear White," which was later released as our second single, the album also included my song "Pride and Devotion," as well as fan favorites "Medication," "There's a Storm Coming," and "Little Sally Tease." The latter song was written by my friend Jim Valley, who at that time was a member of a popular Northwest group called Don and the Goodtimes. Jim would later be known as Harpo of Paul Revere and the Raiders.

Kearney Barton shared his memories of recording the album with writers Chuck Burgess and Bill Nowlin for their book *Love That Dirty Water! The Standells and Their Improbable Red Sox Victory Anthem.* His impression of Ed Cobb was less than flattering, something that evaded me at the time, but was perhaps emblematic of Ed's later idiosyncrasies.

"It was rather a strange session," remembered Barton. "Cobb, to me, was one of the worst producers I ever worked with. So, we started doing the session and all of the sudden the sound was just going berserk and I looked over and he was playing with the equalizers! I said, 'What the hell are you doing?' and he said, 'I don't like the sound on the drums.' I said, 'Well, I usually do the EQ at the end of the thing, when we listen to it back and you can say, "I like that" or "I don't like that – but you don't change it in the middle of a take!' I said, 'If you're looking for EQ on the drums, you can do this…' And he said, 'Oh, that's what I'm looking for.' I said, 'All you've got to do is ask.'"

Kearney also complained about his difficulty getting paid for the session. It took him three months of calls and getting the run-around to finally reach Ed. Shaking his head about the experience, Kearny asked Ed, "What's the story? The record is number two on the national charts in Billboard and we still haven't been paid for this."

Ed responded, "Oh, I thought you'd be so honored to do us that you'd do it for nothing."

To which, Kearney said, "You're out of your cottonpicking mind."

According to Kearney, it was only after threatening to sue that he was finally paid. Ray Harris of Attarack later offered what I thought to be a rather lame and far-fetched excuse for Kearney's treatment. When Cobb returned from Seattle, Harris claimed to have listened to our next single "Sometimes Good Guys Don't Wear White," and told Ed, "We've got distortion here, heavy distortion. How are we going to correct this?" He claimed that using Richie Podolor's American Recording Studios to re-master the song solved the problem, and then made the absurd statement that, "they meshed the distortion on 'Good Guys' into the drumbeats. That's how we did it, total distortion disguised in the drumbeats." [27]

This was a breathtakingly idiotic statement. Not only is it technically impossible to remove distortion, but to also somehow funnel it into the drumbeat, as Harris suggested, was something you'd see in a fictional rock exploitation movie like *Kiss Meets the Phantom of the Park*, which was so dumb even Kiss disowned it.

---

27 *Love That Dirty Water: The Standells and the Improbable Red Sox Victory Anthem* (2008)

In reality, Kearney was a legend in the business and very well-respected. I personally recall that he was an incredible engineer, easy to work with, and most definitely a significant part of rock 'n' roll history. His custom-made console, made for him by Ken Heid using Langevin components, was considered a "classic piece of minimalist engineering," much admired by many producers and performers. Kearney Barton passed away on January 17, 2012. His beloved mixer, responsible for so many hits, was auctioned off on eBay in late April of that year.

We wrapped up the engagement at Club Esquire almost at the same time we finished our album. The club wanted us to renew our contract, but by then "Dirty Water" entered the Billboard Top 100 and Burt had other ideas. He put together a hastily arranged tour, beginning in early May in Orlando, Florida.

At this point, I cannot continue without paying homage to the young women who played such significant roles in rock musicians' lives. Female fans were the lifeblood of musicians. Without them, those long tours would have been boring. Let me first begin by defining them. I have divided them up into three categories:

Ordinary Groupies

Young women who follow rock groups around, sometimes to the point of fanaticism.

Super Groupies or Groupies Extraordinaire

Girls who were on a quest to sleep with as many rock stars as they could.

Perhaps the most famous Super Groupie was Connie Hamzy, who proudly admits to having jumped in bed with an impressive list of rock performers, including members of the Eagles, Led Zeppelin, the Allman Brothers Band, Bad Company, the Doobie Brothers, ZZ Top, and Neil Diamond, plus numerous managers and roadies. She unabashedly remained a groupie until she was well into her 50's. I was not on her achievement list. [28]

I have a good friend, Teri, whom I've known since the sixties. Back then, she worked for Tiger Beat, Flip, and Teen Screen Magazines. She had a lot of *inside* stories. I am affectionately referred to as *Fuckin' Larry*. In fact, she refers to everyone with the same prefix. Back in the 60's she and another girlfriend, who (of all professions) was a talent coordinator for Chuck Barris' The Dating Game, had a contest to see who could lay the most rock musicians within a year's period. As Teri recalls, her friend won the contest with an impressive three hundred eighty conquests; Teri was a close second, with three hundred sixty-five.

Plaster Casters

The Plaster Casters were a very specialized type of groupie who gained celebrity status among many in the music business. Their particular expertise was in collecting plaster casts of rock stars' penises. I'd heard of these enterprising young women back then but never came into contact with them. *No pun intended.*

It all began with Cynthia Albritton, who went by the moniker *Cynthia Plaster Caster*. She was looking for an edge to get into rock stars' rooms, as the competition was very *stiff*. Reportedly, losing her virginity to Mark Lindsey of Paul Revere and the Raiders, she finally came up with the idea of offering to make casts of stars' penises. Cynthia used what could be likened to a

---

28 www.spin.com - *Oldest Living Confederate Groupie Tells All* (2005)

martini-shaker canister filled with alginate, a dental compound. To make a proper cast the specimen had to be at its ideal proportions, so Cynthia's associate, Dianne, was the designated blowjob giver. Cynthia's first and perhaps most famous mold was that of Jimi Hendrix, who was an ideal subject and fully cooperated.

The process of creating the molds was exact. *Just the thought of it gives me the creeps.* The aroused musician had to be willing to dip his schlong into the canister, at which time plaster was poured into the mold. Then it was set to dry. This was not always as easy as it sounds; there were a few virile rock stars that had great difficulty with this procedure. Some even had their roadies test-drive the process before dipping their own dongs.

One such difficult subject, according to Cynthia, was a well-known drummer who had backed up many names such as David Bowie and Dr. Sheets Beck. He wouldn't dip his appendage into the mold until he was "big and beefy enough". This presented quite a problem because it could not meet his satisfaction. *Typical drummer.* According to Cynthia, they wasted a lot of alginate in the process. Yeah, some musicians had inflated views of themselves. I could never imagine going through this excruciating process only to have a sculpture of my best buddy mounted on some groupie's mantle. So, no, I was not included in her collection. Besides, shouldn't there be some kind of licensing arrangement?

Eventually, Cynthia's notoriety caught on, and she and her team were collecting casts of famous penises from all over the world, including MC5's Wayne Kramer, Jello Biafra, John Langford, and Chris Connelly. She amassed an impressive collection of plaster penises, a noteworthy trophy collection for any Groupie.

Twenty-two were made into bronze… busts? So renowned was Cynthia that at least two songs were written about her: *Five Short Minutes* by *Jim Croce* and *Plaster Caster* by *Kiss*. Ms. Plaster Caster is the stuff that legends are made of.

Having such a prize collection really demanded an exhibition in at an art gallery or museum. In 2000, Cynthia was actually able to unveil her masterpieces at a hall in the SoHo district of New York. In 2001, *Plaster Caster,* a documentary, was made which featured Cynthia and many of her Castees. Later, in 2017, Cynthia's second art exhibition was at the world-famous MoMA PS1 in Brooklyn NY. [29] [30] [31]

Having a record on the charts brought sudden dramatic changes to our lives. Going from a nightclub act to overnight rock stars was quite a culture shock for all of us. Embarking on our first tour from Eureka to Florida remarkable in-an-of itself. However, the real shock was about to set in. As the plane taxied up to the Orlando terminal, I was stunned to see a huge crowd of screaming teenagers as well as news media. Some were waving banners with slogans like "Standells 4ever." After deboarding the aircraft, we were guided through a wild throng of teenage girls trying to pull our clothes off into a waiting limousine. We were given star treatment at concerts in Orlando, Fort Lauderdale, and Tampa. What an abrupt introduction into stardom.

It was during this crucial time, when we were at last seeing the fruits of our labors being rewarded, that Gary Lane shock-

29 www.wikipedia.org - *Cynthia Paster Caste*
30 www.mtv.com - MTV News - *Legendary Rock Groupie Displays 'Plaster Caster' Collection* (2000)
31 *Plaster Caster* (2006)

ingly decided to quit the group. He had long been hinting that he would like to lead an ordinary life. In radio interviews when each of us was asked what he eventually wanted to do, we all answered with something connected to the music business. Except Gary, who said very seriously, "I'd like to be a plumber."

He was a very shy and private person. Being in the limelight just wasn't in the cards for Gary, but the deciding factor was that he'd learned while on the road that his wife, Edie, was pregnant. He also hated flying, so he took the train back home.

I didn't understand Gary's abrupt announcement, parting from the group at such a critical juncture, but I never held it against him. Years later, Edie informed me that it had been strictly his own decision. She really loved the group. Although he left us in quite a predicament, I appreciated the fact that family meant so much to Gary that he would sacrifice his career for them. He settled down and learned a new trade, cutting hair for a small barbershop near his home in Sunland Tujunga, where he lived for the rest of his life. We remained friends throughout the years.

We had a short amount of time to find a replacement for Gary, which placed even more pressure on us. After putting the word out around the Orlando area, we finally decided upon Dave Burke, a talented bassist from a group called the Tropics. He was hired as a salaried employee. Because of the abruptness of our decision, I didn't get to know what kind of person Dave was. As it turned out, he had quite a lot of baggage. He was very neurotic with some real behavior problems. For instance, I learned that he'd been stealing money from the purses of girls he slept with. This, to me, was deplorable. There was absolutely no need for him to stoop to such depths; we made enough money. This was one of the major reasons that he ended up being with us for such a short period.

We continued to tour up and down Florida, from Jacksonville to Miami. I remember at one point, we drove by signs alongside a swamp in Orlando saying, "Future Home of Disney World." I said, "Who in their right mind would ever build a theme park way out here in the middle of nowhere?" Of course, Walt Disney would.

Meanwhile, "Dirty Water" continued to slowly climb the charts. Burt was booking jobs as we traveled, one after the other. He expanded our tour into the Southern states and along the East Coast. It got so we didn't know where we were going next. One address we showed up at turned out to be a cow pasture. I guess someone put one over on Burt.

In addition to several other TV shows, we guested on *The Mike Douglas Show*. The episode included co-host Diahann Caroll, singer/ventriloquist Shari Lewis, actor Walter Slezak, and the McGuire Sisters. Back then musical artists would invariably lip-sync to their records, but on The Mike Douglas Show we played live, performing "Dirty Water," "There's a Storm Coming" and "Hey Joe." The producer of the show was a guy called Roger Ailes. Little did I know what a prick he'd turn out to be, as the disgraced ex-CEO womanizer of Fox News.

On the road we mostly played at high schools, radio station concert promotions, and colleges. I can't remember how many cities and states we went to, but after one concert at a town hall in Millbury, Massachusetts, the place mysteriously burned to the ground soon after we departed. I guess you could say that we burned down the house.

Touring the South was especially treacherous back then. With our long hair, we represented something un-American and unpatriotic in the minds of rednecks. Whenever we walked into a restaurant, it was like the scene out of the 1969 movie *Easy Rider*. Suddenly the place would get quiet, then the chuckles would begin, followed by a few wolf whistles with smooching sounds.

In a hotel lobby in Alabama, a woman went out of her way to lambast me for my long-haired scruffy appearance. She found out what room I was staying in and stealthily hung the paper band from a bar of soap around my doorknob. I found out what room she was staying in and hung a $1,000 money band around her doorknob. I don't know if she got the allegory, but there weren't any more unpleasant contacts from her.

In another hotel, several overweight businessmen verbally assaulted us about our appearance.

"You shoulda talk," Tony responded. "Go look in the mirror. Big ponza."

At that, we all laughed.

In Mississippi, we entered a small market where Ku Klux Klan material was prominently displayed. I couldn't believe the amount of hatred these people had against blacks, and how openly they expressed it. Seemingly they hated us just as much. On numerous occasions we were even threatened with violence.

We were traveling through Tennessee one night on a deserted highway in the pitch dark, doing about 80 MPH. Tony was driving. Suddenly red lights flashed behind us. Tony pulled the car over to the side of the road and stopped. Behind us, a potbellied Smoky stepped out of his police vehicle and slowly ambled up to our rented car.

He leaned over, and with a bulbous chaw in his cheek said to Tony, "War-you-goin-to-boy-a-fire?" Mind you, this thick Southern draw had to be filtered through an Italian brain that thought "Surfin' USA" was recorded by the *Bitch* Boys.

Trying to be polite, Tony answered with a smile "Yes."

The cop didn't take Tony's response the way it was intended, and almost swallowed his chewing tobacco in anger.

"Oh looky here," he snarled. "We got us a wiseass Yankee." He demanded Tony's driver's license.

Discovering that we were from Los Angeles, California, it only further enraged him. He stuck the license in his shirt pocket and angrily snapped, "Turn around and foller me."

While driving back to whatever doom awaited us, we had visions of wearing striped outfits, and working in the rock piles for the next few decades. We finally arrived at a small building, conveniently invisible from the highway. As we pulled to a stop, we noticed the writing on the building's face: "Police Station, Justice of the Peace, Mortician, and Legal Services." I assumed that our soon-to-be captor held all of those titles.

As we were escorted into the office, we couldn't help noticing the jail cells located on either side of the hallway, attached to the office like in Mayberry RFD.

"Pallamini," remarked Tony.

The cop looked squarely at him and responded, "I don't give a flying leap whose pal you are, boy. Here that ain't gonna get you diddly squat."

I immediately intervened. "Pallamini, it's an Italian expression. He just said that it's a nice office."

We were now directly under a glaring light where the officer/judge/mortician could take a good look at us. Sizing us up, he asked, "Are you boys in some kinda rock 'n' roll group?"

I knew that this could carry even heavier weight on our sentencing than just the long hair, but Tony broke the silence, "Yes."

Now I was convinced we were headed straight to jail.

"What's the name of your group?" the lawman surprisingly asked next.

At this point, I was convinced that there was nothing I could do or say that would make any difference, so I said, "The Standells"

The grimace on his face softened a bit, then showed some signs of recognition. "Did you say the STANDELLS?"

Oh shit, I thought, *was there an APB out on us?*

"Yes," I admitted, while the other guys grimaced.

To my astonishment, his face broke out into a wide grin. "Good Golly! My daughter's a big fan of yours!"

It took us a few seconds to realize that the miracle of miracles had just occurred.

After almost picking myself up off the floor, I smiled "Great." Then after collecting my thoughts, added, "I think we have an album we can autograph for her."

Suddenly he was like putty in our hands. I ran out to the car and returned with the *Dirty Water* album. He shyly asked, "Could ya'll sign it to Sissy?"

"You bet," I replied enthusiastically. I then decided to push our luck. "We only ask one favor from you."

But by then, the Smoky was so elated that he looked up from the album and happily responded, "Name it."

Our car slowly pulled away from the building, the happy cop waving goodbye to us with the autographed album tucked under his beefy arm and resting atop his gun holster. Before long, we were sailing along the highway, with Sergeant Barns' "Get Out of Jail Free" card on our dashboard, knowing at least that there would be no more Smoky episodes in Tennessee, elated that the gods had smiled upon us once again.

Leaving the South and heading into Yankee territory, things were bound to get better, right? Well, not quite. We had reserved rooms in a swanky hotel in Chicago. When we arrived, they refused to admit us because of our appearance. We knew for a fact that Smokey Robinson and the Miracles were staying there at the time (I loved Smokey Robinson), but it seems we were deemed unsuitable because of our long hair. I later found out that the Yardbirds were thrown out of a hotel for the same reason, even though that hotel was housing a mule!

By the time we completed our first exhausting tour, "Dirty Water" had climbed as high as #45 in the Billboard charts. We returned home on June 19th, reeling from our instant national fame from "Dirty Water," the adoring crowds that flooded our concerts, along with a newfound appreciation of groupies, and the other trappings of stardom. We were running on adrenalin; it seemed as if nothing could top the euphoria we were experiencing until we were called into Burt's office the following day.

Seated behind his desk, Burt motioned for all of us to sit. A big smile crossed his face. "You guys will never guess what just happened."

We all looked at each other trying to figure out why Burt was beaming from ear-to-ear.

Finally, I said, "Okay…what's up?"

Burt rose from his chair, spread his arms, and announced: "You fucking guys have been signed to be on the Rolling Stones' tour."

After the shock wore off, Tony broke the silence, "No sheet?"

"No fucking way," Dick chimed in.

Dave, in his Southern drawl, drolly added, "The Rolling who?"

All of us leaped out of our chairs and began jumping up and down, clapping ourselves and Burt on the back. I piped in, "How in the hell did you swing it, Burt? Whose leg did you break?" *Okay, a little inside humor.*

Burt laughed. "Actually, their agent called me. You'll be joining the McCoys and Tradewinds on the Rolling Stones' summer tour!"

"When are we leaving?" Dick blurted out.

"Tomorrow."

It took me a while to fully realize that this wasn't my imagination playing tricks on me; it was truly happening! After the Beatles, the Stones were our next favorite group. We had covered their song "19ᵗʰ Nervous Breakdown" on our *Dirty Water* album. Now we would be with them on a whirlwind tour for over a month.

After the meeting, I rushed home and told my mother the exhilarating news. Although I rarely saw her these days, I was still officially living with her.

"I always believed you could do it, Larry," she said as she hugged me.

It was the truth; throughout all the trials and tribulations, even at the lowest points in my life, she'd never lost faith in me.

The next day, we all excitedly boarded the plane bound for New York. We were to rendezvous with the Stones at JFK airport on June 22ⁿᵈ for our first concert in Massachusetts on the 24ᵗʰ. We decided to get new outfits for the tour, so we went shopping in Greenwich Village. We found the perfect matching jackets in a small shop and asked the salesman if any other bands had them. We were assured that no other performers did, that they were unique, and the only four in stock.

After their press conference aboard a yacht in the New York harbor, the Rolling Stones greeted us aboard a chartered Martin 4-0-4 two-engine passenger plane. We were carrying our new suit jackets, still in the original plastic bags. Passing by Mick Jagger, Keith Richards, and Brian Jones, I received little more than cursory acknowledgments of my presence. But that was okay; they were the Stones and we were the Standells.

No sooner did we get seated than the McCoys entered the plane – Rick Derringer and his brother Randy, plus two others. Their record "Hang on Sloopy" had topped the charts in 1965. We were absolutely dumbfounded to see that they had the same exact *unique* suit jackets we did. Later we made an arrangement with them that we'd alternate wearing the jackets.

The Stones' tour manager was Mike Gruber, in my opinion a major asshole. He treated me and most of the other performers like shit. The terminology "What goes around comes around" is very fitting when it comes to Gruber. Several years later he came to me in dire straits, but I showed him respect, unlike the manner in which he'd treated me on the tour. I've seen karma take its course many times during my life.

Their business manager Ron Schneider was quite the opposite, a gem. Ron remains a friend today.

Our first concert at the Manning Bowl in Lynn, Massachusetts, on June 24th was one of the most memorable. "Dirty Water" was a huge hit by then, and the screaming girls let us know how much we were appreciated. Fortunately, there was a barricade that separated us from the wild crowd. In an interview with Greg Prevost for the book *Stones Gear*, Dick remembered, "We started playing 'Dirty Water' as the last song, and it started raining. Everyone went crazy and blamed us for bringing the rain and the water and all that. Then, when the Stones finally went on, Brian was playing the electric Vox Bijou Dulcimer on 'Lady Jane.' The metal folding chair he was sitting on was still a bit damp, and Brian got a shock and bolted out of the chair."

Later in the Stones' set, all hell broke loose. We were behind the stage when they began to perform "Satisfaction." All of a sudden, the crowd surged forward like a tidal wave and broke through the barrier. Some of the girls reached us, and I can say that I'd much rather have faced a pack of lions than a herd of groupies. They were pulling on our hair, clothes – anything they could get hold of. Yeah, that too!

As the police shot off tear gas canisters, the Stones were rushed off the stage by security. It was like a war zone, with clouds of the noxious gas wafting throughout the bowl. The Stones' limousine quickly avoided the fumes, but our bus had to drive through some of it. With tearful eyes, we said farewell to Lynn, Massachusetts, as we drove back to the airport.

We then flew to Pittsburgh, Pennsylvania, and spent the night there for our concert the following day at the Civic Center Arena. That concert went off without a hitch. Now that I had a chance to see Jagger on stage, I observed somewhat of an abnormal bulge in his tight pants. Something that size can only be attributed to padding. However, it certainly had the desired effect on the predominantly female audience.

That evening, we performed at the Cleveland Arena in Cleveland, Ohio. The stadium was packed with screaming teenagers.

After the concert, back in our hotel rooms, we experienced what was commonly known as a groupie stampede. It began as a low distant rumble, slowly gaining in intensity, culminating in a thunderous roar as the girls stormed up and down our hallways. It was frightening. None of us were about to step outside into this frenzy for fear of being trampled to death. Eventually, the calamity subsided, and we were able to venture down to the restaurant. There, inevitably, we found a few strays who wound up in our rooms.

As many girls as I slept with, Tony was the undisputed champ, sometimes having three to four per night. No sooner would he get done with one than he would boot her out and look for another. What an insatiable appetite. He had a line that always seemed to work: "You have beeeeeutiful eyes."

I could never understand the willingness of groupies to jump into bed with musicians. Far be it for me to complain, having reaped the rewards of a surfeit of girls throwing themselves at me. Years later a musician friend described it this way: "You could be the biggest geek, but the minute you picked up a guitar you could guarantee getting laid." Well, I had a Vox keyboard, but I guess the same applied to me. Sometimes when asked by DJ's what instrument I played, I would answer with a straight face, "The female organ." Okay, I admit it, a real dumb response.

After that, many of the concerts and cities became a blur to me; fly-in, bus to the concert, perform, bus to hotel or airport, eat, have sex, and fly out to the next gig. In some cases, we did two cities in a day. For example, on June 26, when we played at the Coliseum in Washington DC in the afternoon, and then performed at the Baltimore Civic Centre in Maryland in the evening.

On June 29, at the Maple Leaf Gardens, in Toronto, Ontario, local Canadian group the Ugly Ducklings opened up the show. When it was our turn to come on, the crowd went wild. David Foley from the *Toronto Star* was so impressed with the Standells performance that he singled us out in his review:

Of the American acts, I thought the Standells were the best. To their act, they added their own brand of humor, especially that too well-known tune 'Gloria' already recorded by Them, Shadows of Knight, and King Beezz.

There was an odd occurrence in our hotel that night. A guy with curly hair who seemed peculiarly out of place suddenly took an interest in being my friend. He appeared to know everyone and had promised to take me to a wild party that evening. However, in coming to my room, he asked, "Hey, do you have any drugs?"

I thought that was a rather strange question, and curtly answered, "No."

But he insisted. "Come on, you gotta have something. Pot? Hash? Acid?"

By then, I was getting uncomfortable, "Look, I don't do drugs."

But he persisted. "I heard you did. Come on, Larry."

"If that's why you came up here, you're wasting your fucking time," I responded angrily. "I'm not bullshitting you. I don't do drugs." I wasn't lying. The guy was really beginning to annoy me. After pausing for a moment, I added, "Hey, come to think of it, why don't you go to the party without me? I'm a little tired now."

He left without a word. I didn't think much about it until the following day when Dick told me the guy was an undercover cop, commonly referred to as a narc. He'd heard it from some of the others on the tour. I guess I looked like a druggie, or on second thought perhaps still suffered from the Impaired Pupillary Light Reflex that I'd had since I was a teenager. This may have been one of the reasons I continued to stay away from drugs.

One concert that stuck out in my mind was at the Forum in Montreal, Quebec on June 30th. An audience of 12,000 was on hand. Instead of police, they had about thirty bouncers. "Huge blokes," according to Mick Jagger. "After the Stones finished, kids rushed on stage, and the bouncers began to beat the shit out of them. I was even roughed up by one of them backstage who mistakenly thought I was a fan that had broken through the barrier." Jagger later said that he was scared and disgusted. [32]

Afterward, in the hotel lobby, there were hundreds of girls waiting to come up into our rooms. You know the expression "Too much of a good thing"? It sure seems to have applied there. Above the lobby was a balcony where we could step out and view everyone without getting mauled. Unbelievably, the performers would select the girls they wanted: "I'll take you, the blond with the red mini skirt," "I'll take the redhead over there," and so on, almost as though they were ordering ala carte. One of the roadies would then escort the selected girls up to our rooms, and after giving of themselves munificently they politely left. Some of the guys would return out to the balcony and choose more. Once again, no one could top Tony; his thirst for girls was unquenchable.

July was a banner month for the Standells. Not only were we in the midst of our tour with the Rolling Stones, but "Dirty Water" peaked on Billboard at #11 in the charts, on Cashbox at #8, and on Record World at #1. Meanwhile, our newest single, "Sometimes Good Guys Don't Wear White," had just broken into the Top 100. When we performed our songs, the audience went crazy, and girls sometimes even threw themselves on the stage. For the July 2nd concert at the Forest Hills Tennis Stadium in Queens, New York, the local opening act performed the Stones' songs. They were stopped immediately and thrown

---

32 www.time is on our side.com - *The Rolling Stones Chronicle* (1966)

off the stage. When they were backstage, I overheard one of the band members grumbling "Who the fuck do they think they are?"

I stepped up to the young guy and said, "They are the fucking Rolling Stones, that's who."

Sadly, he didn't get that they had committed a cardinal sin. To anyone who has the opportunity to perform with a major act, this is rule #1: DO NOT PERFORM STAR'S MATERIAL.

Afterward, I was invited to have dinner with the Stones in one of their suites at the hotel, and while visiting small talk ensued. I was famished by the time the catered dinner arrived. The main course was New York Strip steaks. As they were being served, I made the unforgivable mistake of asking for ketchup. I had to have ketchup on everything back in those days. To any European, this was sacrilege. As soon as I uttered the request, the room became deathly silent. It was Mick Jagger who finally broke the stillness with "Fuckin' Yank." At which point everyone laughed, adding to my total embarrassment.

The Stones got into some trouble for their July 6th concert in the War Memorial Hall in Syracuse, New York. According to a later article in *The Post Standard*, "Mick Jagger was angry at the Syracuse police. He thought officers had used excessive force to grab a fan who got too close to the Rolling Stones."

"They're a bunch of Nazis, that's what they are," Jagger told a Syracuse University student newspaper reporter who was scribbling notes. "This is unbelievable. Just like Nazi Germany."

More trouble occurred when Brian Jones pulled down an American flag that was hanging in a tunnel in the building and attempted to walk off with it. According to Ron Schneider, Jones took the flag and "wrapped around himself like a cloak. The cops realized he meant no harm. I had run back to the office they had him in ...not a jail, just an office, and the cops were letting him go as I got there."

Sometimes the air travel was lengthy and exhausting. But drugs were plentiful. At the time, in addition to smoking pot, the Stones loved to sniff amyl nitrate, more commonly referred to as "poppers." They were intended for use to revive heart patients, but some people used them to get high. The plane could have flown without the engines. As mentioned, I didn't do drugs back then, but even I was getting a contact high. On one flight, the co-pilot entered the cabin and asked everyone to cut back. It seems the pot smoke was seeping into the cockpit, and our pilots were finding it difficult to fly the plane. Also, it was during this tour that I began to notice Dick's heavy use of drugs, something which got worse as time went on.

After our concert on July 12th in St Louis, Missouri, I had a surprise visit from Linda. We had broken it off and I hadn't seen her in a couple of months, so I was shocked when she showed up at the hotel. After an affair with the lead singer from a Los Angeles group, the East Side Kids (who I coincidentally later produced), she had decided that she was in love with me. Yeah, right, perhaps more in love with my sudden fame! But of course, I didn't see it at that time. The tour had an off day the next day, before going on to Winnipeg on the 14th, so Linda and I went out to dinner, and I foolishly agreed to meet with her once I got back from the tour.

During the flight from Winnipeg to Omaha, Nebraska, on July 15th, we came close to a catastrophe. The plane was cruising at 20,000 feet. Suddenly, the window next to Brian Jones developed a large crack. I've never seen anyone sober up so quickly – Brian leaped over Mick and Keith and into the aisle. Fortunately, with all commercial aircraft there are inner and outer panes on each window. The inner pane had cracked, lowering the cabin pressure somewhat, but not to the point of sucking us all out of the plane. However, we assumed the worst. The pilot put the plane into a steep dive, at which time everyone else in the cabin miraculously sobered up.

No one knew the extent of the emergency, and there were a lot of fearful screams. I don't know why, but I was more amused at Brian's reaction than frightened by what caused it. Sitting next to me was Tony, and he wasn't in much better shape. He clung to his armrests for dear life, mumbling, "Sheet, thees ees not good."

After what seemed like an eternity, the plane leveled out at 5,000 feet, and we were able to safely complete the flight to our concert that night at the Omaha Civic Auditorium. This should have been an omen. As luck would have it, we had several days off, so that repairs could be made without interrupting the tour schedule. It gave us some time to relax before another long flight to the Pacific National Exhibition Forum Park in Vancouver, BC.

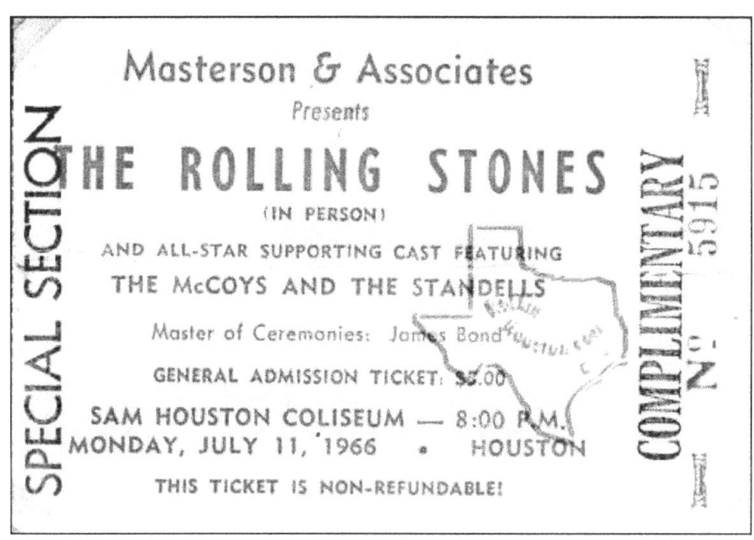

Rolling Stones concert ticket stub, July 11, 1966

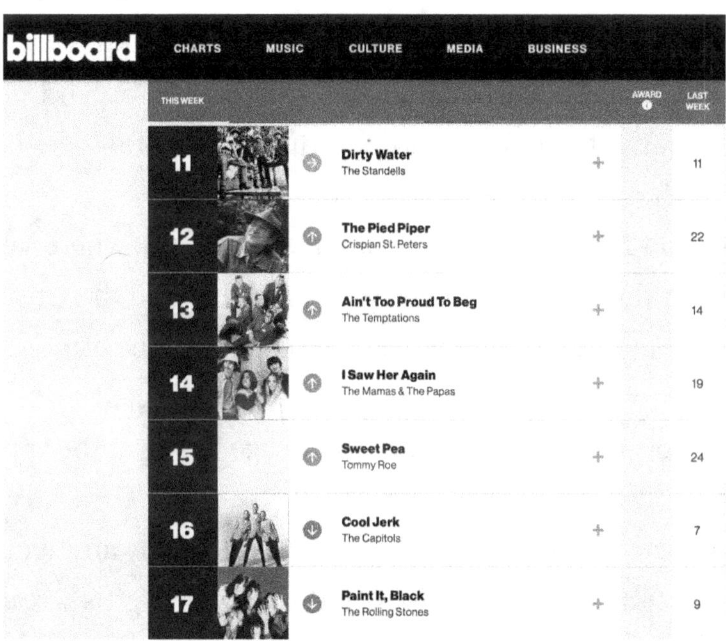

Billboard Hot 100, July 16, 1966

On at least one occasion, we found ourselves jamming backstage with the Stones. That was how we socialized back then. When listening to them perform on stage through the small backstage monitors, I realized that they weren't nearly as good as their records. But I guess that's rock 'n' roll. The amps we used, along with the McCoys, were mostly Fender Twin Reverbs and Vox AC-30s, with an AC-100 on bass. They sounded great in most concert halls. The mics were mostly on the vocals, and none were on the instruments. We had a decent PA, but nothing like the elaborate set-ups of today. No one ever complained about the sound in any of the concerts. According to the book *Stones Gear*, the Stones used their own amps: Keith and Brian had Fender Showmans, and Bill a Vox Foundation bass amp, and of course Charlie had his own Ludwig drum kit, which was set up on a roll-out riser. The Vox Continental organ I played during our set was also used by Brian Jones for part of the Stones' set.

On July 23rd, we flew into Salt Lake City, Utah, where we performed at the Davis County Lagoon, right next to the Great Salt Lake. The most exciting things at the venue were the brine shrimp in the lake. After playing for riots, being subjected to tear gas and groupie fanatics, the crowd at the Lagoon was at the opposite extreme. "It was during the day, a matinee show," Dick later said. "Everyone was really quiet. There would be hardly any applause, and almost no screaming. The whole tour was all girls screaming and chaos and all that. Here they would walk up, take a picture, sit down. It was frustrating for everyone, because we were used to everyone going crazy!"

Our performance, as well as that of the Rolling Stones, was met with polite applause. Afterward, we could hear Mick cussing up a storm about the "fuckin' Mormons."

On July 24, we performed at Bakersfield Civic Auditorium, followed by a show the Hollywood Bowl that evening, a real thrill for me. It was one of the iconic landmarks of Hollywood; I had dreamed about performing there all of my life. At one time Russ lived behind the Bowl, and we would walk up to the ledge of the canyon over the bowl and watch the concerts from there.

The Standells arrived at the Bowl by limo instead of the usual bus. Along with us on the show was a new group, the Buffalo Springfield, which included Neil Young, Steven Stills, Richie Furay, Bruce Palmer, and our old drummer, Dewey Martin. I was glad to see that Dewey had ended up with them. What a terrific show!

The only thing I didn't care for was the smug attitude of the host of the show, Bill Drake, program director of KHJ, the number one radio station in the city at the time. Even though "Dirty Water" had reached #1 on KHJ, he barely spoke to us. Also, unbeknownst to us, they had instigated a "no guest" policy and refused to allow my mother and other performers' relatives into the concert. Even though the audience treated us as superstars for being a local band who achieved national success, being the top radio station seemed to have gone to Drake's head. Even though I had many air personality friends at KHJ, my opinion of Drake never changed – he was an arrogant asshole.

The tour for us culminated at the Cow Palace in San Francisco on July 26th. With 11,000 screaming teenagers, it was one of my favorite concerts. Interestingly, this was one show when the audience seemed more stoned than the bands on stage. Also, on the bill was yet another new group, the Jefferson Airplane, featuring Grace Slick. Grace had a magical quality to her voice which cut right through to my soul, especially in their song "White Rabbit." That song introduced me to psychedelic rock. I ran into Grace several years later at Electra Records' recording studio. She brought a briefcase filled with drugs, all compartmentalized in glass enclosures. Very impressive – except I still wasn't into drugs.

At the show but not performing was Joan Baez, the renowned folk singer, composer, and activist. Backstage, she approached me, and we struck up a conversation. At that time, she was at the forefront of the Civil Rights movement. She is perhaps best known for her rendition of "We Shall Overcome," the song written by Pete Seeger and Guy Carawan. It was performed at the 1963 March on Washington for Jobs and Freedom. I was awe-struck at how intelligent and articulate yet down-to-earth she was. One of her famous quotes that always stuck with me was "You don't get to choose how you're going to die, or when. You can only decide how you're going to live."

This chance meeting with Joan Baez was a moment I shall never forget.

During the tour, I had become good friends with Stones bassist Bill Wyman and drummer Charlie Watts. Charlie was very down-to-earth. He was happily married to his wife Shirley and didn't take to the revelry of the other band members. At an early age, he took an interest in the drums and was a major jazz enthusiast. Charlie and I remained friends for several years after that tour.

Like Charlie, Bill Wyman was also very approachable and yet didn't socialize too much with the others. When the Aftermath tour ended, Bill asked me to line him up with a girl. Linda and I had patched up our relationship by then. I happened to mention Bill's request to Linda, and she discussed it with her girlfriend, Janet, who agreed to a blind date with him. Right before we all met up, Bill asked me if Janet "put out." I told him that I didn't know if she did or didn't. We picked up Bill in my Ford Fairlane and went to a swanky restaurant for dinner. Afterward, we returned to the Beverly Hills Hotel, when we all went up to his suite. Bill led Janet into the bedroom while Linda and I remained in the living room. As it turned out, Janet didn't "put out." When they both emerged from the bedroom later, Bill was quite pissed. He gave me a disgusted look like it was my fault. I hadn't realized that pimping was a requirement for my friendship.

I shrugged it off. Like they say in Russia, "Tough Shitsky." It can happen to the best of us. I never spoke to Bill Wyman again after that.

After returning from the Stones tour, the Standells performed "Dirty Water" on Dick Clark's *Where the Action Is*. The show featured popular acts clowning around while lip-syncing to their hits in various locations. We shot our bit at a slot car arcade. We did the song using mops, brooms and a bucket as props, no instruments except for the harmonica that Tony picked up out of the bucket to play the solo. At first, I thought the segment was rather amateurish, but now that I've seen it again on YouTube, I think it's hilarious. I did my fleeting best to emulate my childhood idols, Laurel and Hardy. *Where the Action Is* was really where Paul Revere and the Raiders got their big break. Before that, they were relatively unknown, but with the constant TV exposure, they quickly became popular and scored their first hit, "Just Like Me" in 1965. In my opinion, with the exception of Paul Revere and the Raiders, most performers looked rather silly and out of place trying to ham it up.

We then began another tour, this time on our own. I had kept in touch with my childhood friend, Anthony, and happened to mention to him that we were looking for a roadie. He agreed to give it a try. Another one of my major mistakes. As troubled as he was as a kid, he was much more so as a young man. His angular face was now more chiseled and defined, with a prominent nose. He could have been Tommy Lee Jones' brother.

Almost immediately, he and Tony took a dislike to each other.

We had purchased a new 1966 Chevy van, which featured a mid-mounted engine between and behind the front two seats. We seemed to always have the most bizarre things happen when traveling at night, especially when Tony was driving. Such was the case one night traveling from Las Vegas. We thought we'd take a short cut going to Reno by taking Highway 375. Somehow, we got off the highway and ended up on a small road, which I believe is now called Mailbox Road.

We were doing a good clip down the road when all at once the van began to violently shake and the engine completely shut down. All of the electricity went out, shutting off the headlights and instrument panel. Tony miraculously avoided skidding off into a ditch. We finally came to a stop, everyone heaving a sigh of relief. After catching our collective breath, we piled out of the van, relieved that we were all in one piece. We noticed a few lights far off in the desert, on the far side of a barbed-wire fence, but there was nothing else around. We climbed back inside the van, grabbed a flashlight, raised the engine cowling, and were completely taken aback by what we saw.

Tony gasped. "Whathefuck happeened?"

All of the wires had melted, including the spark plug cables, leaving a massive rubber glob of spaghetti covering the engine. We sat there with our mouths wide open.

"They sure as hell don't make them like they used to," I exclaimed, "A brand new van. Fucking General Motors."

We again climbed out of the van and tried flagging down a few passing cars. They weren't about to stop for a group of hippies out on a deserted highway. Dick pointed to some lights, off in the desert in the distance. "Hey, maybe we can get some help."

I agreed, "We gotta do something."

Our situation was becoming more desperate by the minute. We had a gig the following day. Out of desperation, Anthony began signaling to the lights. After about fifteen minutes, our signaling paid off. I pointed, "Look!"

Approaching us from the distance on the other side of the fence was a pair of headlights. It wasn't long before a military truck pulled up to the other side of the fence, loaded with soldiers. They jumped out, aiming their assault weapons at us. We were scared shitless!

The commanding officer yelled out, "Get your hands in the air where we can see them!"

We didn't hesitate to comply.

"I deedn't do nuthin!" screamed Tony.

The soldiers climbed the fence, still pointing their weapons at us. The C.O. slowly walked up to us. "What are y'all doing out here?"

"Our van broke down," I explained.

"We were trying to get help," Dick added.

We fearfully explained what had led us into this odd set of circumstances and were taken aback when they all looked at each other and laughed, especially at the part about our cables melting. Still shaking from the experience, we weren't able to laugh along with them. However, that wasn't the end of it. Pretty soon, a bunch of emergency vehicles approached the area, including police, paramedics, and fire trucks. When they arrived, they demanded to know where the accident and bodies were. They had somehow received a message that there was a big accident with lots of casualties. In his eagerness to get help, Anthony had signaled SOS with his flashlight. Leave it to roadies to come up with spectacular lapses in judgment. Evidently, a rambunctious corporal had called it in as a life-and-death situation. The two sides began to argue with each other while we sat in the van, bewildered. The whole thing was so bizarre; we honestly thought there would be a big shoot-out.

After what seemed like an eternity, a tow truck was dispatched. We were once again by ourselves, waiting for it to arrive. When he finally pulled up, Marty the tow truck driver took one look at us and chuckled, "Man, breaking into Area 51, huh?"

At the mention of the famous name, I excitedly asked, "This is Area 51?"

"Is the Pope Catholic?" He belched, then scratched his ear, "No one's ever broken in and lived to tell about it." Okay, he might have been stretching the truth a bit. "You guys almost got yourselves into a shitload of trouble. Man, there's been all sorts of mysterious shit out here."

"Wow, have you lived here long?" I inquired

He nodded, "My whole life. The folks out here have seen everything, flying saucers, bug-eyed green aliens." Marty climbed into the van, opened the cowling, looked back at us. "You guys got zapped, didn't ya?"

"What are you talking about?" Dick responded with a puzzled look on his face.

Marty belched again, "That's a brand-new Chevy engine. There ain't nothing that would melt the wires like that, 'cept a blaster."

Tony's face became ghostly white, "You theenk they shoot us weeth a ray gun?"

Marty turned back to Tony, "What the hell else could it have been, Pisano, a BB gun?"

Tony nervously looked at the rest of us. "I theenk we need to geet out fuck out of here ."

We all piled back in the van, and Marty towed us back to Vegas.

This was not the only time that the band had an unearthly experience in that part of the Nevada desert. In 1969, we were in a caravan with several groups, along with our equipment truck loaded with amplifiers and the sound system. We all decided to take a break from driving and pulled a good distance off the highway in Indian Springs. No buildings or other forms of civilization were visible. We gathered around a small campfire, drinking beer and smoking a few joints, gazing up into the bright starlit night. Suddenly off in the distance I noticed what appeared to be a bright red light, and brought it to the attention of the others. The object drew closer. Here we were, a bunch of hippies in a secluded area in the middle of nowhere, filled not with fear but uncontrollable laughter.

Several people began calling out, "Hey, Mr. Spaceman! Come on down and party!"

The huge craft came within about 500 feet, stopped in midair and hovered. It must have been at that point that the ship's alien occupants had taken a good look at the crazed Earthlings yelping and dancing around the fire, beckoning them to join in what certainly appeared to be a peculiar Earthling rite of passage. The ship almost instantaneously shot up into space and disappeared.

The history of the extra-terrestrial phenomenon associated with Area 51 is quite widely known. In his series of *Millennial Hospitably* books, author Charles James Hall, a USAF weather observer, talks extensively in his memoirs about encounters at Indian Springs with extraterrestrials he deemed "Tall Whites," along with some of the advanced alien technology he witnessed. Many other Air Force personnel also observed these beings but assumed they were mutated animals. In January of 1951, $300,000,000 was spent on what was described as an immense hanger built in Indian Springs, the purpose of which was cloaked in secrecy. Hall claimed that it was used as a hanger base to accommodate Tall Whites and their starships. Charles was stationed at Nellis Air Force base in Las Vegas during the period the Standells first stumbled upon the site. His story was corroborated by three witnesses also stationed with him at Nellis. Was he a crackpot? Hardly. Hall went on to become a nuclear physicist, and today is a noted authority on the mystery surrounding Area 51. [33] [34]

My manager, Mike Copley, was stationed temporarily at Nellis. As he explained, they used to fly into Area 51 in unmarked planes every day, "to a place that didn't exist." He informed me that the military was experimenting with microwaves at the time, which could have been responsible for our engine getting fried back then.

Did we get hit by a microwave beam or ray gun? It sure as hell was something out of the ordinary, which is status quo for me and my otherworldly life experiences.

After the 1966 Area 51 experience, we spent the night in Las Vegas, and took a flight to our next gig in Reno, while Anthony stayed and waited for the van to get repaired.

What else could happen? Plenty!

From Reno, it was a whirlwind of cities and states. In August alone we performed at seventeen venues, from Colorado Springs, Colorado on the 3rd, and ending up in Terra Haute IN on 28th. During this time "Sometimes Good Guys Don't Wear White" reached #43 on the Billboard charts. Many fans have wondered

---

33 www.bibliotecapleyades.net - *Further Investigation of Charles Hall and Tall Whites at Nellis Airforce Base* (2005)
34 *Millennial Hospitality* (2003)

why the song did not go any higher. Ray Harris explained that it was just bad timing; most radio stations across the country supposedly had either adopted KFWB'S Good Guys format or KHJ's Boss Jocks format.

"If you were a Good Guy station, they would play the song. If you were not a Good Guy station, then they wouldn't play it."

Small market radio stations were very competitive in those days. There was one story told to us by a DJ that one station received a very nice chocolate cake, addressed to them from "Grandma Kelly." All of the DJs had a slice, only to later discover that the chocolate layer was in fact made with Ex-Lax. Listeners were subjected to records playing all the way through, but where the DJ would normally switch to another record, they were met with silence… along with the sound of the needle repeatedly hitting the exit groove, "ftttt, ftttt, ftttt."

I can't tell you how many small radio stations we appeared at – they all seemed to be the same – but one particular station was out in the middle of a cow pasture. The DJ was what they call a Combo-man. I noticed a small run-down floral sofa, which must have been where he slept. In addition to running the broadcast functions, he was also in charge of the transmitter, which in this case was a 250-watt non-directional on-site transmitter. He also had numerous formats he had to run, including classical and country. I couldn't help but think *a few years earlier, that could have been me.*

I thought of course that rock was his thing. Typical of most of these small stations, the DJ's were young beginners, referred to in the business as "gulpers." By throwing their voice in such a manner, they believed it made them sound more professional. This particular guy couldn't have been more than 19 years old. I noticed that when he was doing the news, the tone of his voice was the same as when he was doing Top 40. Even worse, he was reading a traffic alert in the same voice, announcing a tragic accident! "Five people killed, and three others injured on Highway 15."

Then, without skipping a beat, he introduced us: "Today we have with us the guys that have the #1 song this week on Tom's Toppers, the Shondells and their hit 'Muddy Water'!"

Wow, what an introduction. All right, people make mistakes. Misinterpreting our song for the blues legend Muddy Waters was done every once-in-a-while. But this clown's confusion with Tommy James and the Shondells was more than I could take.

I replied to him in the same gulper voice. "Well, Tom, it's the STANDELLS, and we recorded 'DIRTY WATER.' 'Hanky Panky' and Tommy James are not part of this group."

Without so much as an apology, Tom continued. "So, tell me guys, how did you come up with the name Standells?"

This was perhaps one of the most oft-asked questions. I used the standard reply: "We got it from standing around booking agents' offices trying to get work."

The next question was a duplicate of one we'd answered so many times, and Tom so far was batting 1000. "So, for a bunch of guys from Boston, how does it feel to have a hit record about your home town?"

"Actually Tom, we're not from Boston, we're from Los Angeles"

This threw him off. "B-b-but…"

Tom had completely lost his train of thought. He tried to recover. Before spinning our record, he uttered, "Uh, thanks Hondells for being with us today."

I couldn't help responding. "You're welcome, Ted," intentionally getting his name wrong. We'd done so many of these kinds of interviews, and most weren't much better than this.

For the next two months, we crisscrossed the country doing countless gigs. However, I noticed that the animosity between Anthony and Tony had grown to unmanageable proportions. The two Italians were often at each other's throats. Admittedly, Tony did seem to treat Anthony more as a servant than a roadie, often demanding he perform duties that he could have done himself, like carry his guitar and luggage. For many who knew Tony, this officious and arrogant behavior had become more and more evident over the years.

On October 21st, we performed with the Beach Boys at the Jenison Fieldhouse, Michigan State University in East Lansing, followed by a show on October 22nd at the University of Michigan, Ann Arbor. We didn't know it, but the Beach Boys concert was being recorded. Rumor has it that someone must have been behind the controls when we went on stage, and that someone was none other than Brian Wilson. As the story goes, he was in the sound truck when we went on stage and recorded us to more-or-less balance the mics.

We never knew that this recording existed until later in 2000, when we were approached by Sundazed who had gotten hold of the tape. Why this tape never found its way into the hands of our record company, I'll never know. The songs included "Dirty

Water," "Sometimes Good Guys Don't Wear White, *Mr. Nobody,* *Good Lovin, Why Did You Hurt Me, Sunny Afternoon, Gloria, Why Pick on Me, Please Please Please*, and *Midnight Hour. Gloria* was a rather raunchy version of the song, and would typify the type of material and jokes we would do at college concerts.

The Standells LIVE on Tour 1966 is considered by music critics and fans to be one of our best albums, and perhaps one of our most important. It captured us at the pinnacle of our career. There was no sweetening or overdubs. What a pleasure it was to discover it, almost like stepping into a time machine to re-live our performance back then. I am deeply indebted to our friends at Sundazed for unearthing this treasure. [35]

After that, we went on to do a string of gigs at various events and colleges, including Oklahoma University, the home of Oklahoma Sooners football. By then, our bawdy reputation was catching up with us. We were asked not to use any questionable material on the show, but we drew the line with "Gloria." That's the way we'd been doing it, and we weren't about to change the arrangement. Besides, we had a certain "bad boy" image to live up to. We had our usual college show, with plenty of football jokes and skits. The students loved it, but the school officials weren't too pleased.

Finally, after traveling with the group across the country, Anthony could take no more of Tony's abusive behavior, and quit. I couldn't blame him. Something had changed in Tony. Perhaps stardom had gone to his head, or at the very least perceived stardom. I felt responsible for bringing Anthony into the situation

---

35 Sundazed Music, *Live On Tour* (2015)

and was afraid that Tony had ruined my lifelong friendship with him. I thought that I'd never hear from him again, only to be surprised by a call years later under the most bizarre circumstances.

I wish I had a nickel for every plane we flew on. One particular airline in the Midwest we frequently traveled on was Allegheny Airlines. They were mostly puddle jumpers; quick hops from one city to another. I remember one flight we took was in an old DC-3. I'm not exaggerating when I say that the plane tried three times to take off, only to have engine trouble and a flat tire, before we were finally able to become airborne. Once again, these flights went over with Tony about as well as pasta without Parmesan. He was a frightful mess when he arrived at the hotels. But he was generally able to shake it off by bedding a groupie, always with the pick-up line, "You beeeeeutiful eyes." Perhaps it was the Continental accent, but it always seemed to work.

CHAPTER 9

We returned to Los Angeles to record our second album. Although "Sometimes Good Guys Don't Wear White" had already been included on the *Dirty Water* album, since it was our most recent single it was also included on the new album. As with the *Dirty Water* album, almost all of the songs had been chosen for us. In addition to Ed Cobb's two songs "Why Pick on Me," and "Have You Ever Spent the Night in Jail," and the Stones' "Paint it Black," we laid down what I think were some very good original songs, like "Mainline" and "Black Hearted Woman." Also included were two songs I wrote and sang, "Girl and the Moon" and "Mr. Nobody." Last of all was a song that Tony wrote and sang, "Mi Hai Fatto Innamorare." I didn't think it was a good fit, but Tony insisted we do the song. The album was released almost as soon as it was completed with the impossibly long and clunky title. *Why Pick On Me – Sometimes Good Guys Don't Wear White*. We were not consulted on the title, and I couldn't imagine a customer asking for the album by name.

The cover photo was shot in the Capitol Records building. It was a very striking and effective shot of us all dressed in black against a white background. It went on to become an iconic image, imitated frequently by later generations of punk and garage rock bands.

"Why Pick On Me," written by Ed Cobb, was released as our third Tower single around the same time with "Mr. Nobody" on the flip side. Ed and I sang most of the background harmonies, and he chose to use a sexual innuendo during the chorus, singing instead "Why ball ball me" – a little-known fact about Ed's idiosyncrasies in the studio. To promote the new single, we appeared on *Hollywood Palace* along with comedians Norm Crosby; Dan Rowan and Dick Martin; Peter Nero; acrobats Otto and Anna; and singer/dancer Juliet Prouse. Many entertainers chose to wear tuxedos on the show, and, against my better judgment, the Standells chose to do the same. We had them custom-made; I considered it to be a waste of money, but I was out voted by the other band members. Like *Saturday Night Live* later, the format of the show was to have a different host every week. On our particular episode, the star of *Ben Casey*, Vince Edwards, was the host. We performed a medley of "Dirty Water" and "Why Pick on Me." The show was aired on November 19th, 1966. That month "Why Pick on Me," reached a disappointing #54 on the Billboard charts, even lower than "Sometimes Good Guys Don't Wear White."

Why Pick on Me, Sometimes Good Guys
Don't Wear White press release

Hollywood Palac

In order to get more coverage in the press, Burt our manager worked a deal the female editor of one of the popular teen magazines. In return for a front-page article, she could have Dick for stud services (managers did those things). Not a bad deal for either side. She was an attractive woman, in her early thirties and Dick was…well, Dick – a young, handsome, virile rock star. I never heard how it went, but we did receive a huge spread in the magazine, and the editor was extraordinarily pleased the next time Burt saw her. We continued to perform on various TV shows, including Sam Riddle's *9th Street West* and *Boss City*, and Casey Kasem's *Shebang*. Additionally, we managed to tape four episodes of Dick Clark's *Where the Action Is*. On one *Boss City* taping, Dick was so stoned that he kept sliding off his drum stool. No sooner did we pick him up and prop him back on the stool than he would slide right back off again. That's when I began to notice that, aside from his incredible talents, he had a proclivity for self-destruction.

We also kept busy by appearing at the Hullabaloo Club on Sunset Boulevard, along with the Buffalo Springfield and other local groups. It was considered a teen club since no drinks were served. Formerly the Moulin Rouge, the large facility featured a revolving stage. While one band performed, another would set up on the opposite side of the stage. We appeared there on multiple occasions throughout the rest of that year and the following one.

On our nights off, we often visited the Sunset Strip to check out many of the groups who performed at clubs like the Whisky A Go-Go, Pandora's Box, and Gazzarri's. Back then the music scene was always fresh, with constantly changing faces, clothing styles, along with new and exciting sounds, like the Doors, Frank Zappa and the Mothers of Invention, Love, Grass Roots, Electric Prunes, and the Leaves.

During this time, we were called into the studio to record another album. In their rush to come out with a follow-up album to *Why Pick on Me – Sometimes Good Guys Don't Wear White*, Attarack had the idea for us to make an album called *The Hot Ones*, consisting solely of other people's hits (except for "Dirty Water"). My initial opinion was that *The Hot Ones* album was not well-conceived. Back then, no one did an album consisting of other people's songs. It was an attempt by Attarack to put as much material out on the market as possible. Attarack, as music critic Ritchie Unterberger later observed, "didn't apply intelligent long-range planning to the band's career, issuing too many albums at once." However, today *The Hot Ones* album has gained a considerable following, and cuts from it get quite a lot of play on Internet radio. [36]

1966 was such an action-packed year for the Standells that, looking back, it's hard to imagine how we managed to fit so much work into such a small space of time. In late October we embarked on another national tour, this time headlined by Paul Revere and the Raiders. Also on the bill was my good friend, Ian Whitcomb, who was also on Tower Records and had a campy hit record called "You Turn Me On," and the Robbs, who didn't have a hit record but were featured regularly on *Where the Action Is*.

Most of the tour was done by bus. Two buses were involved: one for the Raiders, and one for the rest of us. The Raiders' bus was a lot more luxuriously equipped, with beds, TVs and a stereo. Ours had none of the above. Anyone who's ever been on one of these tours can tell you how boring those long drives can be. The hijinks aboard the buses sometimes got out of hand, like the time we gave a full moon broadside to a car filled with old ladies on their way to church. Now that I think of it, they might have gotten a thrill out of it.

To say the least, it was a wild tour. We'd pull into one city, perform, and then out the next morning. Some of the more enterprising groupies followed the tour and became very familiar with most of the band members. One young woman knocked on my door late at night clothed only in a towel. What was I going to do, leave her out in the cold?

---

36 www.allmusic.com - *Artist Biography by Richie Unterberger*

Speaking of young women, sometimes they could be problematic. In Greenville, South Carolina, it seems that some of the hometown boys got jealous of the fact that many of the local girls were spending their time in our rooms. So, they decided to take out their revenge on the long hairs by circling the hotel with their 22's and shooting at random rooms. Finally, the police arrived. If they hadn't been shooting at a Holiday Inn, the cops might not have shown up at all. Fortunately, no one from the tour was injured. It ended up with a police pursuit and car crash with some injuries to the troublemakers. It was all because they were jealous of a bunch of musicians having their way with the girls when they couldn't. In reality, most of us were having too much fun to even notice what was taking place in the outside world.

In some instances, we flew to gigs. At Dallas Love Field, a couple of drunken businessmen were going to a great deal of trouble to mock all of the musicians on the tour. The Raiders road manager was big Mark "Hoss" Amans, who wore a ten-gallon hat, thus his likening to Dan Blocker's Hoss of *Bonanza* fame. Hoss walked up to the two men, pulled out a pair of scissors and cut off both of their ties. It was almost as if the snipping was an allegory to cutting off their penises; it sobered them up pretty quickly. Hoss was a lovable and endearing man, almost as popular as the members of the Raiders.

One evening in Houston, Texas, Tony and I had a couple of girls in the bed in our hotel room. Suddenly, to our shock and horror, in walked a deputy sheriff. I had no idea how he'd gotten in the room, but was stunned to see the intimidating dude with the badge. Clothes were strewn all over the room. With a triumphant look, he walked over to the TV set and picked up a bra with his baton. Once again, my only thought was, *Oh shit, I've had it this time.* By now all four of us were sitting up with the sheets draped around us.

The cop was the first to speak. "Caught in the act, and this here is evidence!" he said, brandishing the bra on the end of his baton.

Tony attempted to come up with a lame excuse, "Thees ees not what eet looks like."

The officer gazed cynically down at Tony: "Then tell me what y'all were doing under the sheets."

I tried to jump to Tony's defense. "You see, these girls came into the room, and we were just having some fun. There can't be a law against that, can there?"

He turned his attention from Tony to me. "Oh, I can think of plenty of laws ya broke here."

If we were not already scared shitless by the lawman's sudden appearance, we were absolutely dumbfounded by his next comment: "But shit, who am I to interfere with an orgy?" His face suddenly broke into a wide grin. "Had ya, didn't I?"

It took us all a few seconds to realize this guy was for real, a rarity as far as Texas cops were concerned. We all began to laugh, joined in by the deputy.

"I know'd who you were all along," he grinned. "The Standells. I love that 'Dirty Water.' Hey, would ya'll like some hooch to make it a real party?"

I couldn't believe my ears. "Yeah, but all of the liquor stores are closed, aren't they?"

"Leave it to me. Jonesy's the name. It's the least I can do after scaring the shit out of ya." He began to chuckle again, as he walked out of the room, closing the door behind him.

About a half-hour later, the deputy returned with a bottle of Jim Beam, some ice, and plastic cups. We asked Jonesy if he'd like to join us, but he said he couldn't while on duty. It was difficult for me to believe that he had gone out of his way to do this for us. We promised him a comp to our concert the following evening, and he was thrilled. On the night of the concert, there was Jonesy with his girlfriend, like everyone else, rocking to the music and having quite a time. In my opinion, Jonesy was one hell of a Texas cop!

Ian Whitcomb was a performer on the tour. Also on Tower Records, he had a number 1 record "You Turn me on". He and I were good friends and hung out a lot. Being British and college-educated, Ian was outspoken about what he perceived as ill-mannered people. One time, we were at a Howard Johnson's restaurant (if I had a dollar for every HoJo's I dined at…). We had a very rude waitress, who obviously disdained our long hair and treated us accordingly. It was a bit like the scene in *Five Easy Pieces* with Jack Nicholson. When she refused a request to make a simple change in the menu, Ian in his proper English dialect let her have it.

"Your behavior madam is unconscionable. You will either adjust your attitude, or I shall demand to talk to your superior."

Without another word, she made the substitution in the menu, her face flushed with anger. I loved Ian. Ian and I remained friends through the years.

We wrapped up the tour in Phoenix. Back at the hotel afterwards, we were invited to a party in one of the other rooms. When we walked in, there was a naked groupie on the bed. It was an orgy, starring a well-known rock 'n' roll performer who shall remain nameless. While Ian and I observed, the guy unveiled his gargantuan appendage and climbed atop the voluptuous woman. When he was finished, one-by-one the musicians from other groups and roadies began to take their turns! Worst of all, she seemed to be enjoying herself.

"Is this really happening?" I asked Ian.

"There does seem to be an assembly line of some sort," he responded drolly.

No, it didn't! And yes, I'm sorry I attended the orgy! Not my most stellar moment.

In her book *Meow! My Groovy Life with Tiger Beat's Teen Idols*, Ann Moses talks about the Paul Revere and the Raiders tour, the Standells, her mad crush on Dick Dodd, and about a particularly disturbing episode with Tony.

In early November, I flew into Columbus, Georgia, where I met the Standells: Dick Dodd, Tony Valentino, Larry Tamblyn, and John Fleck. I was immediately drawn to Dick, the lead singer and drummer for the band. He was, as I described him in my first Tiger Beat article on the group, so "un-Hollywood." Tall and slender, he had warm brown eyes and irresistible dimples when he smiled. I didn't realize that he had such beautiful brown skin because his mother was Mexican. I only knew I couldn't keep my eyes off him. We sat together a lot on the tour bus that week. It wasn't crazy love, but it was definitely a major crush.

On our third night, there was a knock on my door. I was hoping it would be Dick, but instead, it was his cocky bandmate, Tony Valentino. I was dressed in my baby doll PJs, but I invited him in, naively thinking he just wanted to talk. We hadn't spent any time together, so what else could he want? I didn't know Tony considered himself the Casanova of the group. I grabbed a note pad and pen, sat on my bed, and began writing notes in longhand. I figured we were doing an interview, but Tony had something else in mind. Before I knew what was happening, he'd unzipped his pants, pulled out a couple of inches of his penis, which wasn't even fully erect, climbed onto the bed, and tried to pull aside my pajama bottoms. "What the hell are you doing?" I hollered, and pushed him away before he could actually touch me. He looked surprised. "I thought we'd just have some fun." I told him to find some "fun" somewhere else and pushed him out the door.

I must say that I was very shocked when I heard about this years later from Ann, who today is a very good friend. If I had known about his behavior, I would have nailed his ass. I've mentioned Tony's insatiable thirst for young women, but until recently had never known that he forced himself on my friend, furthermore one who was a very influential teen magazine publisher who could have done considerable damage to the Standells. As many girls as I slept with, I personally never forced myself on any of them, and certainly knew that "no" means "no." There was even one situation when a young woman refused to go any further, then had the audacity to shower in my room, parading by me complete nude.

In her book, Ann went on to say that Dick was the one she lost her virginity to – willingly. That's the way it was back in those days. Many a girl lost her cherry to a rock star. I guess it came with the territory. [37]

Not all gigs were groupies and glory. After the completion of the tour in late November, oddly enough, we were booked in a small club in Scottsdale, Arizona. What a letdown. Although the pay was really good, we hadn't played in a nightclub since Seattle. There was also something damned fishy about this gig. As I later learned, my instincts were right-on.

During our opening set, the club manager, who was pudgy with a bulbous nose, a bad toupee, and dressed in a suit and tie, demanded that we turn down the level of our amplifiers. We did so, cutting the levels in half. But that didn't stop him from returning quite frequently during the set, forcefully demanding we lower the volume, even though members of the audience seemed to be enjoying themselves. By the end of the set, our instruments could barely be heard.

Backstage afterwards, the meddlesome prick rushed in, grabbed hold of my shirt and shouted, "Didn't you hear me, punk? I said you're way too fucking loud!"

At that point, I completely lost it. I batted aside his meaty hand and shoved him, knocking him flat on the floor. Others stepped in to separate us, but the damage had been done. We were thrown out of the club. And of course, they refused to pay us.

It wasn't until the following day that I realized their sinister plan. Throughout the weekend, they continued to advertise that the Standells were performing at the club, in the process drawing

---

37 *Meow! My Groovy Life with Tiger Beat's Teen Idols* (2017)

in large crowds. Another band was there posing as us – for considerably less money.

We later took the matter up with the Musicians Union and laid out our case that the club had malicious intentions all along. But it was our word against theirs. Because I had shoved the guy, and the club's insistence that it was "unprovoked," all part of their scheme, we lost the case. You took your chances in those days. There were some real scumbags out there.

Before returning home, we played a gig in Dallas, and afterwards were invited to a party in our honor. Dave Burke claimed he wasn't feeling well, so we attended the party without him. We made a brief appearance then returned to the hotel to check up on Dave to see how he was feeling. He opened the door, somewhat embarrassed because there was a naked girl in his bed. I must say it's pretty bad when you get terminated from a rock group, but Dave had the distinction of being fired on the spot. The news announcement said that he got drafted into the army. It's a real shame, because I really liked Dave as a performer, and thought he added a lot to the group.

After returning to LA, we held auditions for a new bass player at American Recording Studios, Richie Podolor and Bill Cooper's place in Studio City. We took our time, going through many decent bassists before finally deciding on John Fleckenstein, who went by the stage name John Fleck. Having once been a member of the excellent group *Love*, John seemed to be the perfect fit. Not only was he an accomplished musician, but also a talented songwriter.

While we'd been away on the road, there'd been a lot happening in our hometown. On the Sunset Strip, the authorities had been clamping down on the teenagers who crowded the sidewalks every night, drawn by the night life around clubs like Pandora's Box and the Whisky A Go Go. Police began vociferously enforcing curfew and loitering laws and this in turn led to tensions and protests. On November 12, 1966, more than a thousand demonstrators gathered outside Pandora's Box, including celebrities like Peter Fonda, Jack Nicholson, and our one-time producer Sonny Bono, and there were hundreds of arrests. The "Sunset Strip Riots," as the media dubbed them, continued off and on through the end of the year.

As always, Hollywood moviemakers were quick to cash-in on the protests, seeing them as an opportunity to tap into the youth market represented by the emerging hippie counterculture. Towards the end of the year, Burt was approached by producer Sam Katzman for the Standells to appear in a new movie to be titled *Riot on Sunset Strip*. Having worked with Katzman before, we were aware of his low budget reputation. *Riot on Sunset Strip* was to be no exception: an exploitation film based on the recent teenage "riots." Katzman wanted the Standells to write and perform the title song.

I began to write a song, while unbeknownst to me John and Tony were working on another. They were stuck on one line that John wrote: "I'm not on a stay home trip tonight."

Tony just didn't seem to pick up on the slang. According to John, he asked, "Whatsa thees treep?"

John had to explain it the colloquialism to him. As it turned out, once I heard their song, I immediately shelved mine, only to re-write the lyrics as "Get Away From Here," which was the second number we performed in the movie.

The movie was written and rushed to completion within months of the November riots. To me, *Riot on Sunset Strip* was much akin to the movies *Reefer Madness* and *Plan 9 from Outer Space*; so bad that it was good! The idea that a virginal young girl – played by Mimsy Farmer – could meet some hippy friends on the Strip who were bad influences was corny enough; that she could take a hit of acid and suddenly participate in a gang bang, much like the one on the Raiders tour, was ludicrous. Her dance, while she was supposedly high, was more like a choreographed striptease routine. Much of the dialog was about as clichéd as you could get, with obligatory lectures on the dangers of pot. It was written by someone who obviously didn't have a clue about hippies and the drug culture. To give it a little authenticity, Katzman integrated some of the news footage of the protests into the film.

Appropriately, the Standells appeared in the movie during the first several minutes, performing the title song, right after an enraged senior citizen says, "Officer, it's getting worse every night. I've never seen so much riffraff. The authorities ought to do something about it."

It was the perfect introduction for the Standells. The second song comes a little later on in the film.

We recorded our music on the studio soundstage, which was rather primitive for rock 'n' roll. What's worse, they decided to make a soundtrack album, and we weren't invited to the mix-down for it. That's the reason that two of the recorded tracks were accidentally omitted from "Get Away from Here," which happened to be drums and guitar, plus one of the background vocal tracks, meaning the song was only a shadow of how I had envisioned it.

Riot on Sunset Strip was filmed and released within four months after the November riots. [38]

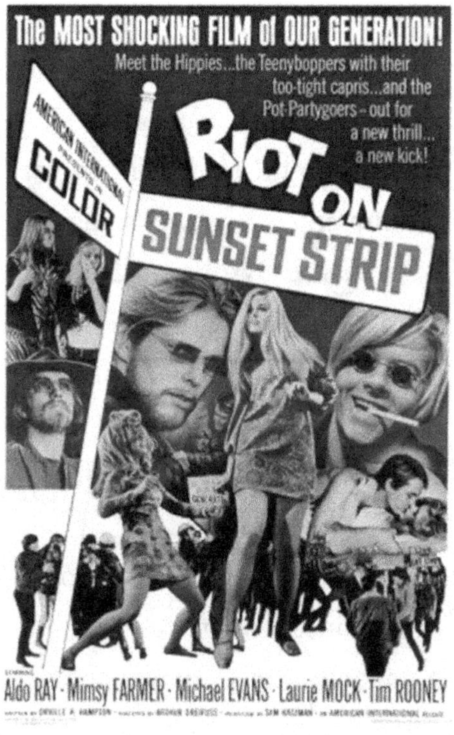

Riot on Sunset Strip lobby card

On December 17, 1966, I finally married Linda. Again, it was not one of the smartest things I ever did. Linda and I were both too young, and not ready for marriage. Keeping with her theme that nothing I did was good enough; Linda decided the wedding ring I purchased wasn't to her liking and had it altered. She had the stones removed from a diamond ring given to her by one of her

---

38 *Riot on Sunset Strip* (1967)

wealthy boyfriends and transplanted onto the ring I gave her. I thought nothing of it at the time. At least I had found another use for the custom tuxedo I had made for *Hollywood Palace*. We had a decent-sized wedding at the Chapel in the Canyon, in Canoga Park. A lot of friends attended.

We settled down in the lower portion of a condo in Laurel Canyon. Above us was Danny Hutton, who would become a member of Three Dog Night. I should have at least had a clue about what a sham our union was on the day after our marriage when Chris Hillman of the Byrds knocked on our door. Linda had just returned from a walk. She'd flirted with him, and he'd followed her back home. He was really surprised when I answered the door. I couldn't blame him; I would be also.

On the positive side, this marriage produced my oldest lovely daughter, Lisa.

It was in that condo that I composed a song called "Where is Mary." Danny Hutton must have gotten sick of hearing me practicing it on the keyboard. The song was totally unlike anything the Standells would ever do, so I brought it to the attention of Eddie Davis, and he had me produce a young group called the Back Seat doing my song. It was released on his Linda label in April of 1967.

Like Eddie, I had a special fondness for Latino and Hispanic musicians and would do anything I could to help them. When doing so, I often thought about my friendship with Ritchie Valens and the potential of finding another talent like him. Eddie and I co-produced a single by the Premiers, of "Farmer John" fame, called "Get On This Plane," kind of a psychedelic tune, along with one of my own compositions, "Come On and Dream." It appeared on his Faro label in late 1966. I completely arranged both songs. Unfortunately, Eddie Davis, had such a soft spot for Latino groups, that without my knowledge added co-producing credits to the song to a young Hispanic friend who had absolutely nothing to do with the recording. I also produced a group called the East Side Kids and their song "Listen to the Wise Man" for Eddie's Valhalla label in the fall of 1967. Their lead singer had previously had an affair with Linda, but I was able to put this aside while working with them.

CHAPTER 10

1967was the year of the first heart transplant, the first ATM, the first Super Bowl, and of course the Summer of Love. Jimi Hendrix burned his guitar onstage at the Monterey International Pop Music Festival, the Beatles released their groundbreaking album *Sgt. Pepper's Lonely Hearts Club Band*, and a rail-thin British model named Twiggy was all the rage.

In January of that year, the Standells played a concert at the Santa Monica Civic Auditorium with Count V, the Seeds, the Turtles, and Love, John's former group. I knew that lead singer Arthur Lee held some animosity towards John for leaving his group, but I didn't know to what extent he would take it. We were set to go on, the announcer said, "And here are the Standells!" We kicked into our first number – and only the drums could be heard. Right before our opening song, Arthur had stealthy unplugged all of our amplifiers. Today, I always rib my good friend Love guitarist Johnny Echols about this.

On January 28th, we again appeared on Dick Clark's *American Bandstand* doing "Dirty Water" and our upcoming single, "Try It." The show also featured a telephone interview with the Monkees' Davy Jones. We also appeared again on Dick Clark's *Where the Action Is*. Of all songs, we performed Tony's "Mi Hai Fatto Imnnomarare." The theme that day was boats in the water. After Neil Diamond performed his song "The Boat That I Row" on a cabin cruiser, naturally we followed in a small boat with Tony as the gondolier, singing his song. It was most certainly not one of our more memorable performances. In February we appeared again on the show, but this time we did one of my favorites, Ed Cobb's "Have You Ever Spent the Night in Jail. "We were all dressed up in striped prison uniforms, much like I had envisioned wearing after being pulled over by that smoky in Tennessee.

Also, in February we did a one-week engagement at the Ice House in Pasadena. It was our first extended show since Seattle in 1966, a fun gig, and it was nice to stay in one venue for a change. We also tried something new: putting Dick out front of the group on several songs while Tony played drums. It was something that Dick always wanted, and I was willing to give it a try. However, as good as he was behind the drums, he was a terrible front man, lacking the charisma and stage presence of more famous lead singers like Mick Jagger and Jim Morrison. Quite frankly, he looked rather stiff. You wouldn't think so with his background as a dancer with the Mickey Mouse Club. I thought that maybe he just needed more experience in this role, so we tried the front man routine several more times at the Ice House, sadly with little improvement.

On March 11th, we appeared on the Sam Riddle Show concert at the Valley Music Theater in Woodland Hills, California. Also on the bill were the Electric Prunes, Harper's Bizarre, the Nitty Gritty Dirt Band, the Merry-Go-Round and DJ the Real Don Steele.

After the show, we immediately left for a tour with the UK duo Chad and Jeremy, performing mostly at colleges. We started on March 12th at Boise College, Idaho, and ended on April 7th at California State Polytechnic College, San Luis Obispo. Chad Stuart and Jeremy Clyde were wonderful to work with and we had a great time performing together. Coincidentally, Ian Whitcomb was also part of this tour and acted as MC. Although his hit record was "You Turn Me on" was rock, Ian had a love for ragtime and jazz. With a ukulele as his accompaniment, he would try to combine the two during the concerts. Sometimes it didn't go over well with the teenage audience. On one occasion, the crowd began to boo Ian. Instead of taking it in stride, Ian let the crowd know how rude he thought they were, which egged them on even more. A little-known fact is that the very talented James Guercio was their combination road manager and bass player. James was a session musician who had played on several of their recordings. He also wrote their top Top 30 hit "Distant Shores." Later, in 1967 Guercio produced the Buckinghams, and helped to create their Top Ten hits "Don't You Care" and "Mercy, Mercy, Mercy."

Our new single, "Try It," was released in February. We loved it. A hard-driving rocker, it was closer to our gritty style of music. Also, Ed Cobb didn't write it, which was a welcome change in direction; it was written by Joey Levine and Marc Bellack. As soon as we recorded it, we were convinced that "Try It" would be a hit. Billboard magazine reviewed it and stated, "Right up the alley of the teen buying market, this hard-driving rocker should put the Standells back in the 'Dirty Water' selling bag. Exposure could skyrocket it up the chart."

As soon as the record was released, many radio stations picked up on it. All looked rosy until radio tycoon Gordon McLendon stepped into the picture and brought our "hit" to a screeching halt.

McLendon, a born-again Christian, owned a communications empire that included radio stations across the United States. In addition to KLIF, he owned KNUS-FM in Dallas, KOST in Los Angeles, WYNR (later WNUS), & WNUS-FM in Chicago, WWWW-FM in Detroit, KEEL in Shreveport, WAKY, in Louisville, KABL in Oakland, KABL-FM in San Francisco, KILT in Houston, KTSA in San Antonio, and KELP in El Paso. On April 8th he declared war against questionable lyrics in rock songs, and targeted "Try It" as "smutty." He claimed that it encouraged young girls to have sexual intercourse.

The Rolling Stones' hit single at the time was "Let's Spend the Night Together," but it was our record "Try It" that was singled out as the centerpiece of his moral crusade. In a full-page ad on *Billboard* magazine, McLendon declared: "Frankly, we're tired – Tired of today's new releases coming through rife with 'raunchy' lyrics." He demanded broadcasters follow his "Code of Record Standards" and refuse to play any music with questionable lyrics. He ended the ad with a veiled threat of "regulatory action" if record companies and broadcasters didn't take action. [39]

McLendon embarked on a national crusade, appearing on TV news stations throughout the country, including a major station in Los Angeles. He held up a copy of "Try It," and, making sure that the camera got a close-up of the record jacket and label, went on to say that the record contained salacious lyrics and advised all radio stations not to play it.

---

39 www.mc.com - *Motor City Flashbacks, Gordon McClendon: An Open Letter to the Music Industry* (1967)

KRLA's station manager John Barrett refused to subscribe to McLendon's code, which he claimed, "relies upon abstraction which I doubt could withstand logical examination." He also went on to say, "I personally admire much of what is being done by young people today." Lee Sherwood, director of WQAM, Miami Beach, FL, felt that the intentions were "too idealistic." He mentioned "Love for Sale" by Cole Porter, which was considered pretty raunchy in its day, and asked, "Who sets the standards?" However, more than a hundred radio stations agreed to abide by McLendon's code of Record Standards.

"Try It" went to #1 on the LA Charts, yet KHJ followed McLendon's threats and refused to play it, adding to my disdain for Bill Drake. It shot up to #1 on WQAM, Miami, and WHOO, Orlando, Top 10 on WLLL in Lynchburg, Virginia, and KSVN, Ogden, Utah, KFLY, Corvallis, Oregon, and Top 40 on WCOL, Columbus, Ohio. Since the vast majority of radio stations refused to play the song, however, "Try It" barely made the national charts.[40]

Bud Frazier, the president of our label, Tower Records, stated to the press that there were no consumer complaints received by Tower or the stations airing "Try It," and that he was "confused" by McLendon's actions.

Learning that McLendon banned our record was like having the rug pulled out from under us. We all were convinced that the song was going to be a hit, but now, its climb in the charts was brought to a screeching halt.

---

40 www.books.google.com - *Billboard Magazine, Pages 28 & 34, McLendon Anti-Filth Drive Stirs Rhubarb* (1967)

McLendon's claims were patently false. He wanted to exert his power in the industry, and he purposely chose the Standells because we weren't as big as the Rolling Stones. Plus, he must have been aware that we were on a weak record label that would do nothing to stop him. He knew he could crush us.

It was obvious that McLendon had tapped into broadcasters' natural fear of the FCC. All of McLendon's stations immediately stopped playing the record, and many others across the nation joined in the boycott.

Reb Foster, Program Director at KRLA chose to play "Try It," in spite of the McLendon threat about questionable lyrics. I assume he was referring to words like "action," "sweet love" and "satisfaction" – which, coincidently, was the name of a huge hit by the Rolling Stones! That was about as racy as it got.

Try It *lyrics*
Marc Bellack and Joe Levine

(Spoken): All right, baby it's all right
    I'm gonna tell you somethin' and you'd better listen
    By the way you look I can tell that you want some action
    Action is my middle name
    Come over here, pretty girl, I'll give you satisfaction
    But two are needed for this game
    I'll give you sweet love you never had before, yeah
    You think you've seen it all but you don't know
    what's in store

C'mon, try it (mmm-mmm)
Try it (mmm-mmm)
Try it (mmm-mmm)
Try it (mmm-mmm)

You look excited and you figure that it's just a bluff - huh
A-don't you dare walk away
I'll get you, tough little chick, before you fall in love
Come here, girl, what do you say
Just say the word and my good lovin' will start
I'll serve a feverish pitch that's headed straight for your heart

Girl, once you've made up your mind
You're gonna see that I'm not lyin'
Come on, try it (mmm-mmm)
Try it (mmm-mmm) Try it
Try it, baby
Try it
Aww, come on, try it
Oh, try it
Oh, try it
Come on, come on, come on

During its last few years, the CBS television show *Art Linkletter's House Party* had a special segment called "Let's Talk," where he would invite different factions on camera to debate each other. He'd heard about the ban on "Try It" and decided to have us on the show along with McLendon.

While on a short tour appearing in Wichita Falls, Texas, and then at a radio station concert in Dallas, we decided to use our downtime between gigs to do some research. In doing so, we discovered that the puritanical McLendon had some skeletons in his closet. His employees at KLIF and elsewhere willingly gave us plenty of ammunition, much of which we couldn't use because it couldn't be substantiated, and our sources could get fired.

I've always said that if you want to find the real scumbag, just follow the pointing finger up the arm. I would later learn that according to authors Warren Hinkle and William W. Turner in their book *Deadly Secrets*, along with author Peter Dale Scott, McLendon might have even played a role in the John F. Kennedy assassination. It was well-known that Jack Ruby, the man who killed Lee Harvey Oswald, was a listener and admirer of McLendon's. He was known to both the KLIF staff and McLendon. It is also said that McLendon was the first person that Ruby asked to consult with after his arrest. McLendon was also a member of the secretive right-wing Suite 8F Group, which also included notorious wealthy conservatives H.L. Hunt, Clint Murchison Sr. and Bobby Baker. Furthermore, Scott claimed that McLendon made a secret trip to Mexico just before the assassination. [41]

On May 27th, the "Let's Talk" debate was set up at the Hullaballoo Club, which was filled to the brim with teenagers. Our management was not satisfied with just stacking the deck; they wanted to make certain that McLendon would be massacred and fed pertinent information to some members of the audience.

------

41 www.spartacus-educational.com - *American History, The Assissination of JFK, Gordon McLendon*

Also, there that day, taping another segment, was Christine Jorgensen, the person widely known in America to have a sex reassignment operation. She came backstage and visited with us, and I found her to be very friendly and talkative. I don't know how the subject got onto Amelia Earhart, but Christine proclaimed herself to be "more of a woman than Amelia."

From behind the stage, we saw McLendon march in with an army of suits, all appearing very much like the CIA. Eventually, it was time for the debate. Lined up on stage, from left to right, was McLendon, Linkletter, me; and further to the right were John, Dick, and Tony. Linkletter handled the introductions perfectly, and when he introduced McLendon the chorus of boos was heard all the way back to Texas.

AN OPEN LETTER TO: The Music Industry

Frankly, We're tired . . .

. . . TIRED of today's new releases coming through rife with "raunchy" lyrics, et cetra. In the past month, six records which were on the national charts far overstepped the boundaries of good taste, and we were forced to ban them.

. . . TIRED of "policing" your industry. It is time consuming, not our responsibility, and an outright imposition—on all broadcasters.

. . . TIRED of answering complaints from our listeners, civic groups, and civic leaders who blame us for your poor judgment on what is, and what is not, in good taste.

. . . TIRED of sincerely promising the FCC that we will do everything to elevate the needs, tastes and desires of the community—only to have one or two records threaten to tear it all down.

Therefore, we intend to

. . . 1 REFUSE to review effective May 15, 1967 any record submitted to us for air play unless it is accompanied by a valid and actual lyric sheet for both sides.

. . . 2 REFUSE to play record releases which continue, through "gimmicks" intonations, and nuances to either innocently or intentionally offend public morals, dignity or taste.

. . . 3 REFUSE consideration of both sides of a record if one side is adjudged unfit for airplay.

. . . 4 URGE ALL RESPONSIBLE BROADCASTERS TO FOLLOW THIS "CODE OF RECORD STANDARDS" IN REVIEWING RECORDS IN THE FUTURE.

Frankly, we are tired. We want to be fair. But our success, after all, is often dependent on your success as record producers; but conversely, your success is predicated on radio airplay of your product. Please, let's work together. Clean things up before some unnecessary regulatory action is taken or before the broadcasters' listening audience indignantly tunes out.

THE McLendon STATIONS

McLendon Open letter to Music Industry

Trade Magazine article regarding Try It

Looking our way, Linkletter began with the statement, "Mr. McLendon claims that your record is not suitable for the teenage listener. What do you boys think of that?"

"Shouldn't that be left up to the teenagers?" I responded, which was met with a thunderous round of cheers.

McLendon countered, "We're talking about our youth, and we as adults need to set an example for them, certainly not by feeding them filth in music."

"What's so filthy about our song?" asked John Fleck.

Again, the audience roared. One member yelled out "What about your niece, McLendon?" To which Gordon's face became noticeably red, and caused him to gaze out into the audience.

"Well, the song encourages young girls to have sex," he sputtered.

I then recited some of the lyrics to the song, and asked, "Where does it say anything about sex?"

"Well," he responded, "it says 'try it.'"

Dick jumped in. "It's talking about love!"

"It's certainly no worse than songs of your day, Mr. McLendon," I interjected.

Gordon quickly regained his composure and demanded, "State your example," thinking he had me cornered.

I'd been waiting for the right moment to spring this one on him, and replied with a hint of a smile, "What does the phrase 'birds do it, bees do it' mean?" blithely referring to the 1928 Cole Porter song "Let's Do it, Let's Fall in Love."

"Well, that's different," he angrily responded.

"How so?" asked John, beginning to smile.

"Well, it's talking about love."

We wasted no time. In unison, we said, "So are we!"

The crowd at this point was roaring.

Art Linkletter interrupted with "We'll be right back after this message," ruining what would have been our finest moment.

McLendon tried to force a smile during the commercial break.

Linkletter came back in, "So the Standells are saying, Mr. McLendon, that you have falsely accused them of putting out a smutty record. How do you respond?"

Gordon was ready, "Well it *is* smutty."

"Come now, is it really that bad?" asked Linkletter.

McLendon stood his ground. "Yes, my lyric-testing panel has deemed it as being dirty."

Unfortunately, no one bothered to grill Gordon about his panel. I later learned that it was composed of "prostitutes, ex-prostitutes, junkies, and ex-addicts," chosen for their fields of expertise. In other words, he was putting the foxes in charge of the henhouse, an unholy alliance of right-wing Christian evangelists and those very people he supposedly detested. It was a classic example of the phrase, "The enemy of my enemy is my friend." I couldn't help thinking that these people were giving McLendon the answers he wanted to hear. [42]

McLendon mentioned the Byrds' hit "Eight Miles High" as glorifying drug use. It was a golden moment. So perfect, yet I had to destroy it with, "Mr. McLendon, you even had a drug song back in your day"

McLendon feigned outrage. "And what might that be?"

I smiled, "The High and the Mighty."

Right, it was a false equivalency and overkill, but the crowd loved it. If I'd done my homework better, I could have been far more effective citing the Cole Porter song, "I Get a Kick Out of You," where the phrase "Some get a kick out of cocaine" was used.

The debate finally ended with resounding applause from the teenage audience. We were surprised when Gordon came backstage afterwards and shook our hands, looking relieved that the ordeal was over. Our manager Burt Jacobs and Ray Harris of Greengrass Productions embraced us. We thought we had won a major victory, certainly making a fool of this hypocrite, and ensuring that the ban on our song would be reversed.

Until we saw the airing of the show on May 27th.

Thanks to creative editing, gone were the brilliant comebacks, like "Birds do it, bees do it" and McLendon's inability to respond to allegations of treating the Standells unfairly. It was apparent that the network executives were not happy with the lop-sided victory, especially over someone who was so powerfully connected in the broadcast industry. So, they thought they'd

---

42 www.books.google.com - Billboard Magazine - *Anti-Smut McLendon to Set Up a "Fringe" Panel* (1967)

make it look more even-handed. The result was that we made some points and Gordon made some points (which appeared to be unanswered), hardly something we could use to get our record back on the air.

Infuriated, we set up a meeting with our Burt and Ray.

"Burt, you know me, and I wouldn't bullshit you," I told him.

"Of course, Larry. Bullshit you are not."

"This thing with McLendon is going to destroy us if we don't do something."

"What do you suggest?" Ray asked calmly. "You know how powerful McLendon is. There's not a whole lot we can do."

"Fuck McLendon!" I shouted. "He can't dictate what gets played on the radio. He's a fascist."

Burt jumped in, "Larry's got a point. Isn't there something we can do to salvage this, Ray?"

Ray threw up his hands. "We can try to make a deal with him on the next record."

"If he kills this, there *is* no next record!" I shot back.

Tony nodded in agreement, "McLendon can't fuck weeth us like thees."

Dick's face got red. "This was supposed to be our next hit, now we're royally screwed."

I jumped in. "Ray, we've got to sue this guy for libel. He can't do this shit."

Ray looked shocked. "You're suggesting we sue the man who could turn around and kill the Standells for good?" Left unsaid was that McLendon could also kill Attarack, Tower Records and some of their other acts.

"If he succeeds, we're already dead," I responded. "Besides, if we sued him, can you imagine the publicity wc could gct out of it? It could be a landmark case, like *To Kill a Mockingbird.*" (Okay, a slight exaggeration.)

Ray finally agreed to discuss the situation with Tower. It took a week before Burt got back to us and called us into a meeting. Like the broadcasters and most everyone else, they were scared to death of McLendon and the potential damage that a lawsuit could do them, as well as all of the other Tower acts.

When I learned of their decision I screamed, "This is fucking bullshit! They're scared to death of him!"

I thoroughly believed that if it had been a larger record label or a bigger band name, the lawsuit would have gone forward. McLendon's banning of "Eight Miles High" didn't seem to hurt the Byrds' airplay or record sales. Instead of #1, it reached #14 on the Billboard charts. We could only wish for that kind of hurt.

As it turned out, "Try It" was later covered by the bubble-gum group Ohio Express, who had a hit with "Yummy Yummy Yummy." Their version was an almost carbon copy of the Standells' recording, with the exception of some of the lyrics. As ludicrous as it sounds, "action" and "satisfaction" were replaced with "kissing" and "missing." Raunchy words, huh? The song was performed by one of the original writers, Joey Levine. I guess Joey thought the word substitution might be more palatable to the likes of McLendon; maybe he was just as confused as we were. Regardless, the song was more successful the second time around.

Many years later, "Try It" has become one of the Standells' best-selling records.

During May, the movie *Riot on Sunset Strip* was released in theaters throughout the United States and elsewhere. About one month after filming the movie, we'd gone into the studio and re-recorded the theme song. The original, recorded on the studio sound stage, was rather sluggish and didn't have good enough sound quality for a finished recording. It was released as a single at about the same time as the movie was launched, with "Black Hearted Woman" on the other side.

We had another single released in early 1967 under the name "The Sllednats," which is Standells spelled backwards. For some reason Ed chose one of Tony's songs, "Don't Tell Me What to Do." It was awful. No matter how much we tried, we just couldn't make anything of it until I came up with the idea of doing a vaudevillian parody. I sang it as comically as I could, including an overacted narration in the middle. The flip side was the old Leadbelly song "When I was a Cowboy." It was a big mistake. Most people realized that it was us but didn't understand the comedy take on it.

CHAPTER 11

On December 10, 1966, Scottish singer and songwriter Donovan had a hit record, Mellow Yellow, which was #8 on the Billboard charts. The song was rumored to be about smoking dried banana skins. It created quite a sensation because –supposedly- smoking the skins had a hallucinogenic effect. At that time, hippies were trying to find an inexpensive way to get high, mainly because the costs of marijuana were beyond what many could afford. The Local East Village newspaper was supposedly where the craze began. According to Paul Krassner, the paper's publisher, in a 2012 article, several editors were discussing the hallucinogenic effects of LSD and serotonin in the brain and wondered if there was a more natural way to stimulate the hormone. According to the article, some druggies put two and two together. Realizing that bananas contained serotonin, they conjectured that by smoking them, one could get high.

Of course, Donovan's song *Mellow Yellow* fit right into the scenario. In the March 1967 issue of the Berkeley Barb, writer Ed Denson presented the "Recipe of the week". In the article, he put forth the method of preparing banana peels for smoking. The directions called for scraping out the white pith, drying it in the oven, and rolling it up into a Zig-Zag paper to smoke. My friend and colleague Joe McDonald, of Country Joe and the Fish, was the man who began the rumor by handing out 500 banana peel joints at a concert.

According to Eric Grundhauser, From there, it spread like wildfire "thanks to the Underground Press Syndicate, which allowed small papers, such as the Barb, to freely share content with one another. The Barb continued to report on the supposed effects of banana peels, running stories with titles such as *Pick Your Load, Banana or Toad* and *Mellow Yellow Future Bright,* which included spurious claims regarding the various substances contained in bananas that gave them psychedelic effects."

By the end of 1967, banana smoking graced the pages of the New York Times and the Wall Street Journal. Some stores and markets began to put limitations on the purchase of bananas. Unbelievably, to purchase them one had to be over the age of 18, and a limit of two bananas was allowed per customer.

In the Anarchist's Cookbook, author William Powell had a more laborious recipe that called for one to "peel scrapings that must then be reduced further into a powder." He wildly claimed that bananas contained a compound called *Bananadine,* and this is from where the bananas reportedly got their psychedelic effects. I must conjecture that Powell was on acid when he wrote this because *Bananadine* did not exist.

Everyone at some point tried doing as the song suggested, including the Standells. As directed, we slowly baked the white layer from the peels until they were dried. Then we meshed up the remains into some Zig Zag's and all of us attempted to smoke them. The results: We'd been had; smoking banana joints was one of the biggest drug hoaxes ever. In truth, bananas do contain a certain amount of serotonin, *but too slight to cross the blood-brain barrier* for any kind of high.

I often wonder if Chiquita Bananas might have been the real culprit behind this con job. Donovan admitted in the Rolling Stone Illustrated Encyclopedia of Rock and Roll that *Mellow Yellow* had nothing to do with real bananas; it was more to do with *electrical bananas*, AKA lady's vibrators. One only had to listen to the opening lyrics to make the connection. *I'm just mad about saffron, and saffron's mad about me.* I guess it created a different kind of buzz than what the hippies had intended. [43]

If I haven't already mentioned it, I loved to play pranks on others, the nastier the better. Once, in Texas, we were in a small motel. We dared John to drink a quart of prune juice after eating half of a watermelon. John was a good-natured guy and went along with the dare. Of course, there was sinister planning at work. While in the bathroom for the umpteenth time, we snuck in his room and put itching powder in his bed. Tony and I went back to our room, waiting to hear about the results.

As we were later told, John, exhausted from his ordeal, slipped in between the sheets, ready for a good night's slumber. As he stretched out, his arm began to itch, followed by his other arm. Next, were his feet. Soon the rest of his body followed suit, in a twisting pulsating mass under the sheets. Finally, John jumped out of bed in solid rage. He didn't have to guess who the culprit was, at which point he stormed out of the room with nothing but his undies on.

Even though we expected John's wrath, we had no idea to what extent. It began with pounding on the door. Having been a

43 www.atlasobscura.com - *Smoking Banana Peels is the Greatest Drug Hoax of All time* (2017)

high school quarterback with a good physique, we weren't about to be on the receiving end of his rage. We refused to answer the door. The pounding became even more intense, to where we could see the door pulsating with each knock. We still weren't about to budge. Finally, with a thunderous crash, the door split in two! As the dust settled, there was John, fists clenched and ready to rumble!

Oh God, I was beginning to realize that this time I had gone too far. I was about to be torn from limb to limb. John stepped into the room, and said, "That wasn't funny". To our total surprise and relief, he turned around a stomped back to his room. Thank God, he had taken his anger out on the door instead of us!

There we were with a broken door, with the knowledge we were going to have to pay for it. That's when I came up with my second brilliant scheme of the evening. We decided to walk to a nearby coffee shop, and as we walked by the motel office, we made sure he heard comments like "nice evening for a walk", "I'm hungry", and "there's a place up the street". Later, when we returned to our room, we made a big ruckus at learning that *someone had broken into the room*. One of the guys went and got the manager, who upon seeing the damage to our door, scratched his head, "I've never seen anything like this before". To make it more authentic, we had scattered our things around the room and pointed to the mess. I said, "It must have been some crazy fan."

Without question, the manager moved Tony and me into another room, and we thought we'd gotten away with this until the following morning. The closets had pre-made metal enclosures which included a hanging rod and shelves. They were bolted to the ceiling and wall. We were packing our things, and wouldn't you know the entire enclosure came crashing down. When we called the manager to report the damage and that we were perfectly innocent of any wrongdoing, we were told they weren't going for it. And we had to pay for the damages. Damn, Karma's a bitch!

Later in Houston, I was taking a nice hot shower, when a bucket of cold ice was dumped on me. Okay, I deserved it, especially coming from John.

In Seattle, we performed several shows at the Seattle Teen Spectacular. We had some time in-between gigs, so we set up one of the most elaborate pranks ever played, even hiring an actress named Tina to play the role of one of Tony's former conquests - a rather young-looking girl named Marsha. We remembered her from Texas because she seemed to be exceptionally young. We gave her a catalog of information on Tony, including the name of his girlfriend at the time Danielle. It was brilliant and couldn't have gone better (or worse).

Tony had been working on one particular girl for what was an extraordinary amount of time – 2 days. He finally had her in his room, on the bed. He was in the process of removing her clothing when he received the telephone call from hell.

Tony hurriedly picked up the phone. "Chaio"

The voice on the other end anxiously responded, "Tony, I've been trying so hard to reach you"

Tony's bushy eyebrows angled in a frown, "Whosa thees?"

Tina, with a perfect Texan drawl, responded, "After all those wonderful things you said, I thought y'all would know my voice."

Tony, having been interrupted from his lovemaking said, "I'm beezy right now. I call you back."

Tina then took it to the next level, "I'm in the lobby and I need to see you."

"Whaaat you want?" Tony exclaimed, as he quickly sat up.

Now she had his full attention, and sprang it on him, "I just wanted to tell you the good news, you and I are going have a baby.

Having now completely lost his erection, Tony hastily gathered the girl's clothes and threw them at her. "Sorry, but someting's come up (or could it have been down?). You gotta leave."

Disheartened by the interruption, She suggested, "Maybe I can come back".

Tony had a major problem, and was no longer thinking with his penis, "No, geet out, now!"

The alluring blond sadly put on her clothes and exited the room, perhaps one of the wisest things she had ever done in her life.

One thing about Tony was when he got nervous his accent thickened. He then anxiously returned to his phone conversation. "I don't know who you are."

Tina had been prepared for this. "Before you took away my virginity, you said 'Marsha' I love you so much. I believed you, and I let you have me. And when I learned that I was pregnant, I was so anxious to tell you, I called your home and spoke to your housekeeper, Danielle."

Learning that she had talked with Tony's girlfriend, the blood began to drain from his face, "You-u-u talked weeth Danielle?

"Yes, and she was such a nice person, so understanding. I told her the entire story. She said she thought that I was taken advantage of, but she knew that you would make things right. And she told me to tell you that she would be moving out of your home." By now, Tony was beside himself. This was when Tina pulled the coup de grâce, "I also told someone else about the wonderful news".

Tony's shaky voice managed to croak out, "Who-o-o-o deed you tell?"

"My daddy, he's a deputy here in Dallas. When I told him how much we were in love, he finally understood. He's flying out to meet with you tomorrow to talk about our wedding plans."

Okay, this might have been overkill, but when used in this context it was pure genius.

Tony told her to wait for him to come down to get her. Meanwhile, he walked over to my room and knocked on the door. I answered, and when I saw his pale face, his panicked expression, and rubbing his hands, I played it perfectly, "Tony you look like you've seen a ghost".

He looked both ways, up and down the hall, then entered my room and slowly shut the door. Rubbing his hands together, another nervous habit of Tony's, he sobbed, "Oh *Leddy* (the closest pronunciation he could get to my name), I reeely fuck up, I reeely fuck up."

Again, I played the reaction perfectly, "My God, Tony, what happened. Are you being audited by the IRS?"

"No, no, eet's much worse"

"What can be worse than an audit?"

"I reeely deed it this time. Mamma Mia, I swear I never do eet again."

"Calm down, it can't be that bad."

Tony grabbed me by my shoulders, "Do you remember thees girl named Masha in Dallas?"

I looked puzzled for a minute, and then as if suddenly recollecting her, I said, "You mean the 14-year-old you were with?" That was stretching it quite a bit to make a point. I was pretty sure she was older.

Tony scowled, "I deedn't know her age, I never check ID."

"What about her?"

"Sheeeee's pregnant!"

"Holy Shit. That's statutory rape."

Meanwhile, the other guys entered the room to listen while Tony explained his sorrowful story, how she had contacted Danielle, and finally the part about her daddy flying in. The whole time we managed to appear very concerned, Tony even receiving pats on the back by Dick and John. I managed to chime in, "Tony, I told you this might happen someday. Didn't you even use a condom?"

"I deedn't think I had to. I pull out on time"

"You know that doesn't always work", added Dick somberly.

"I know eet now" I promise I never do eet again." Tony then walked to the phone and picked it up. "I call Sy." Sy Cohen could do anything. After all he defended Burt when he was a bookie! Tony began to dial Sy's number, and that's when none of us could contain it anymore. We began rolling on the floor with laughter. Tony stopped dialing the number and looked at us, "What's so funny, thees is not funny eet's serious". We continued to laugh, even harder.

Finally, I said, "Tony, it's all a joke."

He looked at us suspiciously, "Whaaaat?"

In unison, we said, "A JOKE"

His expression began to change, "But what about Marsha?"

I said, "An actor. The deputy dad was a nice touch, huh?"

"And she deedn't call Danielle?"

We roared with laughter, and Tony immediately started to pound on my back "You sonomobitch", while laughing from relief.

I said, "Tony, from now on be a little more careful where you stick that *Braunschweiger*."

He then gave us a solemn oath, "I learn my lesson, never again, never again". This was the great thing about Tony: When you pulled such a rotten joke on him, he was instantly forgiving. It's a shame that part of him has disappeared over the years.

Sure enough, the following day Tony was back pursuing the girls like nothing ever happened. That was the Tony I loved back then.

CHAPTER 12

In addition to his being a disc jockey on KRLA and having a TV dance show, Casey Kasem was also the promoter for several concerts throughout the Los Angeles area. We played a number of shows throughout the LA area for Casey, and he often had his good friend drive for us. One night a horrible event occurred that still haunts me to this day. I've kept mostly silent about it, only sharing it with family members.

We were on the 101 Freeway on the way to one of these gigs when Casey's friend made a sudden change into the left lane. I don't know exactly what happened, but we heard a screech of tires. Looking out the rear window, we saw that the car behind us had veered and crashed into the center divider. We pleaded with Casey's friend to stop, but he wouldn't because it would make us late to the gig.

I wanted to tell Casey about what happened as soon as we arrived, but I felt that it was up to his friend to do so. It was very difficult playing the gig that night. The next day, I read in the newspaper about a wreck on the 101. A man driving a car was cut off by another car, and as a result his wife was killed. I wanted to call the police, but was told to keep silent because Casey was our friend. I was also unsure of exactly what happened. I don't know if the other driver was driving at a safe speed. None of the other guys wanted to be involved. I know I should have taken charge, but I didn't. That was my problem back then, I let things slide.

This tragedy has stayed with me since, and I often think of it. My heart goes out to that man. I can only imagine the grief that he felt. Had it been today, I wouldn't have made the same decision to keep silent. I did remain friends with Casey over the years until his death, but I just never could find the nerve to tell him about the incident with his close friend.

On July 5, 1967, we played a show with the Doors and the Coasters at Lowell High School in La Habra, California. At that time there were a few different versions of the Coasters working throughout the US, so I had no way of knowing which franchise was performing. Regardless, they were terrific. For me, however, what took place pre-show was the most memorable. We were all visiting backstage, and it was very noisy. I was talking to one of our fan club presidents at the time when suddenly everything grew quiet. Jim Morrison had stepped into the room through the backstage door. He'd most certainly captured everyone's attention because we all turned to look at him… Not so much because of his aura, but his BO. He was wearing a tight leather outfit, in which, judging by the stench, he must have permanently resided.

The show itself was wild. During the Doors' set, Jim swung from the rafters on the gymnasium ropes and ended up on the basketball hoop. How could anyone top that? I certainly wasn't about to try.

We took many more photos. One in particular that comes to mind was taken by Peter Fonda, showing us along with the female rock group the Clingers. Besides acting, photography was one of Peter's other talents.

We continued our busy schedule of concerts and shows, appearing again at the Hullaballoo Club, and several concerts with Sam Riddle who at that time was with KHJ radio. We razzed him a couple of times for not playing "Try It," but of course he had no control over the station manager's decisions on playlists.

On September 1st and 2nd, we performed at the Fort Worth Teen Fair & Mardi Gras Festival, the Will Rogers Exhibit Building, Fort Worth, Texas. It ran from August 28th through September 4th. The festival also featured the Doors, the Box Tops, the Seeds, the Grass Roots, Every Mother's Son, the McCoys, the Electric Prunes, and Sonny and Cher. Admission was a whopping $2.00, which was average for those days. Today's ticket prices for the same type of event with name acts would probably be in the neighborhood of $500.00. We returned home and did a second one-week engagement at the Ice House in Glendale, a show at the Del Amo Mall in Torrance, and a concert at the Rainbow Ballroom in Fresno. Also, we were guests on the *Woody Woodbury Show* along with Janet Blair and Dick Kallman, broadcast on September 15th.

Around this time, Tony was dating a girl named Ondine who seemed to have a certain mystique. Every time he had some sort of misfortune, she was involved. For example, the time Tony was driving a Jaguar XKE with her and was pulled over for a speeding ticket. The irony was that she also had a black cat, which I ended up adopting. Before long the guys began to jokingly associate our bad luck with Ondine's supposed sorcery. Without my knowledge, Tony passed this information on to Ray Harris and

Ed Cobb. We were later told by Ondine that Ray and Ed had contacted her, set up a meeting, and pleaded with her to stop casting her evil spells. When Ondine told Dick and me, she was laughing hysterically. I can't say that I blame her. She was only guilty of being a good friend.

We returned to wrapping up the album we had started working on before the McLendon fiasco. Once collaborative and approachable, Ed Cobb was now withdrawn and dictatorial, and increasingly difficult to work with. Obviously, he had bought into the hype from Attarack that he was a superstar producer like Phil Spector and that he was solely responsible for the Standells' success. Again, we were also not given a choice in the music we recorded. He brought in Ethen McElroy and Don Bennett, two black R&B composers and arrangers, who completely changed the sound of the group, bringing in other black musicians to replace us. I really liked Ethen and Don, and I worshipped black entertainers, but this was not the Standells sound.

One of the songs they wrote was a soul number called "Can't Help But Love You." As we stood watching other musicians record the track, I turned to Ed and asked why we couldn't play on it instead. His response, which still floors me even to this day, was, "These guys sound more like the Standells than you do." Even Dick's singing was not the same.

"Trip to Paradise" was another song Ethen and Don wrote and arranged for the album, complete with strings. I liked it, but thought it was out of place. During that session, without my knowledge, the string players were also used to add orchestration to a song I wrote and sang called "Summer Clothes". Like my other songs, Ed never gave me any direction. Even though all of the Standells performed on the song, with the strings added it sounded very pop-oriented and completely unlike the Standells. Unlike "Trip to Paradise," they did not include it in the album, but released it instead as a single on Sunburst Records, the artist listed as "Larry."

Except for the R&B songs like "Can't Help But Love You" and "Ninety Nine and a Half," and the orchestral "Trip to Paradise," the album *Try It* was, in reality, a pretty decent record. To capitalize on the McLendon ordeal, Tower plastered "BANNED!" across the front of the album jacket in a bold red cargo-style font. Again, if they'd had any pull in the record industry, they might have milked this for a lot more than they did.

Many of the other songs on the album went on to become very popular with Standells fans. "All Fall Down," written by John Fleck and Dick Dodd, showed us experimenting with psychedelia, and the hard-driving rocker "Barracuda" inspired a band in England in the late 1970s to name themselves after the song, the Barracudas. Either of these songs would have been good for our next single release. I'm also quite proud of our version of "St. James Infirmary," not because I sang it, but because of all of the airplay and favorable comments that the song has received over the years.

Some people have compared "All Fall Down," to Pink Floyd, whose debut album, *The Piper at the Gates of Dawn*, was released on Tower in the USA not long before our *Try It* album. They were signed to EMI Columbia in Europe, who had a distribution deal with Tower in the States.

I briefly met them outside the *9ᵗʰ Street West* KHJ TV studios after a taping. Their mercurial singer and guitarist Syd Barrett seemed to be spaced out, not unlike our own Dick Dodd at the time. Apparently, Barrett had been diagnosed as having depression. What I observed was that he was stoned on drugs. He exhibited the same behavior during the taping of the Dick Clark and Pat Boone shows in November. Syd refused to answer questions or even move his lips when lip-syncing "See Emily Play" on the Boone Show. This must have confounded Boone, who had no tolerance for drugs. Little did I know that this would be the last couple of months he would be a performing member of the group. It wasn't until a few years later that Pink Floyd finally earned the acknowledgment they deserved in the US, with *Dark Side of the Moon.*

Interestingly, Tower did not make use of the powerful Capitol Records EMI distribution team. Even though they were located in the Capitol Records building in Hollywood, Tower operated independently from Capitol. Thus, many of the Standells recordings received absolutely no coverage in Europe. For the same reason, Tower lacked the power to carry the Standells through the McLendon fiasco.

As in the past with Lincoln Mayorga and "Dirty Water," Ed seemed to form outside alliances, then impose them on our group. As I later discovered, he also did this with some of his other acts. Our supposed bad luck was derived not from Ondine, but from the bone-headed decisions made by our producer. The latest one was to release "Can't Help but Love You" as our next single, rather than one of the other excellent cuts from the album. It sounded more like a white dude trying to sing like James Brown than the

Standells. Even the back-up vocals were done be Ethen McElroy and Don Bennett.

Ed Cobb was not the same guy I had met just a few years earlier in 1965. Without our knowledge, he had decided that the band would spotlight Dick Dodd with the rest of us relegated to sidemen. He had lost all respect for our artistic integrity. Although I have no direct evidence, other than Ray Harris' earlier statement, I believe that a deal was struck with McLendon. Attarack had given McLendon credibility by not pursuing a lawsuit. In return, he would play our next record release. All of McLendon's stations immediately jumped "Can't Help but Love You," and it jumped up to #78 on the Billboard charts. However, because it bore no resemblance to the Standells sound fans were familiar with, it quickly lost momentum and was soon forgotten about.

We continued to tour throughout the country, with our next gig scheduled in Santa Fe, New Mexico. Our roadie Bruno took John and went on ahead, planning to meet the three of us there with the equipment. We elected to fly instead. As it turned out, we missed our Western Airlines flight from LAX to Albuquerque and had to take a later flight. The only catch was that there was no connecting flight to Santa Fe. No problem, we decided to charter a plane so that we could make the connection. It looked good on paper.

When we arrived in Albuquerque, we took a cab over to the other side of the airport to where the small aircraft were kept. We met the pilot in a rundown office, and were led to an old single-engine aircraft. We didn't believe the plane was airworthy, but the pilot assured us that it was. So the three of us piled into the plane. He started it up and taxied to the end of the runway.

We hardly noticed the dark clouds in the distance. As the plane slowly took off, the pilot's door flew open. He casually reached over and shut it. No big deal – to him!

The further we traveled toward Santa Fe, the darker the sky became. Soon we found ourselves smack-dab in the middle of a thunder and lightning storm. The aircraft was tossed about in the storm like a paper glider, Fortunately, it was stocked with liquor, and we wasted no time in the downing a few of the mini bottles. Even so, it didn't stop Tony from screaming "Thees is fuckeeng crazy!" and "Big Pallamini!" every time a lightning bolt exploded nearby.

By a wing and a prayer, we found the Santa Fe runway, and fortunately, it was large enough to give us enough opportunity to make our final approach. After fighting with severe winds, the pilot made a bumpy landing. By then, Dick and I were so soused that we hardly noticed we were on the ground. Tony was holding his rosary and mumbling, "Nel nome del Padre, e del iglio, e dello Spirito Santo."

Bruno was there to pick us up. We were late for the gig and rushed to the concert hall. When we arrived, we hurried into our green room, changed, and then rushed out onto the stage where John was patiently waiting. In spite of our terrifying journey, the concert turned out to be one of our best. At least Bruno told me so. Dick, Tony and I couldn't remember much of it.

In November we appeared on the show *Groovy*, which was shown on the local LA TV station KHJ. It was hosted by actor Michael Blodgett, later known for his role in the film *Beyond the Valley of the Dolls*, and taped on the beach in Santa Monica. We were featured along with Thee Midnighters, who had the hit "Whittier Blvd." They were another Chicano rock band that I admired.

The show regularly featured a bikini contest, and when we finished doing "Try It," I was asked to judge it. One of the contestants was none other than Tony's girlfriend Danielle. Just before the contest, Tony pleaded with me to pick Danielle to be the winner, putting me in an untenable situation. Granted, it was completely unethical, but being loyal to Tony I did as he wished. Afterward, he brought Danielle up to thank me. I wanted to hide, but there was no place to run. One of the other contestants came up to me and let me know in no uncertain terms that I had favored Danielle solely because she was a friend, and that it was completely unfair. I silently agreed.

Later that year, along with Sebastian Cabot, Dennis Day, Sandra Dee, and Ralph Pope, we performed on *The Joey Bishop Show*, which was broadcast on December 7th. The show's co-host was Regis Philbin, with whom we had guested on *That Regis Philbin Show* back in 1963. Both Joey and Regis were very complimentary of the group. Sebastian Cabot was surprisingly easy to talk to and had a ton of showbiz stories he shared with me. I didn't get a chance to catch up with Sandra Dee about the time she came to my high school hop back in the fifties, unfortunately. She probably wouldn't have remembered anyway!

Our group returned to the studio to record several more songs. Although he was still very difficult to communicate with, perhaps Ed Cobb was beginning to see the error of his ways. One of the new songs presented to us was "Animal Girl," a ballad that I thought under different circumstances could have been a hit. The other, "Soul Drippin'" was a solid rocker, but I thought the song title sucked and could be misconstrued as yet another soul/R&B pastiche.

During this same session, the English songwriter Graham Gouldman came to the studio. Gouldman, at the time, was best known for a slew of million sellers, like "Listen People," "No Milk Today" and "East West" for Herman's Hermits, "For Your Love," "Heart Full of Soul" and "Evil Hearted You" for the Yardbirds, and "Look Through Any Window" (with Charles Silverman) and "Bus Stop" for the Hollies. He later gained fame as part of the band 10cc.

Graham brought in a song he'd written with the Standells in mind called "Schoolgirl." I loved the song, especially since it was written by Gouldman, who was a proven hit-writer. We made several attempts to record it. However, Tony just couldn't grasp it – perhaps because the song had more than three chords. Exasperated, Graham finally left the studio in disgust before we had a chance to complete it. Embarrassed as I was, I couldn't blame him.

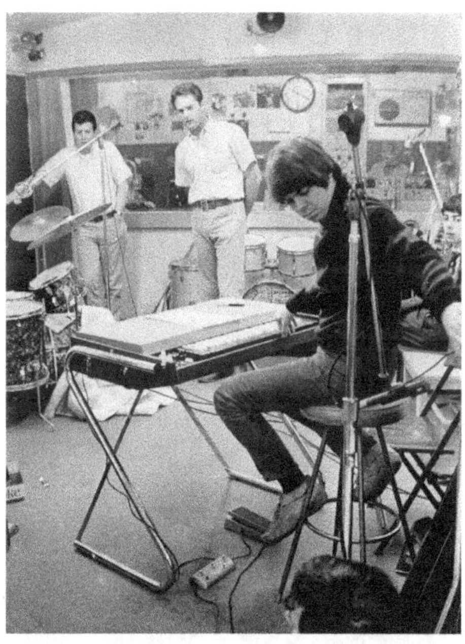

Larry in American Recording Studio, along with Ed Cobb and Ray Harris. On far right is Graham Gouldman

This is perhaps why I was completely surprised to see the song show up decades later, as a bonus track on a CD release of *The Hot Ones* album. In listening to it, it sounds like my keyboard playing, Dick's drumming, and John's bass playing, but that's all. I don't think that was Dick's lead vocal. It had neither Dick's inflections nor the tonality of his voice. I believe that Cobb later put the song together with a different vocalist and guitar player. There are even some rumors that Gouldman himself sang it.

CHAPTER 13

In 1968, Dr. Christian Barnard performed the first heart transplant, and the first Big Mac went on sale at McDonald's for 49 cents. That year also marked the tragic assassinations of Robert Kennedy and Martin Luther King Jr., certainly a dark chapter in American history.

It also was the year that things began to go downhill for the Standells. Our single "Animal Girl" backed with "Soul Drippin'" was released in February and went nowhere. With no records on the charts, our popularity began to dwindle. Music was changing dramatically. It went from the hard-driving sound of the Standells and the Seeds, to psychedelia and acid rock. Within just a few years rock music had been completely transformed. With virtuoso guitarists like Jimi Hendrix, Eric Clapton and Jeff Beck dominating the music scene, Tony Valentino's raw, simple guitar licks suddenly weren't cutting it any longer, while my clean Vox Organ sounds had been superseded by the Hammond B3 organ, Fender Rhodes and other, more sophisticated keyboards. The better-paying gigs began to be few and far between.

Almost as if sensing our disillusionment with Ed Cobb, we were called into a meeting with Burt Jacobs. He informed us, "I'm leaving Attarack. I can't work with them any longer."

Burt then left the choice up to us whether to stay with them or move on. For the first time, we voiced our displeasure at the direction in which our recordings were going with Cobb. We all agreed that the time had come to break our ties with him.

Burt, in the meantime, had partnered with good friend Reb Foster. They had several acts, including Three Dog Night and Steppenwolf, both of whom were successful with ABC Dunhill Records. Burt informed us that the label had expressed an interest in signing us. If we chose to leave Attarack, however, we had to be united. Burt had never led us astray, so we trusted him implicitly. Or at least I thought we did. A letter of noncompliance and termination of our agreement was drafted by Sy Cohen, and sent to Attarack.

We also discovered that we had an accountant who had been controlling our finances wasn't on the up-and-ups. We were turning over half of our income to him without any kind of itemization of expenditures. His odd mannerisms should have tipped us off. He had the bizarre habit of packing down the tobacco in his cigarette on his eyeglasses while carrying on a conversation, which was very disconcerting when trying to carry on a serious conversation about finances. Also, we should have noticed when his office was mysteriously torched, allowing him to collect on an on a lucrative insurance policy, and with the funds purchase a brand-new office building. But it wasn't until our ex-bassist Gary and his wife who retained the accountant's services for personal taxes were in his office one day when the Feds burst in through the front door, handcuffed him and perp-walked him out of the office. Leave it to musicians to innocently fall into these kinds of unsavory relationships.

In January 1968, we were signed once again for a one-week stint at the Ice House in Pasadena, followed by a February 10th concert at the Guitar Center in Hollywood. Next was a concert in Tucson Arizona. We decided it would be easier to charter a plane for this gig. It was an old converted B-25, which was the perfect size to transport us. The flight to Tucson took place without any problems. The gig went well. The return was another story altogether. At the airport, before the flight back home, everyone decided to have a late lunch, but I wasn't hungry – at least for that. I'd met a cute girl named Gracie. While the others were satisfying their appetite, I was satisfying mine with Gracie inside the plane's fuselage. Not the most comfortable place, but as Eddie Davis once said, a certain part of me had no brains! Eventually, the others returned. By then Gracie had exited and they were none the wiser about what had taken place in the cabin. We all piled into the plane and it taxied to the end of the runway.

It was beginning to get dark outside when the plane finally took off. The pilot then informed us that he'd forgotten to tell us one key factor. The heater in the plane was broken. About halfway back to Burbank airport, it began to get uncomfortably cold, and I crawled under a tarp to keep warm.

Finally, we arrived at Burbank, and I returned home to an empty house. Linda was off on one of her trysts.

Linda and I had purchased a new home on Ledgewood Drive in the Hollywood Hills. Our next-door neighbor was Dean Torrance of Jan and Dean. Dean owned what could best be described as a castle, complete with a moat filled with Koi. To enter, one had to transverse a narrow walkway and bridge to get to the medieval front door. He lived there with a few of his buddies.

Dean and I became very good friends, but there was one thing that had been a mystery to me. Every so often at night, I could hear a rather large bell chime. I thought it might be a nearby church, but there were none in the Hollywood Hills. Dean finally provided the answer I'd been seeking. Each time one of the guys got laid, the act would be commemorated by the chiming of the bell. What a unique idea. From then on, whenever I heard the bell it was a carnal-like experience for me. I must admit that even today I cannot hear a church bell without getting a little aroused.

Linda and I had what can be best described as an open relationship. We never discussed our liaisons, and we certainly were not swingers. One very wealthy man used to come over to pick her up at our house and take her up to his ranch to spend the day and evening horseback riding. Yeah, right! On one occasion our dog got injured, and the surgery was very costly. Linda invited the veterinarian over while I was getting ready to do a gig. He stayed there after I left, and oddly enough, the bill was miraculously taken care of afterward. Throughout this, I remained blissfully ignorant.

I was not completely innocent of having affairs either. In addition to several incidents while on tour, I became a conquest of my super groupie friend Teri as part of a contest she was having with a friend to see who could lay the most rock musicians within a year's period. Unbeknownst to me, Dick was also part of that list. I don't really know what number I was, but I had the distinct feeling it was near the end of the tally. Teri made a point of telling me that Tony was not a part of that list, nor was he even considered.

Ice House Poster

In April, we appeared again at the Ice House. Something that evening seemed different. Our concert was not as lively as it had been before. I also observed that all of Dick's family was present. Little did Tony, John and I realize that they were there to see Dick's farewell performance with the Standells. We didn't learn that Dick had quit the group until the following week when Burt called us to his office. There, with absolute shock, we all read the letter from Dick. In it, he wrote that he didn't understand why we left Greengrass Productions, and that he thought Ed had been doing a great job. How odd, since Dick had been in the previous meeting and joined in on the criticism of Cobb, agreeing that a change was necessary.

I was absolutely numb when I realized that we were going to have to cancel a previously scheduled concert the next day at my Alma Mater, Polytechnic High School. I had been looking forward to returning to my old high school for months. We tried calling Dick at his home and then at his parents', with no luck. We later learned he was unreachable because he was spending the week at Ed Cobb's home.

Predictably, Tony reverted to his refrain, "Fuckeeng Mexican," which didn't help matters any.

We filed a complaint with Local 47 of the Musician's Union, claiming that Dick had reneged on his agreement to perform at my high school. The matter was adjudicated at the offices of the Union. Dick was there, along with Ed Cobb and Ray Harris, who were now his guardians. The Union decided in our favor. Dick was fined a whopping $25.00, all of which went to the Union. Some representation!

I have always believed that Ed Cobb failed both the Standells and Dick solely because of his ego. Somewhere during our relationship, he had gone from being the fifth member and collaborator to a self-centered narcissist. In the book *Love That Dirty Water! The Standells and Their Improbable Red Sox Victory Anthem*, Ed Cobb's friend and Four Preps member, Bruce Belland, is quoted as having overheard Ed say, "Well, the Standells were just like every other band. You take them under your wing, you nurture them, you mentor them, you train 'em, you get 'em a hit or two, and then they think they know better than you and they can do it themselves. The next thing you know you never heard of them again." [44]

____

44 *Love That Dirty Water: The Standells and the Improbable Red Sox Victory Anthem* (2007)

When one considers how much the group had already accomplished before even meeting Cobb, his claim was absurd.

Belland went on to say that Cobb had some "very hard feelings about the way the Standells related to him, and what he had done for them as they progressed in their career."

I consider the truth to be quite the opposite. Cobb abandoned the Standells, not the other way around. He would not have had a hit recording of his song "Dirty Water" without the band's contributions. Not surprisingly, Belland claimed that Ed "probably had some degree of satisfaction" that the Standells never had another hit record. For that matter, neither did Ed Cobb as a producer. In retrospect, how nice it would have been if he had stayed the same Ed Cobb we first met.

There were many theories on why Dick left the group at such a critical juncture in our history. A new record deal with ABC Dunhill, one of the hottest record companies at the time, may have provided that spark we needed to get back on top.

According to Ray Harris: "Dick Dodd actually went to Ed and said what [Jacobs and the band] were doing, and I said, 'Oh, boy, I never expected that.'" Harris remembers that Dick then said, "I'm not going to go with that. I don't think it's right."

Dick later told me that Cobb, Harris, and others urged him to cut his ties with us and go solo, telling him, "You don't need the Standells. You're the voice. You can make it on your own."

Dick later expressed remorse at having deceived us, blaming it entirely on the trickery of Ed Cobb and Ray Harris. "It was a dirty thing to do to me, and a dirty thing to do to the Standells," he said. "I will always regret it. I was young and naïve."

To be honest, I think it was both Attarack's and Dick's doing. This was the second time Dick had quit the group, and the only reason he returned the first time was opportunism. Disloyalty was part of a pattern of behavior for Dick.

It was no secret that Dick had long considered himself to be the star of the group. It had also been apparent all along that Ed considered Dick to be the group's centerpiece, and the rest of us to become nothing more than sidemen – once again completely ignoring the group's history prior to his arrival.

For some time, I believed Cobb had lost his consistency as a producer, as well as his ability to be objective. Dick's solo album, which was released on Tower in November, proved me correct. *The First Evolution of Dick Dodd* was a complete change in direction for Dick and totally missed the mark. The album was recorded in Atlanta and produced in association with Bill Lowery. Lowery's fame had been with early rockabilly hits like "Be Bop A Lula" by Gene Vincent and the Blue Caps, and "Young Love" by Sonny James. His later hits were with Georgia-based acts, such as Jerry Reed, Joe South, Ray Stevens, Tommy Roe, Billy Joe Royal, Dennis Yost and the Classics IV, and the Atlanta Rhythm Section. Most all of these acts exemplified the "Atlanta Sound," not the Standells sound. With songs written by Ed Cobb and co-producer Buddy Bowie (a.k.a. Buddy Buie), the album turned out to be an abject failure. Instead of sticking with Dick's talents as a garage/soul singer, a style that Ed had nurtured in Dick over several years, he produced a polished commercial-sounding pop album. Gone was the in-your-face snottiness, replaced by a neutered, finger-snapping Dick. It just wasn't Dick Dodd.

The First Evolution of Dick Dodd album cover

Released on Tower Records, the album's front cover showed Dick dressed all in white standing atop some clouds with the Moon suspended above him, and Earth in the distance. For some reason he was holding a large light bulb. The back cover had a large illustration of a fetus. The entire concept seemed to be intended as a metaphor for Dick's "Evolution." Out of 5 stars, the album received an average of 1 ½ stars from those who purchased the album. One such purchaser later described it as: "Ultra-lightweight, mainstream vocal pop, with horns and orchestration, very reminiscent of Neil Diamond, and just too commercial for my taste."

I can't imagine what Ed Cobb was thinking, or if he was at all. Perhaps he saw something in Dick that none of us did. One thing was for sure: Dick Dodd was no Neil Diamond. [45]

---

45 *First Evolution of Dick Dodd* (1968)

Meanwhile, back in May 1968, Burt dropped a bombshell on us. We were told that ABC Dunhill had been threatened with legal action by Attarack if they signed us, because, they retained ownership of the name. Apparently, since they still had one member under contract, Dick, according to our agreement with them, they owned the name.

This was when we made another fatal mistake. Tony talked me into dropping Burt Jacobs and Reb Foster. The reason was ludicrous: Tony had found a new manager who would supply us with instruments and a PA system, complete with a sound engineer.

When I informed Burt, he was heartbroken. I couldn't blame him. He'd been loyal to us for so many years and had helped guide us to success. In hindsight, it was shortsighted of us to destroy this partnership for such a petty and senseless reason. Once again, I share in the blame; I hadn't stood up for my principles.

In the meantime, the group reformed. We decided that Tony just couldn't cut being lead guitarist any longer, so we first added Daniel Edwards in that capacity, relegating Tony to rhythm. Bill Daffern, later known as Willie Dee, became our new drummer. With a changing roster of band members, we continued to play gigs up and down California.

In August, Lowell George, previously of the Factory, joined the group. George added a new dimension with his classical music education, and solid music background. Lowell had even studied sitar with Ravi Shankar, so we added a sitar segment to our set. I was wowed by his talent. We played several gigs, including one at Pierce College in Van Nuys.

Michael McGeary was our drummer for a while during this time, and he recently shared a few memories with me. "We had a gig at the Indio Date Festival," he remembers "We played in early evening in a big stadium. There was a huge parade just before and about twenty camels in a pen in left field. Mid-set one, then two, then three pairs of camels took up vociferous lovemaking! Man, they were loud! We had to stop. The audience was howling!"

At the time, Lowell seemed to be the perfect fit. However, there was another more dubious fit that I hadn't expected, although I didn't learn about it until after Lowell left the group. It all began with a party I threw at my house. I noticed that Lowell and Linda were spending a lot of time together, mostly away from the main crowd at the party. Months later, Lowell casually told a friend of mine that he'd had an affair with my wife. We'd always had a hard-and-fast rule that no member scored on another's woman.

The relationship between Lowell and I came to a head at a rehearsal in early September, two weeks before our previously booked gig at the Ice House in Pasadena. It was there that Lowell announced his idea for a new direction with the Standells. It was obvious that he had a great deal of contempt not only for me but for the group. Lowell said that we needed to go back what he saw as the origins of the Standells, slick our hair back, and become a greaser band, much like *Sha Na Na* did the following year. Of course, this did not go over very well with Tony, John and me. We were never a greaser band, to begin with. Lowell stuck to his guns, arguing that the Standells would never again amount to anything without the make-over. We continued to be at odds when, at the end of the rehearsal, I announced that Linda and

I had made arrangements to fly to Acapulco over the weekend. This enraged Lowell, perhaps, in retrospect, motivated more by his affair with Linda than anything.

He then brazenly announced, "You'll have to call it off. The band needs more rehearsal time."

"I didn't know you were calling the shots," I angrily responded. "The last time I checked, I was the leader."

To my complete astonishment, he then screamed, "You're fired! Get out!"

It took me by surprise, being fired from the group that I'd created, but I quickly regained my composure. "No, *you're* fired! *You* get out!"

It was a power play, that much was obvious, but fortunately the others chose me over Lowell. I had a history with them, and Lowell didn't. We all stomped out of the meeting. Linda and I went to Acapulco.

From the Standells, Lowell joined Frank Zappa and the Mothers of Invention, going from one extreme to another.

In a 1975 interview in *Zigzag* magazine, George described his Standells experience with utmost distaste. "I replaced Dicky Dodd(s), the lead singer. He quit because he couldn't stand it. And I finally quit because I couldn't stand it either."

That might be so, but several months later he came to one of our rehearsals trying to get us to do one of his songs. Before I could respond, Tony screamed at him "Geet the fuck outta here!"

Lowell turned around and stomped out of the room. That's the last time I ever saw him. Lowell went on to quit the Mothers of Invention and form his band, Little Feat. The rest is history.

Upon returning from Acapulco, the group reformed without Lowell, once again adding Bill Daffern and several others. We signed to tour with Johnny Rivers. One of those concerts was with Burble Faun at the College of Santa Fe. I can remember on a cold snowy day I walked outside my cabin and was hit in the face by a well-aimed snowball thrown by Johnny. It was perhaps the closest we ever came to communication.

We performed at numerous concerts in the Midwest, too many to remember. We also did a concert with the Iron Butterfly, Blue Cheer, and the Byrds at the Arizona State Fairgrounds, October 5th. On October 25th, we performed with Taj Mahal and other acts at the Artists and Models Ball, Century Plaza in Los Angeles.

<h1 style="text-align: center">CHAPTER 14</h1>

In 1969, the world witnessed the crowning achievement of America's space program. The Apollo 11 mission had achieved President John F. Kennedy's dream, successfully landing on the moon, and Neil Armstrong uttered his immortal words "That's one small step for man, one giant leap for mankind." In August, members of the Charles Manson cult senselessly murdered eight people, including actress Sharon Tate and hairstylist Jay Sebring. Woodstock attracted 350,000 music fans to the first super music festival, and the Beatles made their last public performance in a concert on the roof of Apple Records. It was also the beginning of the end of the sixties Standells.

John Fleck decided to go back to filmmaking under his full name, John Fleckenstein. He went on to become one of the top directors of photography and camera operators in the business. His credits include *ET The Extra-Terrestrial* and *Jaws 2*.

At that point, I wanted to take a break from the Standells. That's when I ran into former members of the Knack – not the band who had the hit single "My Sharona," but a completely unrelated group by the same name who had made a handful of singles for Capitol Records in 1966-68. We had first met when they performed at the Hullabaloo teen nightclub. With guitarist and singer Michael "Dink" Kaplan, bassist Larry Gould, and drummer Pug Baker, all from the Knack, we put together a new band called Chakras. I didn't know what to do with Tony, so I appointed him as our manager. As Pug was a solid drummer, we decided to put Bill Daffern up front. Bill was quite a talented singer and a lovable guy. He was also a wild man on stage. However, his style was considerably different than that of the three Knack members, and that led to some animosity from Dink, Larry and Pug. They wanted to oust Bill, but I wouldn't go along with it. I genuinely liked the variety with Bill in it. I stuck to keyboards and didn't do much lead singing with the group. I also changed my first name to "Rocky." Why? I don't know, except perhaps to have some kind of re-birth – and avoid having two Larrys in the group.

We signed with Warners' Reprise label for an unheard-of deal back in those days, including a $10,000 partial advance, paid in monthly installments. We recorded two singles for them, neither of which sold particularly well. However, some of the teen magazines did front-page articles on Chakras, and we also performed two successful concerts at the Whisky A Go-Go. Many thought we were going to be next big supergroup.

Right when I thought the group was about to take off, I was stunned when Dink, Larry and Pug dropped a bombshell on us and told us they were quitting. I couldn't talk them out of it, and neither could the record company. Quite frankly, I think Dink was a legend in his own mind. They walked away from potential superstardom and the remainder of the advance money. [46]

The three of them later formed a new group, Chariot, recorded an album that went nowhere, and were never heard of again – except for Larry Gould who joined a later version of the Standells. Was it a stupid move? Yeah, but sadly, these things are

____

46 www.rateyourmusic.com – *Chakras* (1969)

quite common with rock groups. Remember, Dick Dodd walked away from the Standells and a potentially lucrative deal with a new record company, only to have an unsuccessful solo career. This was perhaps what soured me most about the music business, having to make a living by depending on the whims of others who sometimes let their egos get in the way.

Toward the end of the year, we reformed the Standells. Along with Tony, Bill Daffern (back on drums) and me were new members Paul Downing on guitar and Tim Smyser on bass. Downing and I just simply didn't get along. We performed at Pier 7, a small club in Van Nuys beginning on November 7th.

For me, it was depressing to go back to playing in nightclubs. I had become disgusted and disillusioned with the entire rock group thing. That was when I decided that I could no longer bear dealing with unstable rock musicians to make a living. After a great deal of thought, weighing the pros and cons of continuing, I concluded that I'd finally had enough. I painfully chose to walk away from the only career I had ever known and face the consequences. I gathered up the courage to inform Tony that I would remain with the group for one more week, although even the thought of that was unbearable. From then on, he would take over. He tried to talk me out of it, but my mind was made up.

As the sixties ended, as far as I was concerned, the Standells were dead and buried, cast into oblivion. Not in my wildest imagination did I ever think that several decades later things would change so dramatically.

In 1970, the world saw hope in the completion of the Nuclear Arms Non-Proliferation Treaty. It was also the year that the Apollo

13 mission to the moon was a near disaster, and the often-mis-quoted words "Houston we've had a problem" were uttered as astronauts James Lovell, Jack Swigert and Fred Haise began their perilous but ultimately successful return to earth. It was the year that Ohio National Guards fired into a crowd of unarmed anti-war protesters at Kent State University, killing four and injuring nine students, triggering a nationwide student strike that forced the closure of hundreds of colleges and universities. It was also when Paul McCartney announced that the Beatles had been dissolved. Likewise, my relationship with the Standells had come to an end.

I was still fascinated with the art of making of music, but no longer with performing it. I had an interest in becoming a recording engineer, but back then there were no schools in which one could learn the skills of engineering in a studio. I contacted my old friends Richie Podolor and Bill Cooper, whom we'd worked with so many times with the Standells, and they agreed to let me hang around American Recording Studios to learn the craft. In return, I would set up mics for other groups who recorded there. Richie had now successfully stepped into the producer arena with such groups as Three Dog Night and Steppenwolf.

I happened to be at American Recording Studios when another group he produced Blues Image recorded their hit "Ride Captain Ride." Having Larry Tamblyn of the Standells set up mics for them could have been quite a bragging point, and I was treated with a great deal of respect. Lead singer and guitarist Mike Pinera frankly told to me, "I'm not a star, and I don't intend to be." I guess he knew that you meet the same people on the way up that you do on the way down. After gaining valuable experience at American Recording Studio, I went to work as a recording engineer for my high school friend Fred Piro, as well as a producer for National General Records, for whom I produced several small rock groups, including Dalton, James & Sutton. [47]

My former Chakras bandmates Dink Kaplan, Pug Baker and Larry Gould had by then formed Chariot, and as fate would have it, they were signed to National General. As a salaried engineer, I had no choice but to mix down their album and try not to vomit as I was subjected to Dink's boastful comments throughout the entire session.

It was there, too, that I became reacquainted with a much humbler Ron Gruber, the former Stones tour manager. He was desperate and sought out a job there in a different department. As it turned out, he was hired about the same time I was fired. Life throws you some curves sometimes.

---

47 www.discogs.com - *Dalton, James & Sutton, National General Records* (1970)

CHAPTER 15

In April, my first daughter, Lisa, was born, and my job a National General Records fizzled out. In calling various recording studios around town looking for work, I happened upon a man named Louie Steinman. He was kind of a one-man record company and had a business in an old run-down building in Hollywood. For a fee, Louie would bring in wannabe singers, arrange and record tracks for them, and then press records with a custom label. Kind of a one-stop-shop for hopefuls.

He had created such a recording for Kathy Sheets, the bombshell wife of a prominent eye surgeon, John Sheets, from Odessa, Texas. Dr. Sheets had married her when she was just seventeen years old. After bearing him five children, Kathy suddenly realized that she'd missed out on an important part of her life: stardom! She began performing in Shakespearean plays at the Globe Theater, located at Odessa College. Hard to believe you'd find theater of this caliber in the oil capital of the United States, but there it was: an actual replica of Shakespeare's Globe Theatre in Southwark, London, complete with an authentic Elizabethan stage. However, Kathy had even loftier goals: she wanted to be a recording star. That's where Louie came in.

Dr. Sheets sent her to Hollywood, and Louie produced her records. Returning to Odessa, Sheets then had the two hundred records distributed to record stores throughout Odessa and its twin city Midland. He then proceeded to buy up all of the records, causing Kathy's record to rise to #1 on the Odessa-Midland radio charts.

After catching the show biz bug, Dr. Sheets then got the idea that he would start his own media conglomerate, based on Louie's business model. He went about gathering investors for his new entertainment company, Trans Global Media. By golly, the good folks of Odessa were going to show Hollywood how it was done! The investment funds mostly came from oil money in Odessa and Midland, where the Petroleum Institute of America was located. As part of their mission statement, they planned to franchise recording studios, much like McDonald's franchised fast food restaurants. They would begin by building a large recording studio in Odessa.

That was about the time I had contacted Louie. He put me in touch with Dr. Sheets, who arranged to fly me to Odessa. After arriving, I met with some of the principles of the company, including Senior V.P. Frank Crockett whose expertise was in owning a Chevy dealership. The company also included a local evangelist preacher, the Rev. Pete Cryer, who was the V.P. of Finance. Pete insisted we begin our meeting with a prayer. Also present was the Director of Publicity, Jim Buckley, who had worked for a local radio station in Odessa. Jim was also an avowed John Bircher, who later told me, "Rock and roll is a Communist Conspiracy."

The company also included, of all things, speech therapist Micky Keller. He was genuinely the most pleasant and accommodating member of the company. Unbeknownst to the other principles of Trans Global Media, Micky was a closet gay, much like Corky St. Clair's character in the Christopher Guest movie,

Waiting for Guffman. In fact, this entire adventure in Odessa could be likened to that movie. [48]

Although the partners were from various professions, there was one thing they all had in common: None of them knew what the fuck they were doing. However, being a hopeless optimist and desperate for work, I chose to overlook the disaster-in-the-making and blindly accept their offer. The following day I flew back home. Linda and I packed up as much as we could into a hitched trailer, and shortly thereafter, Linda, the baby, and I headed towards Texas, leaving our home unoccupied – perhaps one of the smarter things I did.

I don't believe in omens. But notwithstanding this eccentric cast of characters with their grandiose plans to take the music business by storm, there were enough clues of biblical proportions on the way to Odessa telling us to turn around and go back home.

The first and most obvious omen came not long after our departure. We were moving to Texas in the heat of the summer, and in Blythe, California, our car's air conditioner stopped working in the sweltering temperatures. If this wasn't bad enough, we were in the midst of – you guessed it – a plague of grasshoppers – millions of them! You could not roll down the car window without having these wretched creatures pour in by the dozens. We had no choice but to stop at the state line, get out and hose down everything, including the car's human and insect occupants, then head back into town for repairs. We stopped at a gas station and were assured by the mechanic that he could have it fixed by the

---

48 *Waiting for Guffman* (1997)

following day. Exhausted, we checked into a motel and quickly fell into a deep slumber. The following morning, we returned to the gas station, only to be told by the mechanic that he wasn't able to fix the problem. The kicker was that even so I owed him for the parts and labor. When I protested, two other bruisers entered the garage, one menacingly slapping a wrench into the palm of his hand. I had no choice but to pay the ransom.

For the remainder of the trip, we traveled at night to avoid the extreme heat. But this presented us with a third problem. Once we crossed the border into Texas, I encountered a marauding truck driver who menacingly tailgated us, passed us, then got in front of us and slowed down. It appeared to me as though he just didn't like folks from California on his highway. Finally, he intentionally ran us off the road, our car narrowly avoiding a collision with a road sign. This was not the first time I experienced this aggressive behavior while driving through Texas. Much like in the scene from the TV movie *Duel*, directed by Steven Spielberg, and starring Dennis Weaver, it was a frightening encounter. Ironically, the writer of the film Richard Matheson was inspired by a similar experience to mine, a terrifying confrontation with a tailgating truck driver.[49]

Even worse, when we neared Odessa, we were treated to a horrific thunder and lightning storm, with lightning bolts crashing around us as we drove. I did say "of biblical proportions," didn't I?

After spending the night in a motel owned by Dr. Sheets, I woke up and decided to stroll out onto the balcony to breath in some of that wonderful, fresh Texas air. Instead, I almost gagged

---

49 *Duel* (1971)

from the smell of hydrogen sulfide being emitted from the nearby oil fields. Rotten eggs were not the most appetizing thing to smell first thing in the morning. As I was to learn, this was something that the locals had grown accustomed to.

The stench didn't get much better. That evening we were invited to a party attended by some of the building's residents. One would think that an event such as this in the middle of the Bumfuck Nowhere would be pretty tame. Hot damn was I mistaken! Who knew that these good ol' boys and their wives were swingers? Yeah, you heard it right. Perhaps it was a way to deal with mundane life in the oil fields, and constantly breathing that hydrogen sulfide. The situation finally became apparent when one of the rednecks grabbed hold of my wife's ass and pulled her toward him. Immediately, I pushed him off and cocked my arm to take a swing at him, but was prevented by the others. I was told that it was a simple misunderstanding. I demanded to know how ass-grabbing can be misunderstood but was the only answer I was given was "No harm intended."

Unsolicited ass-grabbing is clearly acceptable in the land of swingers, but most definitely not in mine. The air was not the only thing rotten in Odessa.

The next day I reported for work and was immediately put in charge of the construction of the studio, a task that stretched the level of my incompetency. At least I was in good company. The building and offices were already completed, but the studio space was just a large empty auditorium. It would be a mammoth undertaking. They were oblivious to the fact that I knew nothing about construction, let alone the acoustical properties that such a facility required. I crammed on every tech book and magazine I could find. In the process, I learned about sound traps, standing waves, and sound isolation. The construction process was slow, but I was going to end up with the perfect studio.

Meanwhile, Dr. Sheets and the others began to be concerned that no potential clients were lining up to record in his as yet unfinished recording studio. Apparently, no one in the organization had ever asked the question "Where would the business come from?" After all, there wasn't a thriving entertainment industry in Odessa – yet!

As if I didn't already have enough to deal with, Frank Crockett then turned me into a salesperson over the weekends, which meant going out and meeting with local musicians to try to drum up business. Of course, it was a next-to-impossible task since we didn't even have a finished studio to show prospective clients.

I was in the middle of designing movable sound baffles when Dr. Sheets excitedly called me into his office.

"Larry!" he exclaimed. "We have decided that we need to create a major event to bring in business."

"Okay," I responded, "I'm game. What did you have in mind?"

"We need to bring in a top name to record here. We're going to put Odessa on the map as a major recording studio and entertainment center."

I thought for a minute, weighing the implausibility of the task. Turning the oil capital into an entertainment capital would be quite an undertaking.

"Let me make some calls," I suggested. "I still have many contacts back in Los Angeles. Maybe even a group like Blues Image."

"Who?" he said.

I thought, *Holy shit. These guys truly are hicks.* "They recorded 'Ride Captain Ride,' which is now a Top 10 hit record. I just worked with them and know how to get in touch."

"No," interjected Frank, who had just entered the room. "It's already been taken care of. I've reached out to a movie producer friend in New York."

"Who's that?" I responded, in total amazement that he knew someone in the film business, let alone someone with a recognizable name.

"Harley Ibsen," he responded proudly.

"Who is he?" I asked, genuinely puzzled. "I've never heard of him. What has he produced?"

"He's with a New York TV station and has produced some big documentaries," Crockett patiently explained, as if Ibsen was a recognizable name other than the famous playwright Henrik Ibsen. As I learned, Harley Ibsen was from a small TV station in upper New York state. I was then told about the "major star" that Harley would be able bring to Odessa. His eyes brightened as he revealed, "Her name is Julie Budd."

I had to pause a few seconds to think about this. "I've never heard of her," I admitted. "What has she recorded?"

"You don't seem to know much, young man," Frank said condescendingly. "She was on the *Ed Sullivan Show.*"

Suddenly, the name rang a bell, although I still couldn't quite place her. I used to watch the *Ed Sullivan Show* faithfully. That's where I saw the Beatles' first performance, plus the Rolling Stones, Dave Clark Five, and the Animals. And of course, my brother had appeared on the show years before. But where had I seen Julie Budd? Then it struck me.

"Now I remember! She was the young girl who looked and sounded like Barbara Streisand. *That's* why she was on the show."

Dr. Sheets piped in, "She's got the star drawing power we need."

I couldn't believe my ears. "Just because she was on *Ed Sullivan*, doesn't make her a star. If that was the case, we could bring in Topo Gigio."

"Don't be a wiseass," Crockett blurted out, with a sneer on his face.

Reverend Cryer had joined us by then, and his face turned beet red from the expletive. I doubt that any of them even knew who Topo the mouse puppet was.

"This is the kind of star we need," Crockett added. [50]

I could not convince them that Budd's appearance on *Ed Sullivan* and other TV variety shows had been solely because she was a young Barbara Streisand look-and-sound-alike, not because of anything she had achieved individually. She was quite remarkable for a sixteen-year-old, but that was it. Julie Budd was not even close to being considered a major name. My years in the business and recognition as a member of the Standells somehow didn't seem amount to much anymore. Dr. Sheets, Frank Crockett, and the others were star-struck over a non-star. They told me that Ibsen was going to be flying in to meet with us over the weekend, and that it was going to be a momentous life-altering event for not only Sheets but everyone in Odessa and Midland. After all, this was a "Big New York Producer."

---

50 www.Imdb.com – IMDb, *Julie Budd Biography*

After the meeting, I cornered Dr. Sheets. "I honestly don't think that a documentary producer is what you're looking for," I told him. "And Julie Budd is a nobody. They're trying to pull something on you."

But Dr. Sheets would have none of it. "You're wrong," he said. "Ibsen knows lots of people in the business. Julie Budd is a major star and I'm convinced they can help make Odessa into a music capital."

Oh boy, I thought, *Ibsen must have smelled the oil money all the way from New York.* At that moment, I realized that my days there were numbered.

The meeting with Harley Ibsen that weekend was even worse than I could ever have imagined. All of the TGM board members were there. Decked in his finest worsted suit, Ibsen announced his grand vision. "I hadn't realized it at the time, but there's quite a story to tell here."

Oh God, I thought, *here it comes.* And I was not let down.

Harley stood up, paced around the room, and spread his arms in a grandiose manner. "We can make this into a television special."

I almost swallowed my chewing gum. Dr. Sheets and Frank Crockett immediately sat straight up. Then Ibsen announced his next gem. Stepping forward and placing his arms on the shoulders of Dr. Sheets, he said, "The story of a big star from New York coming to Odessa would be of national interest. Of course, in addition to Julie Budd, you and your wonderful family would star in the film."

Dr. Sheets's face broke into a broad smile. "Really?"

He was butter in Harley's hands after that, and the producer knew it.

Realizing that this must have been scripted in advance, I could almost guess what Ibsen was going to say next,

"I've got a great name for this film. We can call it *East Meets West.*"

Did Harley intentionally steal this title from the 1936 movie of the same name? The plot summary: *A huckster convincing two countries to bid against each other over a worthless harbor.* The similarity was uncanny. [51]

I thought, who *in their right minds would believe this total crock of shit? A bunch of starry-eyed hicks, that's who.*

Sheets was completely hooked. He was already channeling the stardom this would bring to his family. In his mind's eye, he saw the Sheets name up in lights alongside others like Brando, Hepburn and John Wayne. And, of course, the notoriety this would bring to Odessa.

I could take no more, so at that point, claiming illness, I excused myself. The group hardly noticed as I slipped out.

I'd seen this same scenario before in the movie *After the Fox,* based on the Neal Simon play of the same name. The story involved an escaped thief named Aldo Vanucci, played to perfection by Peter Sellers. Posing as an avant-garde director, he artfully persuaded a small fishing village to smuggle a shipment of stolen gold from Cairo into Italy, convincing them that they would be featured in an epic film about a gold heist. [52]

---

51 *East Meets West* (1936)
52 *After the Fox* (1966)

But this scene playing out before me was not a fictional movie; it was real and taking place right before my very eyes – a classic Ponzi scheme. The dupes, of course, were Dr. Sheets, Frank Crockett, the TGM board of directors, and the cities of Odessa and Midland. I knew the ending of this story before it was even written. I tried several more times to talk Dr. Sheets out of the plan, emphasizing to him that Julie Budd was not a nationally recognized star.

"These are not homefolk," I told him, "they're New Yorkers and you're going to get screwed."

You'd think that my past success in the music business and show-biz family ties would have accounted for something, but I was up against Dr. Sheets' self-aggrandizement being fed by the biggest flim-flam artist since Harold Hill in *The Music Man* selling a line of goods to a bunch of townsfolk in Iowa. My pleas fell on deaf ears. Like Hill, Ibsen was giving these good ol' boys a song-and-a-dance. Sheets and the others were convinced that if Julie Budd had been on *Ed Sullivan*, she was a major celebrity. Of course, he was ignoring the fact that in addition to Topo Gigio, a ventriloquist named Señor Wences, and other oddities also appeared on *Sullivan*.

For her appearance in Odessa, Miss Budd would be accompanied by her music producer/arranger/conductor, Herb Bernstein. To say the least, Bernstein's previous producing and arranging credits were impressive. They included Laura Nyro, John Denver, the Four Seasons, Bob Dylan, and Tony Orlando and Dawn. Song credits such as "See You in September," "Go Away Little Girl," "Knock Three Times," "Leaving on a Jet Plane," and "I Can't

Make It Without You" made the deal even more extraordinary. I had to wonder, though, what could have possibly drawn him to Odessa? The only thing I could think of was money! With film production costs, studio comp-time, rooms and transportation for Julie Budd, Bernstein, Harley Ibsen and his film crew, the budget for this fiasco-in-the-making swelled to over $500,000. To make matters worse, Odessa had no professional orchestra musicians. I brought this up to Dr. Sheets, and he informed me that members of the Odessa/Midland Symphony would be used and paid session fees. At that time, the Symphony was considered a "Metropolitan Orchestra" and was composed mostly of young non-professional musicians. To believe that they were up to the task of doing a major recording session was to believe that pigs can fly.

Meanwhile, it hadn't dawned on any of these "experts" that the recording studio was not completed. Neither did they entertain the fact that even after completion, a certain amount of lag time had to be allowed before the first session to test all of the equipment and give the studio a dry run. As the day approached for Julie Budd's arrival, I feverishly worked day and night on the finishing touches of the studio. The room was nearly completed, with some of the equipment already there, including the Ampex VPR-5200 8-track recorder. But the custom mixing console wasn't due for arrival until Wednesday, three days before the recording session. I tried to postpone the session, but Dr. Sheets and Frank Crockett wouldn't hear of it.

Everyone but me was ready. The local newspapers were full of stories about the big day, with Julie's photo splashed across the headlines. Julie was going to put Odessa's star on the map. Information about the airport arrival time and the scheduled parade through Odessa was posted, encouraging the citizens to be part of this historic event. By Saturday morning the console had been installed and wiring to the tape machine connected. But none of the mics had been unpacked yet. If I hurried, they could be set up before the musicians arrived. This is when Crockett helped to seal my ignominious fate. No matter how much I pleaded, he would not allow me to finish setting everything up and turning the equipment on. Instead I was forced to go to the Midland airport to be part of the "welcoming fans" for Julie Budd.

When I arrived, I was told to go the bleachers behind the fence on the tarmac. The stands were partially filled with about thirty people waiting for Julie Budd's arrival, some with "Welcome Julie Budd" placards. In reality, none of them knew who she was. A reporter from a local TV station was there with a small film camera, perhaps also wondering who she was. On the other side of the fence with a bullhorn in his hand was Jim Buckley. He raised the horn to his mouth and announced. "I'd like to welcome y'all to this historic event. We're naming this Julie Budd Day."

"Now, let me go over the chain of events, today," Jim continued. "The plane will arrive and taxi up to this spot, which we've marked as Site A." He pointed to a chalk-marked area to his right. "This is where Dr. Sheets and his family will be greeting Miss Budd and her producer upon their arrival, giving them a Texas-sized welcome." Then he bellowed out a large "Yeehaw!" waving his Stetson hat in the air. The crowd laughed and applauded.

I couldn't believe what I was hearing. Jim was doing what is normally called a "warm-up" in Hollywood. But this was cornball as hell. Jim concluded his speech by outlining the complete schedule for the day. The first to exit the plane would be the film crew, followed by Herb Bernstein, then Julie Budd. They would then commence a ticker tape parade through the streets of Odessa.

This was a lot to take in, let alone believe that this would be anything other than a total calamity.

Soon the plane landed and taxied up to its marked spot on the tarmac. The first to step off the plane was the film crew – Harley Ibsen with a single camera. *Oh boy,* I thought, *an epic television special in the making – NOT.* Next was Bernstein. I could see his white-capped teeth, contrasted by his in-vogue suntanned face and well-coiffed hair, all the way from the rear of the stands. He was followed by Julie Budd. As scripted, the trio was met by Dr. Sheets and his family, his wife in a breathtakingly low-cut gown, the kids in the hippest clothes they could find in Odessa. All were introduced by Dr. Sheets. They embraced and proceeded over to the parking area where two Chevy convertibles awaited them, donated by Frank Crockett for this special occasion. Ibsen then panned his camera for a shot of the crowd, in which I sat, shielding my face in embarrassment.

This was a major event, unparalleled in Odessa history. Led by a police motorcade, the two open convertibles drove slowly along a parade route on 42nd Street. There was the usual assortment of high school marching bands, baton twirlers, a truck bed filled with Kiwanis club members, Shriners adorned with their red fezzes driving miniature race cars, and hastily assembled floats. Following a car driven by the mayor were the two white Chevy convertibles, luxurious by Odessa standards, but most definitely not by New York standards.

Frank Crockett drove the first vehicle, in which Herb Bernstein comfortably sat alongside Julie Budd who perched atop the rear deck, doing her best attempt at a beauty queen wave to the small handful spectators on either side of the convertible. Behind was the second car in which was seated Kathy Sheets and her five children. Not far behind, was a car with Dr. Sheets and the TGM executives. To his credit, Dr. Sheets would not share in the glory of his wife and children.

Harley walked alongside the two cars with his camera, capturing the full splendor of the event. It was a sight to behold, except for one small detail: There were no people in the streets to cheer them on. Except for a smattering of Odessans jogging or walking their dogs, there was not a single soul viewing the spectacle. Evidently not everyone had been taken in by the hype. I'm sure that quite a few had asked the obvious question, *Who the hell is Julie Budd?*

However, this did not detract from Dr. Sheets' enthusiasm. He was filled with pride at his accomplishment of bringing a "major star" to Odessa and publicizing his buxom wife and family in the process. Nothing I could have said or done would have dissuaded him from this shining moment.

Circumventing the parade route, I made a beeline for the studio, arriving to find members of the orchestra already milling about. Having never recorded anything more than small rock bands, let alone a live orchestra, I must share the blame in the train wreck that was shortly to take place. Running on fumes, exhausted from worry and lack of sleep, I went about trying to seat all of the musicians, going by standard orchestra seating. On the far left were the first violins, next to them second violins, woodwinds in center; on the far-right were double basses, and to the right-front were cellos. To the rear, the grand piano was on the far left, brass section in the center and percussion on the right. All told, about twenty-five musicians were seated. But wait a minute. I had forgotten one important thing…the mics weren't set up!

I crawled under musicians' chairs and feet to connect the cables, then pulled the mics out of their boxes, mounted them on the stands, and attached them to the cables. The Sheets, Bernstein, Budd and the TGM bigwigs all arrived as I was still frantically trying to get everything set-up. Upon seeing this, Bernstein wasted no time in letting loose with some well-crafted expletives, including "Why in the fuck aren't we ready to go?"

I could have said, "Because the engineer was forced to be an extra in your fucking film at the fucking airport," but it would have been useless. Besides, I already had a good idea of what the outcome was going to be. It took another half hour to set up everything and finally turn on the mixer and recording machine. With Julie in the vocal isolation booth, Bernstein then demanded we run through the first song. Except for Julie, it was awful. Instead of criticizing the musicians, Herb concentrated on me. He had an agenda, unobvious to everyone but me. He demanded that I solo each section. And so, I complied. Each was fine until the very last section. One of the mics didn't work. At this point, Bernstein went ballistic. Of course, according to him, the entire thing – musicians and all – was my fault. Then Bernstein threatened to cancel the entire event and go back to New York. This was all part of his script, of course.

Dr. Sheets saw his dream begin to crumble before his eyes and desperately pleaded with Bernstein to stay. "Herb what can we do to make this work?"

Here it comes, I thought.

Bernstein wasted no time in responding, "I want my own engineer."

Unsurprisingly, I was fired on the spot. But the inevitable came more as a relief.

Dr. Sheets gave me the usual "You're like a son to me" speech, and wrote and issued my severance check, which I immediately took to the bank and cashed. It just so happened to be the same bank that I used as well.

The teller, who happened to be a friend and an old Standells fan, said in confidence, "Larry they're writing checks with money they don't have. It's a good thing you cashed it now. They're going to start bouncing."

It took Linda and me three days to pack. Before we left, we stopped by to see Micky Keller, who updated us on what was transpiring at TGM. According to Micky, Bernstein wasn't happy with just replacing me. He also demanded to bring in some key session musicians from New York, at triple scale plus housing and transportation. No doubt, this had been part of Herb's master plan all along. I can't say that I blamed him. There was no way this project stood a chance without the additional musicians.

As for me, I guess I just wasn't ready for the big time in Odessa. It was smooth sailing all the way back home. None of the omens we faced coming to Odessa stood in our way: no mechanical failures, no swarms of locusts, no thunder or lightning, or murderous truckers. Even though I was out of a job, we were relieved to be back home in Hollywood. To hell with homefolk, sulfur, swingers, and wannabe celebrities.

I didn't know or care about what became of Dr. Sheets and his wife after that. In the back of my mind, I knew it would somehow end up tragically. My suspicions turned out be spot-on. About a year later, out of the blue, I received a telephone call from Dr. Sheets.

He spoke in much more somber voice than when we'd last talked. "Hi Larry, I don't s'pose you ever thought you'd ever hear from me again."

"Well, this is quite a surprise," I admitted, then asked him a stupid question. "How are things with Trans Global Media?"

After a few beats, he responded woefully in a much slower twang than I remembered, "Quite frankly, not very well."

"I'm terribly sorry to hear that," I replied, sensing that Sheets' story was heading in the direction that I had predicted a year earlier.

"I just called to say that I should have listened to you," he lamented.

It was indeed a tragic tale, one of greater ramifications than I could ever have imagined. I had long since put behind my disillusionment with Sheets, Ibsen, Bernstein, Budd, Crockett and the entire Odessa/Midand experience. In fact, since returning I had gotten into an entirely new field of employment. Dr. Sheets went on to tell me that, as I had suspected would happen, the costs of the film and recording session had skyrocketed. All of his partners in the business bailed out, leaving him holding the bag. This, in turn, required him to take out a home equity loan to pay for it. Even that wasn't enough money to cover the expenses, which caused him to take out some high interest loans. In the end, it all came crashing down around his shoulders. He was forced to declare bankruptcy.

"Gee," I said, "I'm so sorry. At least you have your family."

"That's the most painful part of this," he despondently continued.

God, I thought. *How could it get much worse?* But it did. Sheets told me that his wife had run off with a local disc jockey, leaving him and his five children behind.

We talked a little more, and before hanging up I told him once again how sorry I was for the way everything turned out. Yeah, there were many opportunities to blurt out, "I told you so," and "you deserve what you got," but I didn't. The fact was that he loved his wife and family and wanted the best for them. Nobody deserves this kind of pay-back.

After hanging up the phone, I relayed the sad story to Linda, who was not as forgiving as me.

"Serves the bastard right," she said.

I could find no solace in having been proved right, knowing that Sheets did all of this for his wife and family only to be kicked in the face for his efforts. I never heard from him again, and years later learned of his passing.

On his tombstone was written: "He was a loving and wonderful husband, father, and friend, who was a pioneer and a visionary in his life and his profession. We love you and miss you."

Somebody had loved and appreciated him. That's all any of us can ask.

CHAPTER 16

On February 9, 1971, the Sylmar earthquake struck. Registering 6.5 on the Richter Scale and centered in the San Gabriel Mountains, it was, to say the least, a nightmare – or I should say a continuation of one I was about to have in real life.

In the dream I was smack dab in the middle of a hurricane. The wind was blowing so fiercely that I was hanging perpendicularly onto a telephone pole. Right then, the Sylmar earthquake hit. My first thought was *It's the end of the world!* Glass was breaking, dogs were barking, electric cables arcing… a real, honest-to-god nightmare. Surviving this was perhaps why I was so receptive to shaking up my career.

After scouring the classifieds for leads, an ad in the *LA Times* caught my eye. Mattel Toys was looking for a children's producer. I made an appointment and drove to Mattel's El Segundo headquarters to apply. I found out later that Mattel had over 4,000 people apply for the job.

I was interviewed by the Human Resources Director and, admittedly lied my way into the testing process. I told the director that I had written several children's stories.

Little did I know what was in store for me next.

I was given a stopwatch, a stack of lined notebook paper, and three of Mattel's products – a stuffed bear, a horse, and a Barbie doll. The young woman led me to a small booth and gave me my assignment: assume each character was a talking doll and write as many phrases for each as I could. The lines had to be created specifically for each character, and they needed to be humorous and interactive, motivating the child to respond in some manner. Why the stopwatch? Due to the mechanics of the Mattel talking dolls, none of the lines could be more than 1.89 seconds. Gulp.

I stepped into the booth and heard the door shut behind me. There I was, alone, looking at the stack of paper, facing three toys, and wondering what in the hell I was doing there. My mind was blank – I could not think of a single thing to write. *Why?* I asked myself.

Well, said my left brain, *it's because you're not a child anymore.*

But what if you were a child? said the right side of my brain. *What cute little phrases could you imagine coming from each of these characters?*

I sat for a few minutes longer, looking at the first piece of lined paper. Slowly it dawned on me that it was just like the paper we used to have in our notebooks in school. So, as I would normally do in class, in the upper right-hand corner I wrote, *Larry Tamblyn, 2nd grade, Age: 7 ½, Teacher: Ms. Gooch.*

But somehow it didn't seem quite right, so I erased it and started over. This time, even though I'm right-handed, I wrote it with my left hand. Voilà! I was transformed back into a seven-and-a-half-year-old boy. Immediately the lines began to flow. "Can you 'paws' for a hug from a Bear?" "'Whinny' me over with a squeeze," and so on.

When I met with the supervisor, Jeff Ehrhart, he astonished me by saying that I had landed the job. He couldn't stop laughing. I nailed the job not necessarily because I had filled a stack of papers with phrases, but because I listed my age as *7 ½* and that I was in *2ⁿᵈ grade*. He said that to create products for children, you had to be like a child.

"You're just as crazy as I am," Jeff told me.

We later became best friends.

Speaking of the Barbie doll, the department head was Gwen Florea, the voice of the talking Barbie Doll. Gwen later co-wrote a book along with another toy designer Glenda Phinney, *Barbie Talks*, about their adventures at Mattel. Gwen became a wonderful friend and mentor. I developed lasting friendships with Gwen and others with whom I worked.

Having no formal education that qualified me for this job, I was working right alongside one PhD and several who held master's degrees in education. One of my co-workers was Gary Grayson. He also moonlighted at the Magic Castle as a magician and looked every bit the part, Van Dyke beard and all. As part of the Research and Design Department, I created some of Mattel's top-selling products, including See & Say, Talking Baseball and Talking Football games, and many more. We used the top voiceover talents in animation films, people like Dal McKennon, the voice of Woody Woodpecker; Hal Smith, the voice of Owl in *Winnie the Pooh*; and Joan Gerber, who worked on a multitude of Saturday morning children's shows. Joanie, as we called her, developed an affectionate name for me – *Baby Tamblyn*, because of my baby face.

All the while, I kept in touch with Tony. He was keeping the Standells going, mostly performing in different nightclubs, mostly in Canada and throughout California. I even went to see them in Las Vegas, though I still had no desire to return to performing. It was during that visit that I visited with not only Tony, but former Knack/Chakras member bassist Larry Gould who had recently joined the Standells. It might have been my imagination, but he seemed a lot humbler. My experience with musicians was that this was very common after promises and dreams failed to materialize.

In 1972, Dick Dodd formed a group called Joshua, who recorded with Ed Cobb. Ed had his own recording studio, Producers Workshop, which churned out hits for an impressive number of popular acts. Joshua was not one of them. Based on what I heard from Tony, Dick had gone downhill because of drugs and alcohol. Even worse, he was in a terrible car wreck while under the influence.

The job at Mattel lasted for about two-and-a-half years, coming to an end in 1973. Gwen Florea had left the company and was replaced by a wretched man named Dale. He had a PhD in music but nothing much to show for it. Between his jealousy of my Standells history – a constant reminder of his failures in music – and his attitude towards my having only a high school education, Dale viewed me condescendingly. He considered me unqualified for the job at Mattel, even though I was one of its top creators. He insisted that I take college classes at night, which I did, even though they were entirely unnecessary.

With all of this as a backdrop, I next made what was one of my stupidest decisions in my life. I received a telephone call from my old friend Fred Piro, asking if I would be interested in producing a new group called Ambrosia. He told me he thought they were going to be a supergroup. I met with guitarist/vocalist David Pack, bassist/vocalist Joe Puerta, keyboardist Christopher North, and drummer Burleigh Drummond in Fred's newly re-built Mama Jo's recording studio, and, decided they were full of themselves. They had every right to be. Ambrosia went on to record several chart records, including "How Much I Feel," "Biggest Part of Me," "You're the Only Woman" and "Holdin' Onto Yesterday." [53]

They must have felt the same way about me. To be honest, my thoughts were elsewhere. I wasn't ready for the long-term commitment it would have taken, and was still very disillusioned with the music business, so I passed on the opportunity. But not long after that I was unceremoniously dumped by Mattel. You can only kick yourself so many times for making irrational decisions such as this. However, at the time, I didn't hadn't the slightest inclination that the Standells legacy would far outlive them. Although I'd been let go by Mattel, my experience and success there led me to a second career in children's products. I landed a job at Superscope Marantz, where I created and produced over a hundred children's audio cassette and book programs labeled as Tele-Story. The products were the most successful of their kind. While at Superscope, I was able to return Jeff Earhart's favor and hire him as a co-producer for the children's stories. I learned from my friend Kit Hudson, who was still at Mattel, that my success at Superscope even further irked Dale. As he saw it, I was not qualified to be successful.

After several years of strong indications, my marriage to Linda finally began to fall apart. After Lisa was born, I'd decided

---

53 www.allmusic.com - *Ambrosia Biography*

to take my vows seriously, whereas Linda did not. I guess it was because in her eyes I was no longer a rock star.

Finally, I could take no more, and in 1973 summoned up the courage to pack up some of my clothes and leave the house. It was perhaps one of the most trying times in my life, moving from our beautiful home in the Hollywood Hills to my brother's home in Topanga Canyon, leaving my beautiful daughter behind. But I knew that it was the right thing to do, especially when I returned a few days later to pack some more of my things. Linda wasn't there, so I let myself in. I went upstairs to the bedroom to discover a strange man, this time a cop, sleeping in my bed.

Not long afterwards, realizing how foolish I'd been to hang on to this marriage for so long, I finally decided that, as painful as it was, divorce was the best thing for both of us.

Going through the divorce was a very dark time in my life, and I found myself in a vulnerable position. Living with Russ and his wife, Elizabeth, was awkward because they were having marital problems of their own. Also, Russ' career had hit the skids. When he could find them, Russ was doing low budget movies like *The Female Bunch* and *Dracula vs. Frankenstein*.

It took me several months, but I finally found an apartment in Brentwood and moved into it.

It had been a long time since I'd heard from my friend Anthony Milano, so I was completely taken by surprise when one evening I received a call from him. What he had to say chilled me to the bone. He told me he desperately needed my help, and that I was the only person who might understand his dire situation. He went on to explain that it had something to do with our childhood. He and his sister had moved back into his old home in North Hollywood, and he pleaded with me to come over. Sensing something ominous, I was hesitant, but Anthony insisted that he needed my help, and I felt obligated to be there for my old friend.

The following day I drove to his home. When I pulled up in his driveway, it was déjà vu. The old Spanish-style adobe bungalow hadn't changed much in twenty years, although the once well-manicured landscape had considerably deteriorated. Rose Milano's prize rose bushes had not been pruned in years and had become a mangled, thorny muddle. Many of the surrounding eucalyptus trees had long since been cut down, revealing only the encompassing, barren, high walls I used to climb as a kid. Anthony and his sister, Mary, met me at the door. Mary had since grown to adulthood, married, then divorced – quite a change from the bratty little sister I remembered. God, where had the time gone? Although both were happy to see me, it was obvious that they were traumatized. I sat in the now-antique child's wooden reclining chair which I remembered as a kid, its once-polished arm rests now scarred and faded. Anthony and Mary took the matching sofa across from me, sending up a noxious cloud of dust when they sat on it, almost like the scene in *The Munsters*. But this dust was real!

Getting straight to the point, Anthony said, "Larry, you remember the situation here, and how awful it was for me as a kid"

"Well, yeah," I admitted. "You went through a lot."

Even though she never suffered like her brother, Mary nodded in agreement. Anthony went on to tell me that his mother had died years earlier, and more recently his father, Sal, had passed away.

"That's when the problems began," he said.

According to the elderly next-door neighbor, before Anthony was born, Sal had an illegitimate child. This news had completely shocked Anthony. "He said that my dad never let his son out of the house because there was something wrong with him."

"What do you mean?" I asked.

"Well, he said that the kid was mentally handicapped."

"That's crazy," I said.

"Yup," Anthony answered, not catching my inadvertent double entendre. "Gus the neighbor said he used to hear the kid crying every day."

"Why didn't he do anything about it?" I asked.

"He eventually did call the police, who did a brief investigation. But by then the crying had stopped, and there was no evidence of a child having ever been in the home. He told Gus that he must have been hearing things."

Next, Anthony shared a story about an incident that happened to him as a kid. He was alone with his father at home one day when he was startled by a thunderous pounding on his front door. Anthony got up and walked toward the door, but his father shoved him aside and opened it. Sal was confronted by an angry Hispanic woman who Anthony had never seen before. She pushed her way into the doorway and let loose a tirade in Spanish at Sal. His father then angrily responded, shoving her back out onto the veranda before slamming the door in her face. She stood outside screaming at the top of her lungs, continuing to pound and kick the door, her screams eventually turning to sobs. "Finally, her crying stopped, and she left. I never saw her again."

Then Anthony pulled out a small aged photo showing he and Mary seated on their expansive front lawn, sharing a toy. Judging by their ages in the snapshot it must have been taken in the early 1950s.

I glanced at the photo. "Yeah, I remember those days. So, what about it?"

"Look closer," he responded, and pointed to an area which was in close proximity to the children. What I saw took my breath away. There floating about a foot above the lawn was the translucent image of a women.

"My god!" I gasped. "You're shitting me. This has got to be fake."

"No," Anthony assured me, "we found this picture yesterday, right before I called you. It's the woman I saw that day, the one my mother had always talked about. The Lady in White. She's the boy's mother."

He then related a series of other terrifying experiences, where Sal's apparition appeared on several different occasions right after his death. One such instance occurred with Anthony's older sister and her husband, who lived on a yacht, docked in a Long Beach harbor. One evening, the couple happened to observe through their cabin window two figures standing on the nearby dock; one large and one small, peering at their ship. She and her husband, a former firefighter, exited the cabin to get a closer look and were shocked by what they saw. Her father was standing alongside a small boy. As they approached, both figures vanished.

More recently, Anthony had witnessed objects mysteriously float across the room. These eerie experiences were increasing in intensity. He said he had recently heard a child's voice in the attic, apparently sitting in a rocking chair, singing "London Bridge is Falling Down." When he and Mary had climbed up into the attic to investigate, all they saw was the chair slowly rocking by itself. Just a few days previously, Mary had been accosted and slapped by an unknown force in her old bedroom.

Anthony and Mary excused themselves and went back into Sal's workshop to look for more evidence. As I sat there alone, I noticed a pad of paper and pen on a small end table next to the recliner. The next thing I knew, for some unknown reason, I had picked them up and began to write. Amazingly, I discovered that I was writing in Spanish – a language I most certainly did not know. The paragraph would later be translated to say, "The mother is coming. She wishes to be with her son and will stop at nothing until they are united again. Only then will they be free to leave this world."

I drove back to my apartment that evening feeling shaken by my experience. I had promised to return the following day, but I truly didn't want to go back. I knew it would certainly not help me in my current state of misery going through the divorce, yet I felt I was obligated to see this through for my friend's sake.

I returned, as promised, and things seemed to be even more intense than the day before. Anthony took me back into the living room. Pointing to the attic, he said, "We've been hearing this all morning."

"What?" I said, before hearing the sound myself: a steady *thump thump thump*, repeated every ten to fifteen seconds. *Holy shit*, I thought. *What the hell have I gotten myself into?*

Anthony and Mary then told me something I found very difficult to believe.

"After you left last night, we decided to try to get some answers from a Ouija Board. We fooled with it for a while, asking what happened with the boy, and this is what we came up with."

Anthony handed me a slip of paper, on which was scribbled, "Look in basement." All of the older homes in the area back then had cellars. He continued, "So we went down to the basement, and I want to show you what we discovered."

They motioned for me to follow them to the hallway door. At first, I refused to go, wanting to take no further part in this macabre event. But Anthony opened the door, and both tugged me past the doorway and down the creaky wooden stairs. The musty smell was overwhelming. I almost choked from the dust on the way down. We reached the foot of the stairs and stepped onto the concrete floor. Mary pointed to the eight-foot square center of the floor, which was never cemented. A large hole had been dug, with dirt piled on either side. I was afraid to look in the hole for fear of seeing the gruesome remains of the long-lost child. I don't think my heart could have taken any more. But Anthony eased my trepidation somewhat, "We didn't find anything."

My relief was short-lived, however, because Anthony led me over to a marble bench that sat beside the hole. The dust had settled around the perfect outlines of a pair of seated bodies with accompanying handprints – those of an adult and child.

Mary assured me that neither she nor Anthony had put them there, nor did their bodies match the outlines.

This story has no clear ending. A body was never found.

I kept in touch with Anthony afterwards. It seems that even though he and his sister moved out of the home, the hauntings continued, following them to their new places of residence. I later learned that the old house had been mysteriously torched and completely burnt down to the ground, leaving nothing but ashes, perhaps in which were the remains of the boy. However, I had a strong impression that those remains were not necessarily in the house. Quite the opposite, maybe the house was the boy. It was his entire existence, the world in which he was kept prisoner. My theory is that neither the boy nor his mother could move on until the ties that bound them to this Earth were destroyed.

I talked to Anthony for the very last time several years later. He had changed considerably. The once intense deeply troubled soul had become a born-again Christian, trading one form of insanity for another. Spouting off biblical passages like a vomit comet, he strongly denied that he'd ever been haunted, or that he had a monster for a father. Perhaps his religion wouldn't allow him to do so. Salvatore, meaning "Savior," was anything but. Mary had since remarried and refused to have further contact with him.

I'd almost forgotten about Anthony, when decades later an old high school friend came to town and wanted to look him up.

None of our childhood contacts had heard from him. He was nowhere to be found. It was as though he'd walked off the face of the Earth. Mary could not be tracked down either. Wherever Anthony is, I do hope that he has finally found peace.

CHAPTER 17

In my attempt to get through this dark period in my life I made another grievous error, I married my second wife Joy. The best thing about this marriage was the five children it produced: Shon, Bleu, Micah, Sheris and Joel.

Because of my previous success with children's entertainment, I was contacted by K-Tel Records. They were looking for a children's album to add to their catalog. A previous attempt by another individual who had no experience in this field had failed miserably. The entire concept was left up to me. After several days of mulling this over, trying to think of names that kids could relate to, I came up with *Lolliwinks*. It sounded catchy to me. Then I imagined what Lolliwinkland would be like. After some thought and imagination, I created the Lolliwinks environment, a magical land between *somewhere* and *nowhere*. The Lolliwinks were characters that could only be seen when you blinked your eyes. You know, those little spots that you see for a microsecond after doing that? After getting together with my artist friend Bob Simmons, the elf-like creatures were brought to life.

The Lolliwinks lived in a forest and each had unique talents. The main characters were Blinky Thinkertinker the mastermind, Rifkin Swiftinbrush, who paints all of the colors, Farfi Fiddlefast, who brings music into the Forest. Last but not least was Erfo Offengoof whose penchant was goofing off. Then I set about writing songs for each one of the characters. I tried to make the songs character-related and positive. It was my goal to teach children about things that are important to them like self-esteem and self-confidence.

Blinky performed tunes like "Planning Ahead."

Did you ever bake a chocolate cake without knowing the recipe?
And you made a mess in the pan because you forgot to plan
Yes planning ahead's the one and only way.

Rifkin sang about art and the importance of color in children's lives with ditties like "If There Were No Colors."

If there were no colors your life would be dull
There would be only Winter, no Autumn or Fall.
There wouldn't be a green-leaf tree
And oranges would not be orange after all.

Farfi sang about the significance of music, nature and sound in such tunes as "Misty Morning".

Traveling through the country in a foggy morning dew
I heard some wonderful music there which brought the day-
light through.
A lonely bird sang the sweetest song and drove the gloomy
weather away.
So we must all be song birds on each and every misty day.

Erfo's character expressed individualism and his mischievous nature in songs such as "When I go Out to Play"

I never listen them 'cause they don't see it my way.
Rules are meant for me to bend when I go out to play.

Erfo provided a nice counterbalance to the other characters. It also made the album less preachy.

The process of songwriting was a real challenge. The only way to make the voices sound animated was to speed them up, like the Chipmunks. But I thought those popular animal characters were overdoing it. Too much of an increase in speed and the individualism of the characters would be lost. So, the songs all had to planned with a moderate speed increase. Doing so required me to write them in a higher key than I normally sang. The technique was to record the voices at a lower speed, then speed them up to the precise pitch that would have the right amount of character and sparkle. I had no recording equipment to test my theory, so it was all guesswork.

It took me a month to write the songs. Then I flew to the United Kingdom to record the music, contracting with arranger Larry Bastian to line up some of the top session musicians in London. Finally, I flew back to the States to record the vocals. Only then, would I find out whether I was capable of singing the songs. Not only did I have to invent the characters' individual style of singing, but emulate Farfi, a girl's voice. Talk about a challenge! Some songs involved more than one individual, and in one tune, "Just Blink," all four Lolliwinks sang in harmony. It was perhaps ideal for someone with multiple personalities, but for me keeping in character was a real chore. I also wrote, produced, and did the voiceover for the thirty- and sixty-second national TV commercials which ran in 1981 on CBS TV.

The end result was the Lolliwinks record album which came with a large poster of the Lolliwinks and their magical land. The album sold over a million copies, and over the years has been deemed a classic children's album. [54]

I had no idea that the Lolliwinks would later garner such a huge following. There are multiple references to the album on the Internet, with hundreds of comments, and it has been streamed on a number of sites such as Last FM. And, like the Standells, the Lolliwinks has developed a cult following.

I also wrote a children's hardcover book during this period, *The Story of Helen Keller: The Power of Overcoming.* [55]

In 1982, I made a shocking discovery: The Garage Rock sound of the Standells had miraculously come back to life with a new generation of groups. When the punk rock movement emerged in the late 1970s, bands like the Ramones, the Dead Boys, and the Zeros cited sixties era bands like the Standells as an influence. British group the Inmates also had covered "Dirty Water" which topped the charts in the UK. To my astonishment, what I'd long thought to be dead and buried was not only dug up from the grave, but suddenly and mysteriously in vogue again. The Standells were now considered to be among the forerunners of punk rock: Sixties Garage Punks. I began to see articles in the music trades and *Los Angeles Times* Calendar section about groups like the Unclaimed, the Pandoras, the Barracudas (whose name was derived from the Standells song of the same name), and the Chesterfield Kings, comparing them to the Stan-

---

54 *Lolliwinks* (1981)
55 *The Story of Helen Keller: The Power of Overcoming* (1989)

dells. A little later even heavy metal groups like Guns N Roses acknowledged the Standells as their inspiration. The impossible had happened.

On the spur of the moment, I called Tony, and we decided to get back together. Against my better judgment, Tony insisted on bringing Dick back in as well.

In 1983, we had our first reunion. Added to the group were lead guitarist Bruce Wallenstein and bassist Eric Wallengren. We happened to share a rehearsal studio at Sound City with Motley Crue, who in my opinion were a perfect fit for their name. It was as if someone had let loose a bunch of chimpanzees; in fact, monkeys would have been much better behaved. It seemed to me that some of these groups thought that heroin abuse and sexual orgies were a prerequisite to being in a rock group.

If this wasn't bad enough, I discovered that Dick was dealing drugs to the rehearsal studio manager. When I angrily confronted Dick about this, I tried to explain to him that if he got busted, he'd be taking me down with him, but it didn't seem to register. He responded with "I'm just trying to earn a living."

I managed to find a booking agent, and the revived Standells proceeded to do a few concerts together, the first being in August at the Club Lingerie. The gig was advertised as the "Old Standells vs. the New Standells." We were paired with the Fleshtones, who were a picture-perfect rendition of the old pre-"Dirty Water" Standells, wearing the matching gray suits with felt lapels and thin ties like we wore on *The Munsters*, right down to an authentic Farfisa organ. There was one major difference, however. I thought they sounded nothing like us.

We were introduced on the show by actor David Carradine, who was unmistakably stoned to the hilt, which I understand was par for the course with him. As I walked by him to enter the stage, he pinched my ass.

We next appeared at the Golden Bear in Huntington Beach, and several other venues. Finally, we ended up doing a week-long gig at Harrah's Casino in Reno, Nevada, which I booked and for considerably more than we'd earned at the previous gigs.

CHAPTER 18

My brother Russ was also going through changes during this period. He married his third wife, Bonnie Murray. Like me, Bonnie had a career in music, as a country singer and songwriter. She wrote the Top 40 country hit "I Hope You Understand When I'm Gone," sung by Dottsy on RCA Records, and as a singer opened for such acts as Dave Mason and Fleetwood Mac. Bonnie has since become the sister I never had. In 1984, Their daughter Amber Rose Tamblyn was born on May 14th. Like her father, Amber went on to become a major star, with featured roles in *General Hospital, Joan of Arcadia* and *Sisterhood of the Traveling Pants*, as well as being a director and renowned book author.

Because of his drug problems, I really wanted nothing more to do with Dick Dodd. In 1984, Tony and I made a Standells record called "60's Band," which I wrote and sang. This was in partnership with his younger brother, who financed the recording session. Tony's officious behavior in the studio made it increasingly difficult to work with him. While trying to lay down the vocal tracks, he openly criticized my singing, even threatening to bring in another singer, making it next to impossible to feel at ease.

As meddlesome as Tony was, his brother was far worse. He was an owner of a motorcycle shop who knew nothing about music and was even more unrestrained than Tony in his verbosity. Arrogance must have run in the family. He also attempted to give me direction, and even had the audacity to perform phrases in a screeching atonal voice the way he thought they should be sung. Anyone who has ever laid down a vocal in a recording studio knows how important it is to feel calm and energized. With the two Sicilians hammering at me – both from completely different perspectives-- I'm surprised I got through the session.

I suddenly discovered that there was a tug-of-war over the leadership of the group. The following year, Tony booked us in a retro-'60s festival at the Glen Helen Regional Park, for which Dick and original bassist Gary Lane rejoined the group. Tony insisted we play his songs at the concert. When I asked why we were doing his original songs at a retro-'60s festival, he threatened to exclude me from the group! He was behaving in an increasingly selfish and pigheaded manner. I'd seen hints of this in the past, but never so blatantly.

At the Glen Helen festival, we performed along with other groups including Peter Noone, the Mamas and the Papas, and my old friend Dewey Martin and his group the Buffalo Springfield Revisited. We suffered through some of Tony's dreadful songs, but also did some of our standards, which were well-received. I suspected that this was nothing more than a vanity concert for Tony – in fact, I believe he looked at most Standells performances in this manner. This theory was confirmed by the ultra-low fees he had agreed to, far less money than we'd ever received in the past. Additionally, later on we had to deal with an unauthorized video of the concert for which we never got paid. After that, I swore that I would never allow Tony to be in charge of another gig.

Tony also became a pain-in-the-ass in other creative areas. I was in touch with an old friend, Jodi Lewis who had been a writer for some of my children's stories. Jodi was also a member of the Screen-writer's Guild, with numerous TV and movie credits. I mentioned to her how great it would be to write a screenplay about the Standells, and she was very receptive, even offering to do a treatment on spec. I set up a meeting with Tony, which turned out to be a disaster.

Jodi came prepared, bringing a tape recorder to capture some of our stories for transcription. I had told Tony about my long relationship with Jodi, and that I considered her to be a good friend. After introducing her to Tony, and reiterating what we intended to do, he flabbergasted me with an off-the-wall question to Jody.

"How do I know I can trust you?"

The brazenness of his question startled Jodi. "What do you mean?"

Not one for tact, Tony continued with his confrontational approach, "Maybe you want to steal thees and make money from it."

Jodi's response was just as abrupt. "I think we're finished here."

She stomped out of the house with me chasing behind her. I apologized to Jodi, as usual trying to cover for Tony's belligerent and insulting demeanor and attempted to explain that he was kind of difficult to deal with at times. But she flat-out told me, "I want nothing more to do with that asshole."

Jodi sat in my car while I went back into talk to Tony.

"What the hell is wrong with you?" I demanded.

"She has bad attitude."

I couldn't believe what I just heard. "Have you examined your own lately?"

And so, ended our foray into a Standells screenplay. I learned that whenever Tony became directly involved, his pugnacious-ness could bring a screeching halt to any further creative efforts.

In the late 1980s, I made a shocking discovery. Ed Cobb and Ray Harris' company, now called American Variety International, had retained rights to the Standells' master recordings. Unbeknownst to me or other members of the group, they made a deal with Rhino Records to release an album in 1983 called *The Best of the Standells*. The liner notes proclaimed gave Ed Cobb far more credit than he deserved.

Earlier in the decade the Standells – Larry Tamblyn, Tony Valentino, Gary Lane and Gary Leeds (who was replaced by Dick Dodd in 1963) – were a clean-living, fun bunch of bananas who laid down the rock hits of the day. After a few recordings of minor notes, their fortunes changed upon meeting producer/songwriter Ed Cobb. The match was perfect. Ed was formerly a member of the super clean Four Preps!

Rather than a combined future in a Disneyland-like middle American Heaven, Ed and the boys pulled a Dr. Jekyll/Mr. Hyde and bounded back with a very seething, resentful, provoking approach that was very influenced by the Rolling Stones. Perhaps the years of growing up squeaky clean had suppressed a lot of angst that unleashed itself in the group's newfound personality. [56]

Once again, Cobb was painted as the Standells' *Svengali*. The description of us being "squeaky clean" until meeting Cobb is complete unadulterated bullshit, as proven by 1963 and 1964 photos of us with long hair.

------

56 *The Best of the Standells* (1983)

As an example of how this kind of misinformation gets circulated as fact, later there was a story floating around about Ed Cobb's song "Tainted Love." The song had originally been released on a single by Grace Jones in 1965, before becoming a massive worldwide hit in 1981 by the group Soft Cell. In his 2006 book *Knocking on Heaven's Door*, rock historian Nick Talevski claimed that "before Jones recorded the song, Cobb had offered it to the Standells whom he managed and produced, but they rejected it." This was a complete fabrication: not only did Cobb not manage us, we were never offered the song.

Meanwhile, back in the eighties, I was dumbfounded to learn that in addition to the *Best of the Standells* album, two further Standells compilations were released on Rhino, Rarities in 1984, and another iteration of The Best of *The Standells* in their "Golden Archive Series" in 1986. When I called Ray Harris to ask why we hadn't received royalties from any of these, he replied, "The albums really aren't selling that well."

"If that's the case," I asked, "why have three of them been released?"

His response sounded fishy to me. "Well, Rhino likes to have this type of material in bulk."

The guys weren't willing to shell out retainer fees for an attorney, but it didn't stop Tony from saying, "They screwing us. We gotta do something."

This seemed to be a constant refrain of Tony's over the years. Never mind the mess he got us into at the Glen Helen Regional Park. Never mind the fact that he never did a thing but complain. He and the others left it up to me to solve. The load was entirely on my shoulders. It took several months to search through old news articles of performers who had similar situations, and their legal remedies, which were very few. I finally happened to stumble upon the case of Richard Berry, the recording artist and composer of classic rock anthem "Louie Louie." In 1957, he had sold the rights to his song for a measly $750.00 to help pay for a wedding. It wasn't until 1963 that the Kingsmen recorded the hit version of this song. The non-profit company who took on Berry's case was Artists Rights Enforcement Corporation. Thirty years later, they assisted Berry in regaining partial ownership of the song. Other artists represented by AREC included B.J. Thomas, the Shirelles, Frankie Lymon, Gene Pitney, and Hank Ballard. The company was responsible for recovering millions of dollars for these artists.

I contacted the AREC's president, Chuck Rubin. We set up a meeting and agreed to have AREC represent us. A lawsuit was filed, and I did most of the legwork on it, meeting in depositions, giving an interview on a legal TV show, and filling out mounds of paperwork – yet I didn't take a dime more than the others. It took until September 1991 for the Standells to settle out of court with AVI for an undisclosed amount. Over the years, this settlement was responsible for putting thousands of dollars in the group members' pockets. Except for Gary, I received not even a thank you or an acknowledgement from either Dick or Tony – except, of course, whining from Tony, "Eets not enough" and of course "They screwing us."

Tony's and Dick complaints were that AREC was getting half of our royalties. How do you explain to someone that *half of something is better than all of nothing?*

Little did I know that I had slowly developed a medical condition, the changes in me so subtle over the years that it was hardly noticeable, causing me to doze off sometimes or act irrationally. Somewhere deep inside I realized that I was living a lie. On a few occasions, I would find myself in tears, not knowing why, but somehow realizing something inside was changing.

In 1990, Joy and I got a divorce.

Mom began having serious medical problems, so I ended up being her caretaker – a very difficult job, but one I've never regretted doing. She had always been in my corner, so for a change I could be in hers. Finally, she became completely bedridden, even to the point of not being able to take a bath without having to hire in-home care. I was forced to place her in a care facility.

In late 1993, I was invited to a small get-together at Russ and Bonnie's home. It was there that I met actress Glenda Chism, who had a featured role as Macaulay Culkin's mother in the film *My Girl*. She had been in a play several years earlier with Russ, and they had remained friends ever since. We hit it off immediately and became instant friends.

However, I had to leave early as I had a previous engagement that evening, a date with a woman I barely knew who had asked me out. After departing from Glenda and the party, I picked up Ellen and went to dinner. Although the meal was delicious, there was very little conversation, which I found opposite from the wonderful time I'd just had with Glenda. I was about to pay the check, so I placed the gratuity on the table. Ellen's face soured and she asked, "Why are you tipping so much money?"

Having not been on the dating scene very much, I thought this question was a bit odd. "Why would you say such a thing?" I inquired.

"The service was shitty," she responded.

This took me by surprise. "I thought it was pretty good. Besides, since I'm paying the bill, shouldn't I be the one to decide the amount?" I was paying the standard fifteen percent tip, which I'd always done, and that was certainly in my opinion not exorbitant.

"As I said, the service sucked," she fired back. "I wouldn't have given them a dime."

I am into women's rights. However, this sure as hell was crossing the line. "Look, no offense, but it's really none of your damn business what I pay."

Ellen jumped up, and in the crowded restaurant screeched, "You're in denial!"

Then she stomped out to the establishment's entrance where she waited for me. I was shocked and embarrassed. Did I do something wrong? Seeing the other restaurant patrons' reaction to this obnoxious woman, I realized that Ellen completely owned this. When I got outside, I was so pissed I bluntly said, "Since you've been such a bitch, you can find your own fucking way home." Her place was only a few blocks away. Unlike my experience with Glenda earlier that evening, this was the date from hell!

Glenda and I saw each other quite often, but she soon had to return to her home in Florida. That's when I was surprised to start receiving calls from Ellen. It seemed that she was turned on by someone who knew their boundaries and had forcefully stood up to her. The calls increased to where it became day and night. I truly didn't care for this woman, but it was flattering to be sought after so vehemently, especially since she was physically attractive. During the next few months, I saw Ellen occasionally, but it always instigated by her and always seemed to be only on her terms. I never really enjoyed being with her. Almost as if emphasizing the shaky relationship with Ellen, we began experiencing nightly earthquake tremblers in Santa Monica. They always came early in the morning and were unsettling at the very least. This culminated in the major Northridge Earthquake on January 17, 1994. It hit us hard in Santa Monica, with broken mirrors and dishes, buildings with large cracks, and rattled nerves on my part. This had been the third major California earthquake I'd experienced. [57]

After checking on my mother to make sure she was okay, I was startled by a car horn. Ellen was outside the apartment demanding to see me. This was very odd. She wanted to tour the damaged areas, almost gloating at people's misery, which to me seemed perverse.

The relationship with Ellen was becoming very like the movie *Fatal Attraction*. [58] She played Glenn Close's character to a tee. Ellen did not appeal to me at all, I had no desire to see her, and yet she was aggressively pursuing me. What finally put the brakes on for me was when we went to her apartment and I noticed some S&M books on her living room shelf. Yup, whips and chains. Ellen was a dominatrix; not my style. After that, I made excuses whenever she called and refused to see her.

---

57 www.history.com - *1994 Northridge earthquake*
58 *Fatal Attraction* (1987)

During this time, I renewed my friendships with some of my old friends at Mattel Toys. Occasionally I got together with my old boss, Gwen Floria, and Charla Moore. I also hung out regularly with my old friend, Jeff Ehrhart, who lived very near to me in Santa Monica. I enjoyed our get-togethers, although I noticed that Jeff now seemed to have some anger management problems. On more than one occasion, he flew off the handle at complete strangers for petty reasons. Jeff, I learned, was in constant pain from a prostatectomy that had gone wrong. After a while, I became uncomfortable with our visits. As with Anthony and Mary, people always seemed to seek me out with their pain and misery.

CHAPTER 19

The bright spot in my life was when Glenda returned from Florida. Like me, she had realized that the two of us had something very special. We picked up where we left off, and in mid-1994 decided to move in together to a small apartment in Palms. Miraculously, Mom's health had improved to such a degree that she was able to move back to her apartment right at the time I moved out. For Glenda and me this was the first time we'd cohabited with someone other than a spouse. We had both been married and divorced twice and were determined not to make the same mistakes again.

I was having a candlelight dinner with Glenda one evening when I received a telephone call from Ellen.

"Larry, I need to see you now!" she demanded.

I'd had it with the constant intrusions into my life by this mad woman. "Look," I snapped at her, "I've been trying to tell you that you need to stop calling me. I have someone in my life now, and we're living together."

However, she didn't want to take no for an answer. "But I need to see you. Can't we at least be friends?"

How odd, I thought, before responding, "We were never really friends." With that, she screamed, "Fuck You!" along with a few other obscenities and hung up.

That wasn't the end of Ellen, not by a long shot. We soon started receiving calls from plumbers, carpenters, and various other small businesses who had messages on their pagers to call me. When I explained that I wasn't responsible for the messages, they politely hung up. However, Ellen continued to leave messages for the same people. When they called back again, they weren't so polite.

"Don't you have any other fucking thing to do besides harassing me?" one contractor said.

Yeah, *Fatal Attraction*, all right. Eventually, the calls diminished. Ellen must have found another guy to torment, maybe one who would even let her try out her chains and whips.

I hadn't heard from Jeff Ehrhart in a while, and then one evening out of the blue I received a call from him. "Hey, Larry, want to go out to a movie?"

I paused for a second before replying, "Hey, I'm sorry, but I'm busy. Can you give me a little more warning the next time?"

Jeff responded, "Yeah," with a dark chuckle, then hung up.

Days later, I received a call from my old friend Kit Hudson, who was now an independent film producer.

"Hi Larry, how are you doing?" His voice was very somber.

"Fine," I responded. "What's new, with you?" I was hoping to hear about one of his latest film projects, but knew it was something far more serious. I wasn't prepared for what came next.

"Jeff has committed suicide."

At first, I was silent then responded, "You're joking, right?"

"I wish I was."

Kit's announcement shook me to my core. When I learned that he had taken his life right after talking to me I was completely mortified, especially learning that he had done so in such a violent manner – putting a gun to his mouth and pulling the trigger. I was the last person he had talked to! This left me gasping for breath. God, could I have prevented his suicide? Could I have been a better friend? I'd been to his apartment on many occasions, and, knowing of Jeff's liberal leanings, I had no idea that he had a gun, let alone intended to use one on himself.

After Kit hung up, I was in tears. Glenda did her best to console me, but it was of little use. How could I have let my friend down?

At Jeff's memorial service, I was still in a state of shock. I felt light-headed and momentarily blacked out. Assuming this was because of my grieving, I paid no further attention to it.

The guilt of Jeff's suicide stayed with me for years afterward. With his weird snicker before hanging up, was it his intention to lay the blame of his suicide on my shoulders? After agonizing over this and talking with others on the subject, I eventually concluded that people have their paths to follow, making their choices and taking ownership of the consequences. I realized that people who take their own lives generally don't consider the effect it has on friends and loved ones, and in some cases will use others as an excuse for their actions. In Jeff's case, meeting with him would have only prolonged the inevitable.

I still think about him quite often, and only hope that wherever he is Jeff has finally found peace.

On Labor Day, September 4, 1995, Glenda and I decided to have my mother spend the week with us at our apartment. It was a most enjoyable day, and everyone there sensed something special about it. Mom played the piano and sang for everyone.

Something in my mind said, *capture this moment of perfection, there will never be another one.* I did, and still vividly remember it today. It was my mother's way of saying farewell. Two days later, she complained of chest pains, and we rushed her to the hospital where she was diagnosed as having had a heart attack. While recovering, on her 81st birthday, on September 8th, she had a stroke. We rushed her to the hospital, and they were able to stabilize her. The following day, though, things took a turn for the worst when she had a massive stroke. We rushed back to the hospital, and we were there embracing her as she passed away. The most difficult part was whispering to her that it was okay to go on. Unable to speak, she squeezed my hand in acknowledgment.

Sally Aileen Tamblyn passed away on September 9, 1995, one day after her 81st birthday. Only at times like these do you remember all that your mother has done for you. An unconditional love that can never be repaid. I was heartbroken. Her death affected me profoundly and continues to do so to this day. I wish I'd spent more quality time with her and have deeply regretted not doing so.

By early 1996, my medical condition was deteriorating rapidly. My personality was changing. I was having bizarre visions, almost like acid trips, and had fainting spells. It culminated late one night when I had a seizure and was rushed to the hospital. My diagnosis came as both a surprise and a relief. I had a pituitary adenoma. These types of tumors are benign and can grow at a very slow rate, sometimes over a decade, and can cause major personality changes like I had experienced. It was a relief to discover why I had been acting so strangely. The adenoma had grown to a considerable size and had to be removed immediately at the USC County Hospital.

Glenda never gave up on me. I wouldn't have blamed her if she did.

Now, the best years were ahead of us. In December of that year, I was hired as an audio engineer and producer by Audio Digest Foundation, a non-profit organization that specializes in continuing education for the medical profession. I had returned to an area of employment in which I felt comfortable. I also moonlighted as an editor for several audio book companies. I ended up being employed by Audio Digest for fifteen years.

On June 6, 1998, my brother Warren passed away at the age of 65 in Phoenix, Arizona, where he was living with his oldest daughter, my niece, Kathleen. His funeral was held in a Mormon church. Along with several of Warren's children, Russ and I were speakers at the memorial service. After listening to a rather mind-numbing speech from a member of the Bishopric of the church, who talked ad nauseam about where one goes after death (who the fuck really knows?), Russ and I both spoke, and I'd like to think that we helped to make the event more palatable by sharing some hilarious stories about Warren. I talked about the time he pulled up in his convertible beside a couple of teenagers, also in a convertible with its top-down, who were blasting rock music. Warren, a classical music enthusiast, in turn, blasted Beethoven's 9th Symphony through his car speakers. I can only imagine what the two youths were thinking.

Beneath his sometimes-irritable personality, Warren had a wonderfully wry sense of humor. Our recollections got a lot of laughs from my nieces and nephews, as well as a few parishioners.

By 1999, Dick Dodd had straightened up considerably, perhaps because his wife Janie kept a very tight leash on him. Tony had since opened a very trendy restaurant, Café Bellissimo, and had gotten married to a young blond waitress who worked for him. She was perceived as a trophy wife by the other band members and would later be the source of Tony's grief, making him even more miserable (and us).

On November 7th of that year, the three Standells had their next reunion at the Cavestomp Festival in New York at the Westbeth Centre Theater, appearing along with the Chocolate Watchband and the Monks. Tony, Dick and I were joined by sideman bassist Peter Stuart, and it was there where we recorded the live album *Ban THIS* [59], a reference to the banning of "Try It" by Gordon McLendon. Glenda graciously acted as our manager and continued in that capacity for the next twelve years. Our fees were considerably better than those of the last fiasco by Tony, and the only reason I agreed to do this.

Unfortunately, the event coincided with the New York Marathon. Accordingly, all of the hotels in the Big Apple were filled, and we had to stay in New Jersey, commuting by train. This did not go over well with Tony, who called and tormented the promoter, Jon Weiss, about the inconvenience. I apologized to Jon, explaining that Tony was tired from the flight; the first of many excuses I had to make for Tony's arrogant behavior that weekend. During our soundcheck and rehearsal, Tony didn't help matters by arguing with me on stage. It was embarrassing, to say the least. At this point, I fully realized that he had completely lost the once

---

59 *The Standells - Ban This! (Live from Cavestomp!)* (2000)

diffident, lovable quality that I had so cherished years ago. This was a different Tony than I had known twenty years earlier. All of a sudden, nothing I did seemed to be good enough for him. Dick, on the other hand, was a pleasure to work with.

In 2000, the changing of the millennium came in with a bang. The threat of the Y2K virus scared the shit out of everyone, after rumors circulated that all computers would stop at the stroke of midnight. That year the State of Vermont passed HB847, legalizing Civil Unions for same-sex couples.

2000 was the first time that all four of the original Standells, including Gary (Lane) McMillan, reunited at the Las Vegas Grind, along with the Remains, and Lyres. [60]

After six years of cohabitating, Glenda and I finally decided to get married. What better way to tie the nuptials than in Las Vegas during the event? This led to what can only be described as absolute bedlam. Everything that could go wrong went wrong.

June 30th was the big day. We'd fly to Las Vegas, tie the knot, and then later that night the Standells would headline the opening night of the Las Vegas Grind.

The night before, I set the alarm clock for 5:30 AM. The following morning, we woke up at 6:30 AM – the alarm didn't go off! We hurriedly gathered our things and bolted for the front door. The plane was due for departure out of LAX at 9:30 AM. Since this was considered part of the July 4th weekend, all of the newscasts advised everyone not to drive to LAX. The traffic was going to be horrendous. So, we instead chose to take the newly opened subway – our next big mistake. At 7:35, we parked the

---

60 www.wikipedia.com - *Las Vegas Grind*

car in the North Hollywood station and rushed inside. The train departed at 7:50. Still plenty of time, right? Wrong! The train had no direct route to LAX. Instead, it took us to Norwalk, where we had to transfer to LAX. At the station, we had to take the escalator to the platform, lugging not only our suitcases but 75 pounds of Standells merchandise which was too wide for the narrow escalator, causing us to have to make several trips. We finally arrived at the airport at 9:15. We could have driven backwards and still beat the time it took us to get there.

Glenda and I rushed into the America West terminal, and were greeted by a huge crowd of travelers, all in an uproar because the airline's computers were all down. By the time we got to the counter it was 9:30. We told the attendant to check us in immediately, and he stifled a laugh. We were informed that our flight had already left the gate and that there was nothing he could do; our seats were already taken. Then he walked off.

"No", I screamed after the man. "We have to be in Las Vegas. Our wedding is at 9:00 PM tonight!"

I think this might have elicited a further chuckle from the man as he exited the room. An attendant named Sonya heard my plea; she must have been moved about the wedding part. We told her the complete story, that in addition to the wedding I was a member of a rock group who was performing that evening.

"We have to be there by 4:00 or our contract with them will be cancelled", I pleaded.

She checked all of the departures and said, "There is no way I can get you out of LAX today."

A man standing next to us who overheard our conversation piped in, "They can't get me out of here for five days."

That sure as hell made me feel better.

Ironically, all of the other group members and their wives had made the flight, including Dick and his wife Janie who drove there from Orange County, forty-two miles distance.

"Is there any other airport we can fly out of?" Glenda desperately asked.

"Let me check something else and see," she responded, then left the desk. I was sure we'd never see her again. Miraculously, she reappeared. "I found you something! It's a flight out of John Wayne Airport. It will be tight, but I can put you on a shuttle to get there. We'll pay for it"

After profoundly thanking Sonya, we hurried out to the passenger loading area where the shuttle was waiting for us. John Wayne airport is in Orange County. On the way there, we passed the exit to Dick's home. The plane arrived at the McCarren International airport in Las Vegas at 1:00 PM. After renting a car, we sped to the hotel, parked, then ran to the auditorium, making it to the sound check with ten minutes to spare. The other guys in the band were already on the stage waiting for us, wondering if we were going to show. The rehearsal went off without a hitch. Afterwards, we rushed to City Hall, only to find out that the County Courthouse was where the wedding licenses were issued, causing us to run four blocks to get there in time.

We arrived back at the hotel at 7:00 PM. By then were famished, so we went to the hotel café, stood in line and finally got seated. Two Standells fans, Fred and Jeff, had just gotten their salads, so we asked them to join us. We then invited them to our wedding, and they were thrilled to be part of it.

At 8:45, the guests arrived, including the Standells and their wives, my brother Russ, his daughter Amber, and my son Micah who lived in Vegas. The wedding went off without a hitch right there in room 921 at the Gold Coast Hotel. Three hours later, at 12:00 midnight, we walked on stage in the packed auditorium. The gig was great. The crowd loved seeing and listening to the original re-united Standells, playing some of their favorite songs.

The following day, our flight was delayed by an hour-and-a-half. When finally arriving home, I discovered that my car had been towed and had to pay a $200 impound fee. An exhausting and stressful weekend, but those are the times you remember the most.

The next month, I was approached by Bob Irwin, president of Sundazed Music, who claimed to have in his possession an unreleased master of a concert we did in 1966 with the Beach Boys at the University of Michigan. They wanted to release it as soon as possible. Since we were under contract to Attarack and Tower Records at the time the recording was made, I told Bob that I wanted to check with our attorney first to see what the legality was. I shared this information with Dick and Tony. Our attorney was out of town, and while I was waiting to hear back from him, Dick contacted Sundazed directly. I found out later that he told them he had the right to negotiate on our behalf. Even though I sang on many of the songs, Dick had bypassed me and cut a deal directly with them. Even worse, he proceeded to collect all of the royalties from the album, never sharing a dime with us. When asked about this, he lied and told us there weren't any. Of course, he was my friend and I believed him.

I was also contacted by a highly regarded Spanish promoter who had seen us at Cavestomp. He offered something I couldn't refuse – a tour in Spain, all expenses paid, plus great fees. We would perform at the very first Go Sinner Go Festival in Madrid, plus several other venues throughout the country. All of the band members initially agreed to go, except for Tony. He couldn't leave his business for that length of time. So, Dick, Gary, and I would have to find another guitarist. All was agreed to, and the promoter began to make travel arrangements.

However, an undercurrent of distrust began to build, spread by none other than Tony. If he couldn't go, nobody could. He complained about me trying to run the group slipshod without consultation from the others, and also voiced absurd fears of being hijacked by terrorists. Eventually he was able to persuade Dick and Gary not to go, forcing us to have to cancel the tour at the last minute. One talent of Tony's I was always aware of was his expertise at the art of manipulation. I felt so betrayed by the group members, especially Tony, that I wrote to them expressing my disgust at their underhanded behavior and telling them how disappointed I was that they had let me down. As far as I was concerned, this was the final chapter of the Standells.

Once again, I was completely mistaken.

At 3:00 PM on Friday, October 22, 2004, I was in my office editing the audio of a boring medical lecture, meticulously removing stutters and miscellaneous obtrusive sounds like mic pops, lip smacks, and even an occasional belch or fart. I was heading toward the end of my work week and looking forward to a relaxing weekend at home. The phone on my desk suddenly buzzed and I answered it, thinking it might be the editorial department head wondering when his project would be finished. But instead, I was met with a young woman's voice.

"Mr. Tamblyn?"

"Yes," I responded.

"This is Sarah McKenna from Dr. Steinberg's office..."

"You probably need to speak to someone in our subscription department," I said, thinking it was a doctor inquiring about enrolling in Audio Digest's continuing education.

"No, you don't understand," she patiently responded. "Dr. Steinberg from the Boston Red Sox."

"Did you say the Red Sox?"

"I'm sorry for the last-minute call, but I just got off the phone with your drummer, Dick Dodd. He referred me to you. How would you feel about performing at the World Series in Boston?"

Color me gobsmacked.

Sarah went on to explain that the Standells song "Dirty Water" was synonymous with Boston winning at home, and that Dr. Steinberg, who was a huge fan, thought it would be terrific to have the group perform at the World Series game.

I couldn't believe my ears. "When?"

"Well, that's the thing," Sarah answered. "We're returning home this weekend, and we'd love to have you there. Nothing gets the fans more fired up than Dirty Water."

I told Sarah I'd call her back. I had to reach the guys first to see if it was okay. That's when I began a marathon of calls to and from band members, making sure that they were all available, then back to Sarah negotiating a fee, then back to the guys.

In Tony's case, I had to go through his trophy wife, and was quite flabbergasted when she asked, "How can I be sure they're going to pay Tony?" As though that's ever been a problem. It seemed as though she had picked up a few of Tony's traits.

"Because it's the fucking Red Sox," I responded, "and it's fucking Larry Tamblyn who's always looked after Tony's best interests, that's how."

I worked until midnight making travel arrangements, booking hotels, and so on, and within twelve hours all of the band members and wives were on their way to Boston.

Our flight to Boston was long but thrilling, knowing what was in store. We were even introduced on the plane and received applause from the passengers, especially the Red Sox fans. We were picked up in a limo and taken to our hotel, which was fairly close to Fenway Park. By the time we checked in to our rooms and unpacked, it was late evening and we were all hungry. We decided to take a walk in the frigid weather (to Californians, anything under 70 degrees is glacial). Finding no restaurants, we stumbled upon a hot dog vendor, to whom I yelled, "Go Sox!"

He replied in his thick Bostonian accent, "They're gonna blow it, they always do."

Their last World Series win was in 1918, before trading Babe Ruth. Because the Red Sox weren't able to capture the title after that, the term "Curse of the Babe" had become widely circulated among Sox fans. So, the vendor's frustration was understandable.

I'd previously been given instructions not to utter that phrase in Fenway; baseball teams are very superstitious.

The next morning, we were taken to Fenway and were met by team officials. We were given a tour of the stadium, then led into hallowed ground, the Red Sox dugout, where the Babe himself once sat. Wow, going from editing belches and farts to sitting in the Red Sox dugout – all within a 24-hour timeframe. Even though we were given strict instructions not to touch the soil, Glenda managed to scoop some of it up in a small container. Today it is kept in a special place in our home.

During a radio interview before the game, I was quite shocked when the interviewer asked who the leader the group was, and Tony responded, "We don't have one."

After all of these years of being referred to as the leader and spokesperson of the Standells, giving countless interviews, of being widely quoted in articles, I was mortified. At that moment, I realized that Tony was no longer my friend, but an adversary. He had done everything in his power to try to diminish my capacity in the group – eliminating my name from the group name, lip-syncing to songs I sang, and second-guessing me at every turn. In so doing, he was self-inflating his own status. I let him finish the interview, cringing at his abrupt responses to questions and lack of elocution, interspersed with an abundance of "uh's and "you know's."

Was this the thanks I got for all of the years of dedication to his well-being, of in many cases placing his needs before those of my own?

The Standells' performance at Game 2 of the World Series will always be etched in my mind. Before a packed stadium, the crowd singing along with every lyric, it was something to behold. Sportswriter Bill Plaschke was there that evening. In his October 31, 2004 *Los Angeles Times* article, he wrote:

"I was sitting in a press area nearby, wondering, with other journalists, why the Red Sox were allowing these old, obscure dudes to handle pregame entertainment before perhaps the most important game in franchise history.

Then they began playing "Dirty Water." And we learned. Everyone began singing. Young, old, ushers, vendors, everyone, waving their arms and singing. Down in the bullpen, the players were dancing. Over in the dugout, bats were tapping. They finished to a standing ovation, left the stage, and flew home to their Southland lives." [61]

The original Standells were brought together at Fenway on three more occasions: 2005, 2006 and 2007. None of us were aware that during this time Dick had ingratiated himself with the Red Sox, going there without the rest of the group on several occasions and even recording a song for the team. I would not even have minded if he still sounded like the Dick Dodd of the sixties, but he was not even close – sounding more like a Ray Charles wannabe. I felt that rather than acting as an ambassador, he had dealt considerable harm to the Standells name.

In 2007 the Red Sox insisted that all of the original members once again be in attendance. It was the opening game of the ALCS playoff series between the Red Sox and the Los Angeles Angels,

---

61   www.latimes.com - *Coming Through with the Big Hit at Fenway* (2004)

Standells at 2004 World Series

and we were asked to sing the National Anthem. We were told that it was to be performed acapella. Realizing that we weren't capable of doing this as a live performance, I had the difficult task of pre-recording the song in four-part harmony. Anyone who heard us perform that day would not have realized that it was me singing all of the harmonies.

We spent a week in Boston, participating in a number of events, including a Red Sox rally at the Boston City Hall Plaza. The fees were considerably more than we'd ever been paid, yet Tony complained in front of several clients. "Eeet's not enough," was by then a favorite refrain of his. He claimed that he could have done better. I had to remind him that the only gig he ever booked was at a fraction of what the Red Sox were paying us. As he aged, his grandiose image of himself seemed to expand exponentially. It was also at this time that we began to notice how wretchedly Tony's wife was treating him. She would go off by herself and drink, avoiding contact with the others. Whenever she did join members of the group and their spouses, she openly criticized and mocked Tony. Both Gary and Dick pulled Tony aside one evening and told him that he really shouldn't tolerate this behavior. As it turned out, Tony's misery turned out to be our misery; if he wasn't already miserable, he became next-to-impossible to work with.

As they did with every postseason game in which the Standells attended, the Red Sox won and went on to win the World Series. We were indeed the Red Sox's good luck charm.

EPILOG

In 2009, the original Standells performed together for the very last time at the Cannery Casino in Las Vegas. Dick and Tony demanded special accommodations for friends and family members, causing extra work on Glenda's part to make arrangements with the hotel. It was all I could do to get the group together for just one rehearsal beforehand, and the concert was a disaster. Gary had practiced at home and was the only one who came prepared. One hour of the soundcheck was taken up almost entirely by Tony, with comments like "I can't hear the guitar," "I don't hear any bass," let alone comments on the sound mix through his floor monitors. This left the band with about one-half hour for an actual soundcheck.

Once again, after pleading with him to sing "Dirty Water" as he did originally, Dick completely changed the melody, intonations, and removed all of the wonderful improvs that made the song famous. The song ended up sounding like an R&B rendition of the original, with a different singer who from years of drug and alcohol abuse had lost the edge in his voice and the snotty in-your-face attitude that sold the song.

Tony appeared to be oblivious to everyone on the stage, and during the harmonica solo he began to play it upside down. What's worse, Dick yelled at Tony throughout most of the set. I was absolutely embarrassed to be there. Over the years, Tony's guitar playing had suffered greatly. He, in fact, even had great difficulty in playing the "Dirty Water" riff. By then, he had gone through the divorce and sold his business, the wife getting most of the proceeds. Perhaps she was much smarter than we all had thought. This couldn't help but have an effect on his guitar playing and his dreadful treatment of me.

After I returned home from the gig, I had decided that I was going to completely break it off with the other band members. However, they beat me to the punch.

Led by Sky Saxon, the Seeds were another LA band from the sixties who had found a new generation of fans with the garage rock revival. Sky's death in June 2009 left a vacuum on an East Coast tour. A promoter approached me about having the Standells fill in. At the same time, I learned that Dick had earlier approached this same promoter about going out as the Standells on his own without my knowledge. When the promoter contacted me, he thought he was getting back to Dick. I confronted Dick with this, and he denied it. However, it didn't matter; he and the other members refused to participate in the tour. I was told by Dick's wife Janie that, because of his health, he could no longer do any kind of extensive touring. This was also acknowledged by Dick.

I was then called by Tony, who informed me, "I can't do thees anymore." When I asked why, he said, "I joined thees group the Icons. They doing my songs."

I couldn't imagine anyone wanting to do Tony's songs, other than to have access to the Standells' name. Furthermore, he said he would only continue with the Standells if he was paid an extraordinary amount of money – much more than he'd ever received for a concert date, even at the height of our popularity.

To me, his logic for leaving the Standells was completely insane, but I gladly accepted his resignation. At that moment, I also checked the Icons YouTube page, Tony was already listed as "Former lead guitarist of the Standells," so evidently Tony had been planning this for quite some time without informing me.

Both Dick and Tony had become completely unreliable, at a time when I strongly felt a resurgence in my enthusiasm for the Standells.

I'd seen signs of Tony's destructive behavior early on. All of the likable aspects of him had completely disappeared. I've come in contact with several people who also have observed a change in Tony over the years. One particular close friend opined that Tony was "clinging to a long-lost past." He said that Tony would be friendly one minute, then with little provocation argumentative and accusatory the next. He attributed this to Tony's marriage to a much younger woman, and the bitter divorce that followed. As many faults as Tony had, he didn't deserve the shabby treatment he received from his wife.

With Dick, I noticed that he had once again fallen into his old habits: While boasting about being a rock star he seemed to be constantly scheming in an underhanded manner, using the Standells name to his advantage, a name he once disowned. He was behaving more like a lowlife than a rock star.

It was during this time that I decided to have the Standells name trademarked, proving that I was its originator and had prior usage of it. I did this for several reasons. First and foremost, the name had to be protected, otherwise I honestly believed that Dick and Tony would have run it into the ground. Because of his limited involvement in the group, Gary was not a consideration. Both Dick and Tony had a history of using the Standells name to suit their own purposes.

As with any trademark filing, the band members had a period of one year in which to challenge it, which they chose not to.

With this business taken care of, I decided to reform the group completely. I started by calling our old bassist, John "Fleck" Fleckenstein. John had been out of the hospital for only two months when I reached him. He had suffered from a form of leukemia, was hospitalized, induced into a coma, and was near death, when, after a worldwide search, a stem cell donor was found. His transplant operation was a success. At the time, I had known nothing of his horrible ordeal. Fleck had enjoyed a long and distinguished film career, but the doctors advised him that the film industry was too strenuous for him, so he jumped at the chance of re-joining the Standells.

We were able to add guitarist Paul Downing, who had been with the group in 1969, along with drummer Greg Burnham. My original intention was not to do much lead singing, because I had lost all confidence in my singing abilities. But in rehearsing with the new group, I was encouraged by the others to re-assume the lead vocal slot. They were also cognizant of the fact that an original lead singer added more value to the group. Once I began singing "Dirty Water," I made an amazing discovery. With Tony out of the picture I had a new-found self-assuredness, and I did very well behind the mic. In addition to tunes I originally sang in the group, I discovered that on the others I sounded more like the sixties Dick Dodd than he did in later years.

In September 2009, the re-organized Standells performed at Amoeba Records in Hollywood, celebrating the inclusion of our song "Riot on Sunset Strip" on the newest Rhino collection, *Where the Action Is*, a CD box set. It was the kick-off song for the entire set, and the album was nominated for a Grammy Award. It was great seeing a lot of old friends there, including Micky Dolenz, P.F. Sloan, and Bobby Hart. I also renewed a friendship with Lance Baker Fenton of the Peanut Butter Conspiracy, who remains a close friend today. Our performance was well-received and was closely followed by another at the Echoplex in Hollywood.

With the finalization of the trademark in January 2010, I was able to approach Sundazed Music who cooperated fully in revealing the original agreement with Dick for the live album, and the royalties paid directly to him since 2000. I was shocked at what I learned. I felt thoroughly betrayed and was dumbfounded at how Dick could do this to his bandmates. He had signed the agreement as "Dick Dodd for the Standells." There was a more sinister aspect to Dick than I had realized. It took considerable thought and effort to finally write to him, informing him that the embezzlement had been uncovered.

After all of these years, I was finally acting responsibly in taking the helm of the Standells, as I should have done originally. Rather than filing embezzlement charges and a lawsuit against Dick, I offered him a simple settlement, which without a word of apology he signed. Here again, I found a further source of income all the while representing Tony's interests. Instead of thanking me, though, Tony turned around and accused me of stealing the

Standells from him. Since he willingly quit the group, I found his claim to be outrageous.

In 2010, the reformed Standells booked a four-week tour in Europe. As fate would have it, our first stop was in Madrid, Spain, at the Go Sinner Go Festival. And wouldn't you know it, just weeks before departing, Tony contacted me and demanded to be included on the tour, playing the very same venue he had turned down in 2000.

Of course, I denied this brazen request for several reasons. Firstly, because all of the preparations had already been made, including flights and hotel arrangements. Secondly, I already had a guitar player who was a much better musician than Tony. Thirdly, and most importantly, I simply couldn't work with Tony any longer.

Instead, I offered him an occasional guest appearance. But he would have none of it. He felt entitled to the name and proceeded to contact the European promoter, demanding to be part of the tour. I was deeply embarrassed. Like me, the promoter was dumbfounded.

We continued on our tour, which covered not only Spain but France, Great Britain, Norway, Greece, and Germany. On returning to the US, Paul Downing left the group and we performed at several more venues with a new guitarist Adam Marsland. On my birthday, February 5, 2011, we did a concert at the Whisky A Go-Go, one that I will not likely forget. I had looked forward to returning to the famed Sunset Strip club. However, instead of being treated as the celebrated rock group who helped bring fame to the Strip with "Riot on Sunset Strip," we were treated with complete disrespect. To add further insult, a no-name group, received the top billing. As I understand it, they had four-walled the event, purchasing their own tickets.

After that, I swore to stay mostly away from Hollywood nightclubs.

CHAPTER 21

The squabbling with Tony continued for several years, with his behavior becoming more and more outrageous, childish, and unreasonable. He even illegally began a Standells website, on which I was deemed to be a "liar" and "cheat." Then Tony contacted Facebook deceiving them by stating that he owned the trademark, and preposterously claiming that I was infringing on it. Based only on these false allegations, Facebook shut down the Standells page. They wouldn't accept any proof from me that I was the actual owner of the trademark. It stayed shut down for over a year. In essence, Tony was cutting off his nose to spite his face, because much of the Facebook site was devoted to him.

After pleading with him to stop his idiotic behavior, I finally had to file a lawsuit against Tony, which cost thousands of dollars in attorney's fees. We ended up in arbitration. In legal documents, Tony completely lied about the facts, claiming that he had spearheaded the group, even denying that I was the original lead singer. This absurdity couldn't have been more evident in the fact that the group was originally billed as "Larry Tamblyn and the Standells." It didn't help that during this period, I had been diagnosed with advanced prostate cancer, and had to undergo a radical prostatectomy and radiation treatment. Because of my illness, I was finally forced to settle in arbitration, and against my better judgment Tony was allowed to be added to the trademark. However, I was granted full control of its usage.

We continued to do various events during 2011, including a performance in San Francisco at The Independent on July 14. In 2012, after doing a small Midwest Tour, I decided to do something I'd been thinking about for a long time – record a new album. I recalled how "Dirty Water" was recorded in a garage studio, and desired to return to that sound. So, we decided to build our own studio in a converted garage behind drummer Greg Burnham's home. It was the perfect solution: we wouldn't be impeded by working within the confines of a regular recording studio. There would be no clocks to watch for running overtime, and no one's schedule to adhere to but our own. We could come and go as we pleased. I was able to act as the producer and recording engineer. Replacing guitarist Adam Marsland with Mark Adrian, the first song laid down was an original I wrote called "Mr. One Percent," an ode to corporate greed. It was the perfect subject matter for a snarly Standells song. The rest of the album was recorded over the next four or five months.

Dick contacted me, expressing concern for my medical condition and remorse for the way he'd behaved. He wanted to make amends. This was the Dick Dodd that I'd known in the sixties, who, despite his other faults, was kind and generous. I made the mistake, once again, of adding him to the group. Yeah, I still had many faults, one of which was being too trusting of others. I also thought it would be cool to include Dick in the album. Yet another error in judgment. He had separated from his wife Janie and returned to drinking and drugs. We included him in previously lined-up gigs. Since Greg was our drummer, we put Dick out front playing guitar and timbales, just like he'd always wanted. Out of respect for Dick, I was even willing to once again give up lead singing the hits.

Our first gig with him was headlining the Monterey Summer of Love Festival on September 30, 2012. Dick was used sparingly, and the event was a success. Next came our performance at the Uptown Nightclub in Oakland on November 12th. Here I discovered that Dick near booze was like having gasoline near a fire. He became so intoxicated that he forgot the lyrics to some of the songs. At one point, he was so schnockered he didn't even know which way to face towards the audience. Even so, the gig was a success. Afterward, Dick tearfully expressed to the other guys how happy he was to once again be part of the group. After returning home, we picked up where we'd left off on the recording sessions. Dick had one song he wanted to do called "Tough Like Boston," which he presented to us as having been written by him. We later learned that the writer was actually his new girlfriend. He also claimed poverty; the money he'd made at the gigs was gone. The band chipped in by giving Dick a car to drive and $1,000 for him to move closer to LA for rehearsals. Instead of using the money as he had promised, he stayed put and spent it on other things. When he did finally show up at the recording studio, he tried to manipulate us, demanding we record instead at a studio located near him in Huntington Beach. We could get it at no cost, because the engineer was a business partner of his girlfriend. I immediately refused. How many problems had we had in the past with wives and girlfriends?

"What would happen if you and your girlfriend broke up?" I asked him. Dick couldn't answer that.

We later found out that she had taken him for every penny he had, the real reason for his poverty. I also felt terrible about the shabby treatment of his wife, Janie, who had sacrificed a great deal for him. Even Dick's close friend Gary McMillan had stopped speaking to him.

After all that, Dick ended up recording only one song for the album. I drew up a contract for him, listing his share accordingly. Meanwhile, the record company was waiting for the release, and Dick held up the deal for two weeks, saying his attorney didn't agree with the terms of the contract. His *attorney*? This, from a guy who had pleaded poverty and received money and a car from the band?

In the end we decided to omit "Tough Like Boston" from the album along with any mention of Dick's involvement. Dealing with him was more trouble than it was worth.

With me now doing most the of the lead singing, *Bump*, the Standells' first record album in over forty-five years was met with critical praise.

At the Blog Critics website, Wesley Britton wrote:

"Bump" isn't a record to pop in when you have seduction on your mind or if you're considering a short period of meditation. On the other hand, it's not a collection so loud and discordant you need to be under 50 to enjoy it. Rather, it really is a time-capsule of what garage rock was all about in 1966, very recognizable as being new tunes recorded to sound like they were being jammed out before the summer of love kicked in. If you liked The Seeds, Electric Prunes,

The Stooges, and the original Standells, this is a fun outing to enjoy even if Boston isn't your home. [62]

"The new album is called "Bump," which by the way I heard for the first time last night, and let me tell you something, I think you guys hit it out of the park. It covered a lot of ground. There are no ballads on it; it's real straight-ahead rock and roll. I think it stays true to your roots, and really kind of in some ways brings me back, but it also brings me forward." [63]

Meanwhile, we had several gigs lined up with Dick included, still months away. The first was in San Diego at the Adams Avenue Street Festival on September 28th and the second was at the Ponderosa Stomp in New Orleans, Louisiana, on October 5th. This is when we began further having problems with Dick. He started doing gigs at small nightclubs, in some cases dives, using the Standells name, even though he'd been warned and had agreed not to. Because we had a lot at stake with the larger venues, I was forced to send out a number of cease and desist letters to the clubs and promoters.

Had this been the extent of Dick's misbehavior, maybe we could have been able to work things out. But then Dick began creating problems with our gig at the Ponderosa Stomp, insisting that he would only fly out of the Long Beach airport, and demanding that some of his supposed friends whom I deemed "drinking buddies" accompany him. The problem was that the rest of us were sched-

---

62 www.logcritics.org - *Music Review: The Standells - 'Bump'* (2013)
63 Stu Robins, WBAI-FM 99.5, New York (2013)

uled to fly out of LAX. When I informed Dick that I wouldn't allow this kind of behavior, he went behind my back and contacted Ponderosa Stomp promoter Dr. Ike and threatened to quit if he didn't have special accommodations. Against my objections, special handling was allowed for Dick, and Dr. Ike assumed all responsibility. This behavior was so unlike the kind and thoughtful Dick that I grew up with. He never demanded special favors as a young band member. But, like Tony, he had changed.

The problems with Dick escalated, culminating with a letter from his attorney informing me "my client no longer wishes to have any association with the Standells." Being quite surprised that Dick could afford and attorney, it was later learned that she was a longtime female friend who really only handled traffic accidents. I was especially angered with an edict from his attorney not to contact Dick directly. Regardless, telephone calls to Dick went unanswered. Since Dr. Ike was decidedly set on having Dick at the Ponderosa Stomp event, it seemed to be a no-win situation. Finally, I offered him a last-minute solution, a double bill with my friend Johnny Echols of Love. He agreed, and both gigs went quite well without Dick.

In a review of the Ponderosa Stomp, Steven W. Terrell wrote, "All too often when you hear old bands play their old songs from decades past, it's sad and cheesy. But these Standells aren't ready for the casino circuit, and hopefully, they never will be. They play like they could start a real riot on Sunset Strip." [64]

Reviews from the Adams Ave. Street Fair were equally as positive. "Legendary garage rockers The Standells, led by original

---

64 www.allmusic.com - *Ponderosa Stomp: The Finale* (2016)

singer-keyboardist Larry Tamblyn, headlined the Adams Avenue Street Fair in San Diego. The Godfathers of Punk Rock didn't disappoint. They tore it up." [65]

My desire to maintain the Standells' image and garage rock sound had been realized. And I had done so without Dick and Tony, which at one time would have seemed to be an impossibility. Perhaps it had been my self-doubt that kept me from realizing this.

Shortly afterward, Dick was hospitalized, his condition considered dire. He had esophageal cancer which had metastasized in his brain.

On November 29, 2013, I received the sad news that Dick had passed away. I was convinced that his condition had caused his odd behavior. I grieved at Dick's passing. It didn't help that I began to be harassed by his friends from Huntington Beach. All of them I considered to be more enablers to Dick's alcoholism and drug abuse. They blamed me for his death, rather than themselves for not intervening and making sure he received medical tests and treatment which I had pleaded with Dick to seek out. To express my remorse, I wrote the following tribute to Dick, which was published throughout the world:

As fate would have it, The Standells were all together, not performing, but enjoying the evening (a rare event) when we received the news that Dick Dodd had passed away at the age of 68. There's also a metaphor in his departing on Black

---

65 Pasadena Star news, Steve Smith, *Adams Avenue Street Fair, Standells Review* (2016)

Friday. Dick always had a wry sense of humor. Unknown until recently, Dick had been suffering from esophageal cancer for quite some time.

I've known Dick since he was about 20 years old. The first time we met was when he walked into P.J.s nightclub to audition for the Standells. He had a tough job to fill; we desperately needed a drummer who could sing, as we were about two weeks away from recording our first record album. Until that time, I had done all of the lead singing, and I needed someone else to share the load. As soon as Dick sat behind the drums and began to sing and play, I knew we had found the right person! Not only did he knock our socks off, but he survived some very lame jokes about his being a former Mouseketeer.

Dick was an incredible talent, both as a drummer and singer! In addition, Dick was a very kind and generous person, always there for his friends when they needed him, and on a number of occasions giving gifts to associates. He also was very caring to his friends. Last year during my bout with prostate cancer, he called me every week offering words of comfort. I understand that he did the same for many of his friends.

Dick is survived by his wife Jane and daughter Nicole. He passed away at 10:00 pm Friday evening, appropriately with drumsticks in his hands. Rest in peace Dick. We miss you but know that you're in a better place!"

After all, I had known Dick for over fifty years, much longer than his supposed friends. He was like a brother to me. How could I not celebrate the good times we had together? I still loved Dick and was hurt deeply when Gary, John and I were prevented by his daughter, Nicole, at the insistence of his friends from seeing him at the hospital or attending his memorial service.

The following year, on November 5, 2014, Gary McMillan died, also from cancer. He and his wife, Edie, had always been good friends to me. I am still close to Edie today, as well as Dick's wife Janey. I have continued to look after their needs as I had their husbands.

I created a memorial video "In Memory of Dick Dodd & Gary (Lane) McMillan," featuring movies and TV shows they had appeared in throughout the years, including our guest episode on *The Munsters*. For the video, I created a special opening orchestral score, incorporating "Dirty Water" and "Sometimes Good Guys Don't Wear White" as a musical fugue. To this day, right around the anniversaries of their deaths, I post the video and offer tribute to Dick and Gary and their contributions. Thousands have seen the video and have shared it with others.

The Standells continued to perform in concerts, in 2014 a national tour covering thirteen states, including the Mayne Stage in Chicago where we recorded a live album *The 60's The Standells* for Sony Music. [66]

That same year, the group performed at Festival Beat, Salsomaggiore Terme, Italy, and on the following year performed live in the Cornerstones of Rock Soundstage on PBS, broadcast worldwide. Out of twenty performers including, the Buckinghams, Cryan Shames, New Colony Six, Shadows of Knight,

------

66 *The 60s the Standells* (2015)

McCoys, American Breed, the Standells portion was used to advertise the show internationally.

In early 2017, the Standells performed at the Cannery Casino in Las Vegas. The last performance as a group was on June 3rd at the Palace Theater in Los Angeles, along with my old friend Rick Derringer from the McCoys.

On October 18, 2017, John Fleckenstein passed away from a re-occurrence of AML leukemia.

As if I was destined to live a life of dealing with the misery from former members, the quarreling between Tony and me continued. In 2018, I tried to make amends with him, but to date we have been unable to reconcile our differences. I might humorously add that Tony is four years senior to me, but throughout recent years he has publicly proclaimed himself to miraculously have become younger than me.

Russ and I are all that's left of our original Tamblyn family. We try to see each other as often as we can. He has also made a comeback in his career, being featured most recently in the return of *Twin Peaks* TV series. I was there on November 15, 2011, during the long-overdue Hand and Footprint Ceremony at the Chinese Theater, along with *West Side Story* cast members George Chakiris and Rita Morino, as well attending other functions honoring his lifetime achievements.

I have managed to recently tell Russ how much I love him, and how important he has been to me, stepping in when Dad passed away, not only as my big brother but my mentor, never judging but always being there when I've needed him.

If nothing else, I've learned to adapt to the vicissitudes of life. It took me all of these years to finally take inventory of myself. In the process, I have discovered that I really don't need to depend on others to gauge my own individual self-worth. I am now doing solo concerts throughout the country.

I've taken ownership of my life, and for the first time, I am at the helm of its course to wherever that journey may take me. More importantly, I've come to realize that I honestly cannot despise my stepfather for his abuse, nor Dick and Tony for their betrayals. In reality, I am the sum total of all of my life experiences, good and bad. If I had to do it all over again, I wouldn't change a thing. I would not be the same person today if any one of the circumstances was altered, and most definitely I would never have been able to say that *I love that Dirty Water.*

THE END

BIBLIOGRAPHY

Standells 1966 Tour with the Rolling Stones

June 24: Manning Bowl, Lynn MA
June 25: Civic Center Arena, Pittsburgh, PA (Afternoon Show)
June 25: Cleveland Arena, Cleveland OH (Evening Show)
June 26: Arena (Washington Coliseum), Washington DC (Afternoon Show)
June 26: Baltimore Civic Centre, Baltimore, MD (Evening Show)
June 27: Dillon Stadium, Hartford, CT
June 28: War Memorial Auditorium, Buffalo, NY
June 29: Maple Leaf Gardens, Toronto, ONT
June 30: Forum, Montreal, QUE
July 1: Steel Pier, Atlantic City, NJ
July 2: Forest Hills Tennis Stadium, Queens, NY
July 3: Convention Hall, Asbury Park, NJ
July 4: Virginia Beach Dome, Virginia Beach, VA
July 5: (Off)
July 6: War Memorial Hall, Syracuse, NY
July 7: (Off)
July 8: Cobo Hall, Detroit, MI
July 8: Indiana State Fairgrounds Coliseum, Indianapolis, NY
July 10: Arie Crown Theater, McCormick Place, Chicago, IL
July 11: Sam Houston Coliseum, Houston, TX
July 12: Kiel Convention Hall, St Louis, MO
July 13: (Off)
July 14: Winnipeg Stadium, Winnipeg, MAN
July 15: Omaha Civic Auditorium, Omaha, NE

July 16-18: (Off)
July 19: Pacific National Exhibition Forum Park, Vancouver, BC
July 20: Seattle Coliseum, Seattle, WA
July 21: Memorial Coliseum, Portland, OR
July 22: Sacramento Memorial Auditorium, Sacramento, CA
July 23: Davis County Lagoon, Salt Lake City, UT
July 24: Bakersfield Civic Auditorium, Bakersfield, CA
July 24: Hollywood Bowl, Los Angeles, CA
July 26: Cow Palace, San Francisco, CA (last date with the Standells)
July 28: Hawaii International Center, Honolulu Hawaii

Standells 1966 Tour with Paul Revere & the Raiders

October 27: Kent Theatre, Des Moines, Iowa
October 28: Milwaukee Auditorium, Milwaukee, Wisconsin
October 29: Freedom Hall, Louisville, Kentucky
October 30: Cincinnati Music Hall, Cincinnati, Ohio
November 01: Ohio State Fairgrounds, Columbus, Ohio
November 02: Indianapolis State Fairgrounds, Indianapolis, Indiana
November 03: Sports Center, Owensboro, Kentucky
November 04: Mid-South Coliseum, Memphis, Tennessee
November 05: Jackson Coliseum—Jackson, Mississippi
November 06: Mobile Municipal Auditorium—Mobile, Alabama
November 07: Travel Day
November 08: Greenville Memorial Auditorium—Greenville, South
    Carolina
November 09: Madison County Coliseum—Huntsville, Alabama
November 10: Knoxville Coliseum—Knoxville, Tennessee
November 11: Travel Day
November 12: Birmingham Municipal Auditorium—Birmingham,
    Alabama

November 13: Nashville Municipal Auditorium—Nashville, Tennessee

November 14: Asheville Auditorium—Asheville, North Carolina

November 15: Travel Day

November 16: Municipal Auditorium—Atlanta, Georgia

November 17: William Bell Memorial Auditorium—Augusta, Georgia

November 18: Columbus Municipal Auditorium—Columbus, Georgia

November 19: Alabama State Coliseum—Montgomery, Alabama

November 20: State Fair Arena—Oklahoma City, Oklahoma

November 21: El Dorado Municipal Auditorium—El Dorado, Arkansas

November 22: Memorial Auditorium—Dallas Texas

November 23: Houston Music Hall—Houston, Texas

November 24: Municipal Auditorium—San Antonio, Texas

November 25: Memorial Coliseum—Corpus Christi, Texas

November 26: City Auditorium—Amarillo, Texas

November 27: Travel Day

November 28: Lubbock Coliseum—Lubbock, Texas

November 29: Municipal Auditorium—Austin, Texas

November 30: Travel Day

December 01: Coliseum—El Paso, Texas

December 02: Albuquerque Civic Center—Albuquerque, New Mexico

December 03: Phoenix Star Theater—Phoenix, Arizona

Discography

Albums

The Standells In Person at PJ's (LP) Liberty (1965)

Dirty Water (2 versions) Tower Records (1966)

Dirty Water (LP, Album, mono) Tower Records (1966)

Dirty Water (CD, mono) Sundazed Music (1994)

Why Pick On Me / Sometimes Good Guys Don't Wear White (4 versions) Tower Records (1966)

Why Pick On Me / Sometimes Good Guys Don't Wear White LP, mono) Sparton (1966)

Why Pick On Me / Sometimes Good Guys Don't Wear White (LP) Tower Records (1966)

Why PIck On Me / Sometimes Good Guys Don't Wear White LP, mono) Tower Records (1966)

Why Pick On Me / Sometimes Good Guys Don't Wear White (LP) Eva Records (1988)

The Hot Ones (2 versions) Tower Records (1966)

The Hot Ones (LP, mono) Tower Records 1966

The Hot Ones (CD, mono) Sundazed Music (1994)

The Standells: Live And Out Of Sight (LP) Sunset Records (1966)

Try It (LP) Tower Records (1967)

Try It (LP, stereo) Eva Records (1988)

Try It (CD, mono) Sundazed Music (1994)

The Best of the Standells (LP) Rhino Records (1983)

Rarities (LP) Rhino Records (1983)

Rarities (CD) Big Beat Records (2009)

Ban THIS (CD) Cavestomp Records (1999)

The Standells Live on Tour (LP and CD) Sundazed Music

Bump (CD) GRA Records (2013)

SINGLES

The Shake (7") Liberty Records 1964

I'll Go Crazy (7") Liberty Records 1964

Linda Lou (7") Liberty Records 1964

The Boy Next Door (7") Vee Jay Records 1965

Dirty Water / Rari (3 versions) Tower Records 1966

Dirty Water / Rari (7") Tower Records 1966

Dirty Water (7") Rhino Records 1984

Dirty Water / Surfin' Bird (7") Trip Records

Why Pick On Me (2 versions) Tower Records 1966

Why Pick On Me (7") Tower Records 1966

Why Pick On Me (7") Uptown Records 1966

Sometimes Good Guys Don't Wear White (7") Tower Records 1966Try It / Poor Shell Of A Man (7") Tower Records 1967

Can't Help But Love You (7") Tower Records 1967

Poor Boys Born In A Rubble (2 versions) Sundazed Music 1995

Poor Boys Born In A Rubble (7" EP, Mono, Pur.) Sundazed Music 1995

Poor Boys Born In A Rubble (7" EP, Mono, Gre.) Sundazed Music 1995

The Live Ones! (10", EP, Mono) Sundazed Music 2001

Barracuda (7", Ltd, EP) Eva Records 1990

Compilations

The Best of the Standells (2 versions) Rhino Records 1989

The Best of the Standells (LP, Comp) Rhino Records 1986

The Best of the Standells (CD, Comp) Rhino Records 1989

Dirty Water + The Hot Ones (CD, Comp, Mono) Eva Records 1990

Dirty Water / Why Pick On Me / Sometimes Good Guys Don't Wear White (CD, comp, RM, Mono) Big Beat Records 1992

The Hot Ones / Try It (CD, Album, Comp) Big Beat Records 1993

Riot On Sunset Strip (LP, Comp, Mono) Eva Records 1990

Dirty Water (LP, Comp, Mono) Eva Records 1990

Where the Action Is: Los Angeles Nuggets 1965-1968 Rhino Records 2010

Dirty Water: The Birth of Punk Attitude Year Zero 2010